Gladwin B. Williams BSc., MA

Financial Matters And The Family

All rights reserved. Written permission must be secured from the author to use or reproduce any part of this book, except in the case of brief quotations embodied in critical reviews or articles.

First Edition Printed and Published in 2003 by Tropical Print Services Ltd., Bridgetown, Barbados.

Second Edition Printed and published in 2014 by CreateSpace
1200 12th Ave South, Suite 1200, Seattle, WA 98144, USA

*Scripture quotations are from New Revised Standard Version Bible, copyright © 1989 National Council of Churches of Christ in the United States of America. Used by permission. All rights reserved.
Front cover photograph downloaded from Microsoft Clip Gallery
Copyright © 2015 Gladwin B. Williams BSc., MA
All rights reserved.
ISBN10: 1514660849
ISBN 13: 978-1514660843
To order additional copies, please contact us.
www.createspace.com

Caps were used to begin words such as His and You as far as possible, when referring to Jehovah, the Holy Spirit and Jesus, while common letter were used for satan and the devil.

Table of Contents

ACKNOWLEDGEMENT v

PREFACE vi

SUMMARY xii

Chapter 1 FUNDAMENTAL PRINCIPLES OF BIBLICAL FINANCE 1

    THE BIBLE & FINANCIAL MANAGEMENT 5

    EXTENDING & RECEIVING FINANCIAL BLESSINGS 13

    IS MONEY THE ROOT TO ALL EVIL? 20

    ACQUIRING AND MANAGING MATERIAL RESOURCES 29

    LENDING & BORROWING 50

    CHALLENGES IN OBTAINAING A LOAN 54

    CHARITY & THE CHRISTIAN FAMILY 64

    LIVING BY FAITH 69

    TIME MANAGEMENT & THE CHRISTIAN FAMILY 72

    CHRISTIANS BENEFIT FROM THE TREASURES OF THE UNRIGHTEOUS 78

    GAMBLING 88

    THE PRE-NATAL PERIOD 99

    EARLY CHILDHOOD 102

    THE MATURING CHILD 108

    HEALTH ISSUES 116

    CAREER GUIDANCE AND PERSONAL DEVELOPMENT 122

    THE CHILD AND FINANCIAL MANAGEMENT 142

    FINANCIAL RESPONSIBILITY OF CHILDREN TO THEIR PARENTS 148

Chapter 3 INVESTMENT OPPORTUNITIES AND THE FAMILY 154

    BANKING AND THE CHRISTIAN FAMILY 155

    INSURANCE COVERAGE 161

    CAPITAL MARKETS 170

    OTHER INTERNATIONAL FINANCIAL OPPORTUNITIES 174

    CHRISTIANS AND BUSINESS 177

    MANAGING THE FAMILY BUSINESS 184

STARTING YOUR OWN BUSINESS 190

RAISING CAPITAL 198

MANAGING TAXATION 202

MANAGING INFLATION 209

MANAGING DEBT 210

MANAGING FINANCIAL CRISES 232

PURCHASING FROM MAIL ORDER SALES AND VIA THE INTERNET 236

CHRISTIANS AND THE LAW, AS IT RELATES   TO FINANCIAL ISSUES 238

Chapter 4 FINANCIAL MANAGEMENTBY THE FAMILY 244

FINANCIAL PREPARATION FOR MARRIAGE 245

THE CHRISTIAN WOMAN AND FINANCE 252

WOMEN BREAKING THE GLASS CEILING IN THE CORPORATE WORLD 266

THE CHRISTIAN MAN AND FINANCE 274

BUDGETING AND THE CHRISTIAN FAMILY 282

FORMULATING AND ACHIEVING GOALS 308

COMMON ATTRIBUTES OF GODLY VISIONARIES 314

GETTING OUT AND STAYING OUT OF POVERTY 316

FINANCIAL IMPLICATIONS OF A DIVORCE 319

Chapter 5 FINANCIAL MANAGEMENT & THE GOLDEN OLD AGE 328

ENJOYING RETIREMENT 329

CONSUMER PROTECTION 331

PENSION PLANS 337

CARING FOR THE ELDERLY 339

RIGHT ENDING ATTITUDES 345

Chapter 6 ENJOYING MORETHAN ENOUGH 351

SELECTED REFERENCES 398

APPENDIX 399

ACKNOWLEDGEMENT

Sincere appreciation is expressed to my loving children, Raule, Paul, James and Candace; my mom, Euranie; brothers, Frank and Oliver; in-laws and their families and the numerous other persons who have contributed in some way to the completion and publication of this book. This includes Sisters Patricia Crichlow, Susana Grant and Michelle Ifill, who have spent valuable time and energy in proof reading the manuscript of this book. Most importantly, all praise and glory belong to my Provider, Jehovah-Jireh.

Dedicated to our second son Mr. Paul A. Williams BSc, MBA – love and proud of you guy.

PREFACE

It is common to find Christians in pursuit of either of two extreme philosophies pertaining to the acquisition and management of material possessions. There are those who are of the view that they need to **relinquish any desire to attain material possessions** which is above their basic needs to sustain themselves and family, contribute to the church, and help the needy. At the other end of the spectrum, we find many preachers and other Christians majoring on what is often referred to as the '**Theology of Prosperity**.' The adapting of the former approach has to a great extent hindered the effectiveness of the ministry of the Word of God from a holistic perspective.

You may be familiar with the '**name and claim**' era in the history of the Christian movement, where many Christians laid their hands on cars, houses and other property with the expectation that God would have granted them these 'desires of their hearts.' Sadly, many Christians who pursued this philosophy were disappointed when their desires were not met. Thankfully, most of us have matured beyond that stage in our Christian lives. On the contrary, persons who adopt a dogmatic approach in shunning all but the most basic material possessions are often distracted from placing the pre-eminence of spiritual matters above a selfish desire for material wealth. The pros and cons of these and other issues are highlighted in the pages of this book.

> Jesus focused on financial issues in sixteen of His thirty-eight parables. This shows the level of importance which God attributes to the management of material resources.

Even though it is necessary to use a few technical financial terms, this book presents simple and practical principles which can be adopted to enable us to manage the material resources with which God has blessed us and of which we are the custodians. It also provides us with a guideline which will enable us to harvest the resources which are realistically within our power to achieve without unnecessary sacrifices and, more importantly, which will complement our spiritual life. For this reason it is important that from early in our Christian life, we recognize the specific calling of God on our lives. What a waste it would be, for example, if a man who is called by God to be a very successful businessman and to assist in the financing of the gospel, decides to spend the greater part of his life functioning in the office of an evangelist because of the glamour which he perceives in this office. Even though the 'misplaced evangelist' may have led a number of persons to Christ, his reward would have been greater with the number of persons whose lives were touched as a result of the amount of finance that he would have given to assist in the financing of the Gospel and in areas such as assisting the poor.

This book focuses on the issue of parents demonstrating to their children the correct principles and attitudes in managing their money and other assets. Children have to be taught to abstain from unhealthy practices such as gambling and stealing, and instead concentrate on careers which will enable them to become citizens who make a valuable contribution to society. Since the home is usually the first place where godly principles are established, parents have a solemn responsibility to lead by godly example. Therefore, issues such as good budgeting techniques and practices, finance and the children, and catering for old age are given extensive coverage. We pray that the issues presented in this book have a profound positive impact on the life of each reader.

Financial Management can be identified simply as **how well we manage the material resources which are at our disposal or which we have been mandated to manage**. This simplified definition can be related to:

(a) The budgeting and utilization of one's personal finances and that of the family,
(b) Issues such as the effective utilization of the money which the beggar receives from those who are charitable among us,
(c) The use of the allowance which a child receives from his parents,
(d) The effective utilization of the financial resources of specialists such as accountants, bankers and other financial analysts in the management of a financial or non-financial institution. This process is usually very complex and they often use computer models and other sophisticated methods to guide them in making prudent financial and other decisions.
(e) The management of national resources of a country,
(f) The management of the impact of international activities on a local economy,

This book is more concerned with the medium between the two spheres of financial management as it relates to issues surrounding the affairs of the family. Even though reference is made to several complex aspects of financial management, the main focus of this book is on using simple illustrations to reiterate the fact that every Christian has the capacity to manage his material resources in order that he can be termed as 'a good stewards' in this vital area of their lives. We should be aware that nothing in this life is inherently tree, thus a price had to be paid, or will have to be paid to achieve the desired level of success. Our primary focus as

Christians should always be on achieving excellence in every area of our lives. Therefore, we should utilize the deposit of the Holy Spirit who dwells in us and all of His positive attributes such as the imparting of wisdom in us and bringing things to our remembrance to enable us to achieve God's best in our lives.

> One of the primary decisions of every human being is choosing between the eternal and the momentary. While the eternal provides gratification on the present earth and for eternity, the latter may provide momentary gratification but the consequence is often detrimental for the present life and for eternity.

Unless one chooses to be a hermit, monk or nun, for example, and chooses to live a life in seclusion, we have to make daily choices on how we manage our financial resources. As a matter of fact, even such persons have to make choices on how to manage the meagre material resources which they choose to live on. The housewife, for example who, by choice or otherwise, allows her husband to manage the major financial resources of the family, still makes decisions which have major financial consequences. She may have to determine what type of food items to purchase from the market or elsewhere from the budget allocated by her husband. In addition, she will choose quantity and quality of food items for cooking. Her method of cooking will also have an important impact on the energy bill of the family and also on the health of the family, and ultimately on the finances, health and general wellbeing of the family.

The importance which a person attributes to personal financial management is dependent on factors such as his outlook on life, the amount of disposable financial resources, the level of development of the society and his projected material targets. In developing countries, for example, where the population of many countries is adversely affected by acute underdevelopment, the primary focus of a large percentage of the population is on the survival of the individual and the family. For persons living in refugee camps because of a war or famine, their survival may be dependent on aid from charitable organizations and individuals and other agencies which are financing the management of the camp. However, even in this situation, the desire of the average refugee is still to live in a peaceful environment and to provide a satisfactory standard of living and a home for his family.

A poorer family living in an affluent society might be able to provide a fairly higher standard of living for their family, such as a comfortable home, education and other essential amenities, in comparison to poorer families living in developing countries. This is so because the poor in developed countries often receive financial assistance from the state and charitable organizations. They may still be unable to maintain a healthy saving balance at a financial institution and engage in speculative financing. Therefore, they have to be very prudent, or even the little that they have is taken away due to inflation, worsening economic conditions and natural disaster.

An upper class family living in an affluent society usually is able to exercise a wide scope of financial choices since they have a large number of financial and other resources at their disposal. The system which is used to perpetuate their wealth may be inconsistent with the principles of the Bible. This often takes the form of indulging in drug trafficking, money laundering, smuggling of arms and ammunitions and other commodities, tax dodging, gambling and other non-scriptural and illegal activities. This, however, does not infer that Christianity is synonymous with poverty, for there is ample room for us to be wealthy materially and still progress in the ways of the Lord. Many Christians choose to live financially humble lives even though they are conscious that the effective spreading of the Gospel demands that we engage in mass evangelism and other outreach programs which are financially demanding. Of course God provides, but, He expects us to achieve high returns from the level of investment which He has placed at our disposal.

This book emphasizes that the fundamental solution for managing money is not vested in the philosophies of the many secular 'financial gurus,' but rather in the pages of the Bible and the observance of the guidelines which are written therein. In fact, many of these philosophies of the 'financial wizards' are extensions of Biblical principles which have been fashioned to modern applications. It is designed to assist Christians to be able to manage their financial affairs in a way which is consistent with the principles of good stewards.

It is recalled that in the Parable of the Stewards, the servants were provided with different amounts of money that is 5, 2 and 1 talents, respectively. One would presume that they were distributed in accordance with the master's assessment of the ability of the individual servants to manage their respective financial resources. In the same way, God has given us various tasks to use in accordance with our ability and capacity to manage them. This does not infer that He will necessarily grant pre-eminence to the person who has generated a higher monetary value or return on resources given. Very often what He requires is that we make the maximum usage of whatever we have at our disposal in addition to our attitude during the process.

> Every financial decision is spiritual in nature, since we are the stewards of God's financial and others resources. We are His, and everything which we have, belongs to Him. We should be in tune with Him for His Guidance before making financial and indeed, every other decision.

SUMMARY

Chapter 1 examines several important aspects of financial management which are highlighted in the Bible. These are practical principles which have been successful, not only in Biblical days but are just as relevant today, even though the level of sophistication of some of them has increased. The Bible often gave room for expansion of some principles even though there are other fundamental issues which are dogmatic.

Chapter 2 reviews several important aspects of financial management as it relates to our relationship with our children. It is vital that parents be adequately educated in Biblical financial matters so that our children will have a firsthand experience of the success of their parents in this vital area of our lives. Even if this is not so in their immediate environment, children, and indeed each person should be aware that the true and lasting answers to money management and other aspects of our lives can be found in the Bible and from our other relationship with the Lord.

Chapter 3 reviews several important issues in financial management which families have to pay particular attention to in order to be classified as prudent stewards. Our call to be the light and salt of the earth is not restricted to 'spiritual' matters but we are to be the leaders in essential areas such as the management of businesses, education, social and other activities in society. We have to show society that we can manage debt and not seek to live like the Jones', for example.

Chapter 4 conducts a micro review of the financial management by married couples. Several prominent psychologists and authorities on religious matters recognize that along with spiritual insecurities, sexuality infidelity and physical health, financial difficulties are a major source of marital conflict. As a matter of fact, the inability of a couple to manage their financial and other material resources may gnaw away at the very fibre of their marriage and infringe on their level of spirituality and other vital areas of their lives as a couple, their relationship as a family and with the wider community.

As the family expands from two to three persons, and in many instances even beyond, so does the need to manage our financial and other resources increase. Chapter 5 examines the importance of conducting efficient budget allocation to adequately cater for the intricate needs of our family, in whom God has invested so much potential. Parents are caretakers of the gems in whom God has invested a unique purpose. Hence, parents have a solemn responsibility to nurture their children in every vital area of their lives to ensure that they grow in conformity with the principles of the Word of God. If we are unable to adequately cater for this God-given responsibility, it is better that we remain childless.

Chapter 5 reviews the important concept of accumulating and yet not hoarding material assets. Hopefully, we are not only 'dancing' in the summer of our lives and expect to have enough to enjoy a financially secured twilight years of our lives. We have a right to enjoy a happy old age. However, it necessitates that we **save and invest prudently** and, of course, have the right relationship with the Lord and those around us.

There is a famous maxim which advocates that 'life begins at forty'. If this is really so, then it necessitates that the responsible Christian should not spend his youthful life like the slothful grasshopper, in the popular children's story, which played and danced during summer instead of storing up food for winter. Therefore, when winter came, he had to go begging for food from the wise and prudent ant. In contrast, the ant worked ardently during the summer and stored up food for the winter. During the winter period he could have afforded to sing and dance, since he was confined to his home with adequate supply of food for himself and family. (A similar incident is highlighted in Proverbs Chapter 6).

Chapter 6 **merges several of the principles which were discussed in previous chapters into a more focused format. Unless we are able from very early in our lives to tap into the area which the Lord wants us to specialize in, we have spent years as underachievers. It is important to identify where we fall in the scale of being able and willing to generate the zero to 100% and higher level of returns in the various areas of our lives, including material affluence. It is also important to recognize the level of returns which would enable us to live a life of what we perceive as being able to enjoy 'more than enough.' Care must be taken that our perceptions and achievements are consistent with the will of the Lord for our lives.**

Gladwin B. Williams BSc., MA

NOTES

****

Chapter 1
FUNDAMENTAL PRINCIPLES OF BIBLICAL FINANCE

INTRODUCTION

This chapter reviews several practical aspects of financial management in the home, at church, on the job and investment opportunities that are available to Christians. It is very restrictive to attempt to confine financial management by Christians to simple budgeting at home. Christians are the light of the world not only in spiritual matters, for we should be the ones who are leading the way in prudent money management and other aspects of our lives.

As Christians, we have to take possession of material resources at our disposal by expanding our personal and/or business assets, the financial resources of the church, community development and other programs. Even when a Christian is 'called' to a life of meager financial standing, he will still have to be wise in financial matters. Even as the late Mother Theresa was dedicated to helping the poor in Calcutta and other impoverished communities, millions of dollars was needed each year to sustain her programs. In addition, money acquired from Christian businesses is often used to support ministries, charitable programs, missionary activities and other worthy causes.

Although special emphasis is focused on reviewing finance from the Christian perspective in this book, even non-Christians who have achieved financial success apply many Biblical principles to their lives. However, there are a number of financial management practices such as tithing which many non-Christians and even Christians deem to be inconsistent with their principles of financial management. It should be noted that Biblical financial management principles are presented as the panacea for eliminating all financial woes. The correct application of several of these important principles will make the management of our material resources more systematic and set us free from unnecessary worry when managing our financial and other resources.

> There is repeated emphasis in the Bible on using money as a vehicle to achieve righteous objectives rather than loving money for itself, as occurs when a person is a miser, or when wealth distracts us from serving the Lord, for example.

Many Churches do not object to Christians engaging in business ventures. In fact, it is commonly believed among Christians that we should generally be the most successful entrepreneurs, who display positive attitude such as honesty, integrity, impeccable character and the wisdom of God to enable us to be prudent and astute in our business and other undertakings. We are expected to be as 'wise as serpents but as gentle as doves.'

There are several successful national and international businesses which are owned and/or managed by Christians. Many of these managers are represented in organizations such as the Full Gospel Businessmen and Full Gospel Businesswomen's Fellowship, which have arms in several countries. Many organizations, such as the Young Men Christian Association (YMCA) and Young Women's Christian Associations (YWCA), Save the Children Fund and Baptist Associations are also involved in promoting entrepreneurship among persons in the communities in which they minister. In addition, most Christians welcome the advancements in science and technology in areas which they can understand and consider which they deem to be directly or indirectly beneficial to humanity, and which are consistent with the principles of the Bible.

This includes the extended use of electricity, motor transportation and life saving medications and operations. However, there are several areas of science and technology that some Christians view with a high degree of scepticism and even condemnation.

Some areas in science and technology that are of concern for many Christians are:

(a) Experiments in an attempt to prove the validity of the theory of evolution,
(b) Several aspects of costly space explorations,
(c) Some aspects of genetic science including areas such as cloning which attempts to reproduce identical human beings, as illustrated in the film 'Boys From Brazil,' and some aspects of Genetically Modified (GM) plants and animals.
(d) Improved abortion techniques and several aspects of the use of stem cells from aborted foetuses,
(e) Several innovations in the technology which facilitate financial transactions,

The last item relates to various aspects of financial innovations, several of which are of concerns to many Christians. Revelation 13: 11 to 18, for example, refer to the formation of a world economic system in which economic transactions will only be conducted via the use of the decoding of the 'Mark of the Beast' (666). This mark will be imprinted on the forehead or hand of persons who have rejected the Gospel and have accepted the leadership of the Anti-Christ. The personal identification code on a person's body will have to be presented to a decoding device for verification. After it is confirmed, they will be able to effect financial and other transactions. Several current practices in the financial system are similar to the principle for the fulfilment of this prophecy. There is the establishment of several economic, political and other alliances which are evident in the single currency, monetary, economic and other unions, such as the European Union. They signal the establishment of the world economic order before the second coming of Christ.

The way the Lord deals with His people is very often different from the worldly interpretation of the management of financial and other issues. We frequently hear of the Lord blessing Christians with much material and other resources, only to instruct them to 'give it all away'. The story does not end there, for as we obey Him, He blesses us, our relatives, the church and others spiritually, financially and otherwise, long beyond the support which was given away. When He finds persons who put Him first in their lives, above wealth, personal aspirations and even their very lives, the Lord is moved to pour into them His bountiful blessings. Indeed there are financial and other blessings which we will derive from giving back of our substance to Him. This principle was highlighted in the lives of Abraham, David and the Apostle Paul, for example. However, the reward is derived in the Lord fulfilling His purpose in that person's life and the other channels which He opens as a result of the willingness of His people to give.

Several types of financial institutions are operating in most countries. They include commercial and other types of banks, insurance companies, building societies, trust companies, the stock market and moneylenders and other traditional saving and lending institutions (particularly in developing countries). The operations of a sample of these institutions are reviewed in this chapter in the light of how their operations affect Christendom.

> Even though we are not all great athletes in the natural, every Christian is a world rated spiritual athlete. Once we follow the Lord, He guarantees that His goodness and mercies will follow us all the days of our lives. His goodness and mercies are overwhelming; therefore, there is no reason why we should not be successful in all endeavors which are consistent with His will.

> Which would you prefer to have? A home where there is much love and contentment, where each member of the family is fulfilling the call of the Lord on their lives, or one in which the family is financially secure and there is no material lack? Christians can have the best of both worlds when we put into practice the philosophy of Joshua, for example, when he stated in Joshua 24: 15(b) "....as for me and my household, we will serve the Lord".

THE BIBLE & FINANCIAL MANAGEMENT

Jesus asked the following question in Luke 9:25: **"25What does it profit them if they gain the whole world, but lose or forfeit themselves?"**

Many Christians have misinterpreted this Scripture to infer that we should not pursue material prosperity or seek to achieve secular prominence. Similarly, it is the view of many Christians that we should not be involved in secular politics, since we are not of this world and our Kingdom is in Heaven. Jesus supported the fact that we are not of this world and that we have a Heavenly Kingdom. However, He noted in Luke 20:25 that we should give (render) to Caesar the things that are Caesar's.

Jesus also demonstrated His obedience to the law of taxation by performing a miracle and He and His disciples secured the money needed to pay their taxes. So, is it a sin if our faith is not strong enough, hence, we choose not to depend on God to perform miracles to enable us to meet all of our financial needs? We are reminded that the Apostle Paul, for example, worked as a tent maker (during his spare time) to support himself and his ministry.

It is not normally sinful to visit a medical doctor and to take medication and even to work to earn a living, unless of course a person is told expressly by the Lord not to do so but to trust Him for their healing. Once we recognize Him as the source of the wisdom of the doctor and the practice by the physician is not contrary to the Word, for example, visiting the doctor is scriptural. However, there are situations such as when the finding of the physicians is that the situation is hopeless, for example, where we may be forced to rely on the miracle-working power of the Lord. Some persons have enough faith and they never visit the doctor, therefore, relying on God to prevent accidents and sickness and healing when they are sick.

Some Christians go to the extent of not visiting a doctor and taking medication, resulting in the death of family members, for example. There are several examples where such parents receive criminal charge when a child or other loved one die when a person is denied access to the necessary medical and other forms of treatment. Secondly, even as we work, we have to recognize that the Lord is the One who guides and protects us as we earn a living. He also grants us special favour with those in authority over us.

> God's desire is that we prosper in every area of our lives, even as our soul prospers. Salvation does not stop with spiritual liberation. It also includes financial, health and the total well being of every aspect of our lives. There are, however, several important principles which we have to adhere to on a consistent basis. They include being in continuous communication with Him, and following His leadership.

We are admonished in 1 Thessalonians 4:11 to work with our hands and not to depend on anyone. We also have a responsibility to encourage the expansion of the Gospel, to pursue financially rewarding careers and to excel in all of our financial and other endeavours.

> If we are to prosper in all things, even as our soul prospers, isn't it an unbalanced life if we are growing in spiritual matters when we are facing 'hell' to pay our bills and meet our other material obligations instead of enjoying at least a comfortable standard of living?

Many prominent preachers have expounded on what they sometimes referred to as the '**theology of prosperity**.' One preacher propagates that:

"**If pimps and 'drug lords' drive fancy cars, live in the best houses, wear the most expensive clothing and eat the best foods, then Christians should enjoy even more.**" His rationale is that our Heavenly Father has riches untold, and as heirs and joint-heirs with Jesus, we should enjoy a part of this fortune on earth. In addition, we have a Heavenly Father who is far more loving and caring than any earthly father. Therefore, according to this theology, poor Christians:

(a) May not be receiving the correct teaching on this important principle,

(b) Lack enough faith to claim what is rightfully ours,

(c) May not be living according to Biblical principles of financial prosperity, unless they deliberately prefer to live materially humble lives,

2 Corinthians 8:4 states: "**⁴For you know the generous acts of our Lord Jesus Christ, that though He was rich, yet for your sakes He became poor, so that by His poverty you might become rich.**"

> Some persons are wealthy, yet they are humble, while others are poor and haughty. Christians, who are wealthy, by their very nature, should also be humble.

The more conservative, and possibly the more popular view, is that we should not be engrossed in acquiring wealth. Luke 18:25 states: "**²⁵Indeed it is easier for a camel to go through the eye of a needle than for someone who is rich to enter the Kingdom of God.**"

This verse confirms that **it is possible** that a materially wealthy person can be a Christian. There are numerous examples of persons in the Bible who served Jehovah who were very wealthy in accordance to the material standards of their day. They included Abraham, Job, King David and King Solomon. Even though Jesus chose not to possess much material assets, His cloak, for example was very expensive. In addition, carpentry was an occupation which commanded high wage and much respect among the community. One also wonders what happened with all of the gifts which Jesus was presented when He was a baby. In addition, several wealthy persons supported Jesus' ministry.

In the early Church, as described in the book of Acts, many believers who had material possessions such as house and land, either shared them where possible, or sold them and shared the proceeds with others. However, there is no evidence to suggest that Christianity is synonymous with living in material poverty. If that were so, how then will we fulfil our obligations to adequately cater to the financial needs of our families, assist the needy and support the financing of the Gospel? The upkeep of ministries and spreading of the gospel have high financial demands. Can we as believers expect the unrighteous to finance the spreading of the gospel; secondly, does it bring glory to God when we have to beg the unsaved to fund the Lord's work? It is true that the Lord often uses the unsaved to provide for His people.

Once we are able to understand that **money is a tool and not a means in itself**, we are on our way to manage money as the Lord expects us to. On a macro level, money (capital) is used to finance the provision of services such as medical, education and other social services, infrastructure facilities such as roads, potable water and other amenities by the government. These facilities are financed from sources such as taxes, the sale of treasury bills, debentures, bonds and other securities. Bilateral, multilateral aid, grants, loans and other contributions may also be provided by international agencies, other governments, Non Government Organizations (NGOs) and other agencies. Money is also important to finance the production of the goods and services which we need.

> 1 Timothy 6:6-10 states: "⁶*Of course, there is great gain in godliness combined with contentment, ⁷for we brought nothing into the world, so that we can take nothing out of it; ⁸but if we have food and clothing, we have to be content with these. ⁹But those who want to be rich fall into temptation and are trapped by many senseless and harmful desires that plunge people into ruin and destruction. ¹⁰For the love of money is a root of all kinds of evil, and in their eagerness to be rich some have wandered away from the faith and pierced themselves with many pains.*"

On the micro level, money is needed by the family to purchase items such as food and clothing and for the payment of services such as utility bills and the cost of transportation. Money is also needed to enable persons to perform spiritual functions such the payment of tithes and the giving of offering, helping the poor and for supporting missionaries and other methods of financing the promotion of the Gospel.

The acquisition of financial wealth can be obtained by several methods. They include unscriptural practices such as:

(a) Engaging in dishonest practices such as the sale of narcotics, illegal arms and ammunition, tax evasion, gambling and the smuggling of precious metals,

(b) Robbing others of their possessions by breaking and entering their homes,

defrauding them, and by coveting the possessions of others,
(c) Stealing from employers and other agencies,
(d) Gambling and prostitution,

Scriptural methods of acquiring material resources include:
(a) Pursuing lucrative career opportunities such as owning and/or managing a well established business entity, a successful career as a musician, actor/actress, established farmers, holding a senior management office and also careers such as a surgeon, judge, senior government official and other offices at the national level,
(b) Enjoying the blessing of inheriting substantial amount of finance and other assets from their parents or others,
(c) Making prudent business decisions and investing money and other assets wisely,

There are many ministers of the gospel who have acquired much wealth as a result of the significant growth of their church and the fact that members are faithful in their giving of finances and other resources to the church, hence, they are paid a handsome salary, receive several fringe benefits such as a furnished house and motor vehicle, possibly paid an attractive annual bonus and receive an attractive pension. A minister may also receive substantial 'love offerings' when he ministers at conferences and at other churches locally and internationally and also use such forums to sell tape, video and/or CDs of his messages, books and other items which they produce or that of other members of their congregation. Some ministries also have a team of aggressive sales personnel who market tapes, CDs, literature and other products of the organization. A ministry may also have a private school, university or other training centres which students have to pay to attend.

The first list highlights a number of methods such as robbing and drug trafficking in which Christians should not be involved since these activities destroy the body and condemns the souls of the perpetrator. Christian should not seek after wealth for selfish reasons and to manipulate others because of the influence which a wealthy person can exhort over the poor. Rather, the wealthy should use their resources as a means of improving the standard of living of their family, the community as a whole, and to spread the Gospel. There are several tangible ways in which the wealthy can assist their community. They include:

(a) Establishing legitimate business ventures which would create jobs for members of the society,
(b) Fund needy causes such as orphanages, homes for the elderly and destitute, and contributing generously to other charitable events,
(c) Establishing scholarships and other programs which would assist poorer persons to improve their standard of living,
(d) Contributing towards the establishment and maintenance of libraries, sports complexes, and other services which would benefit the community,
(e) Paying their taxes and contributing to other funds which will provide the revenue necessary to facilitate infrastructural activities such as health, education and other social services,

An interesting passage to meditate on is Proverbs 10:15, which states: "[15]**The wealth of the rich is their fortress; the poverty of the poor is their ruin.**"

It is no secret that the majority of wealthy persons who are not Christians use their wealth to exploit the poor. This reality is vividly demonstrated in so many historical events and is prevalent in most societies today. The exploitation by the rich of the poor is evident in slavery which existed in several societies in the world. The exploitation of domestic servants, children and women in 'sweat shops' and other occurrences, are examples of the rich exploiting the poor. Many persons have transferred their material wealth into political and other power because of the influence which wealth wheels in most societies. This influence has often been used to pervert the course of justice, where the rich commit crimes and they are able to bribe the jury, judge and other officials and have verdicts made in their favor.

There are many examples which can be referred to attest to the truth of the first part of the above verse. The home of the wealthy are usually constructed with the best building materials which they can purchase. This is not only to make their home fashionable and comfortable but also to protect them from intruders. Some of the features of such homes may include:

(a) Sturdy walls, doors, windows and other protective devices,
(b) Iron grills to reinforce the protection of the occupants,
(c) Very high concrete, chain-link and/or other types of fencing which may be supported by special material at the top which will seriously injure a person who attempts to climb over,
(d) There may be electronically controlled gates and garage doors,
(e) Security personnel may be employed to provide twenty-four hours protection. They may also be surveillance cameras which are constantly monitored by security personnel,
(f) The house may be surrounded by a wide expansion of lawn, where intruders can be easily identified if they were able to enter the estate and approach the house,
(g) The home is usually staffed by servants who would defend the household in the event that an intruder was able to enter the premises,
(h) The wealthy may also be protected by security guards when they are in public places,
(i) The mansions of the wealthy are usually located in exclusive neighborhoods where one would need special security clearance before entering,

The contrast also holds for the poor making one wonder if the two groups are living in the same world and even the same society. It is common to find slums in close proximity to luxury homes and commercial centers. This is a common sight even in affluent countries.

As Christians, we have several financial responsibilities:
- **Spiritual Obligations** such as tithes and offering, helping the poor and needy as onto the Lord,
- **Statutory Requirements to the government** such as the payment of Income Tax, National Insurance and other government contribution from individuals and institutions,
- **Personal and Family Obligations** such as to budgeting wisely and as far as possible spending according to the budget, saving and investing prudently in order to achieve short, medium and long-terms goals,
- **Contributing to the development of our society** such as being good corporate citizens, for example; our contribution to society,

The Lord may not blesses a person materially until he is ready to use the blessing to bless others, unless of course, He is using the situation to demonstrate the extent of His mercies, for example. Hence, as we give, He may replenish and increase what we have so that we can give even more. This is the foundation of the riches of King Solomon, for example, who requested wisdom so that he could be a blessing to the people whom he led. In return God granted him abundant wealth, power and other attributes.

God has blessed each one of us with various resources, even the spastic and mentally retarded and physically challenged have their place of importance in the mosaic of God's beautiful garden. Even though our talent would not lead all of us to extra ordinary amount of wealth, it would not leave us in poverty either. Like the believers after the Day of Pentecost, the rich should assist the poor.

EXTENDING & RECEIVING FINANCIAL BLESSINGS

Proverbs 11:24, 25 admonishes us that: **"²⁴Some give freely, yet grow all the richer, others withhold what is due,** *and only suffer want. ²⁵A generous person will be enriched, and one who gives water will get water."*

I have not come across any scripture passages which prohibit a person from acquiring a substantial amount of material resources once it is obtained and expanded legitimately and it is used in the correct way. As a matter of fact, many of the prophets, kings and other persons whom the Lord classified as being close to Him were enormously wealthy. Examples of such persons are Job, Abraham, King David and Solomon. In contrast, there were also persons such as the widows who were poor and also received special commendation for their faithfulness as demonstrated by the poor widow who gave of her last coin to the Lord (the Parable of the Widow's mite). There are also several examples of wealthy persons in the Bible who misused their wealth and power to exploit others. They include Queen Jezebel. The 'rich young ruler' was also an example of a person who idolized his riches. Some of the primary negative criticisms which are levelled against persons who are wealthy are that:

(a) Wealth is idolized so that their earthly possessions are more important than serving God,

(b) Persons do not give thanks and recognize the source of their wealth and their very lives is Jehovah,

(c) They use their wealth and power to exploit the poor instead of helping others,

(d) They are more attached to the accumulation and expansion of earthly wealth rather that investing their treasury, time and talent for eternal wealth,

There are numerous examples of the tremendous blessings which persons receive when they give freely to others and to the Lord. Many persons are selective in their giving of money and other gifts to some beggars, for example, because of factors such as:

(a) **Some persons would not give money to a male beggar** since they feel that he may have wasted his youthful days on riotous living and as a result he is now being punished for his evil deeds.

(b) **Some persons would not give money to a young beggar** whose eyes and other mannerism may suggest that one may be a drug addict, smokes cigarettes or consumes alcoholic beverages, for example, since they would be contributing to the further destruction of the body and soul of the consumers of these products and to the disadvantage of their families and society as a whole.

(c) It is import to discern the differences between persons with genuine needs versus persons who are 'con-artists' – tricksters, and persons who would use monetary contributions to feed an addiction. A possible solution is to provide a person who is a drug addict, for example, non-monetary gifts such as food. Where possible, assistance can also be extended to offer such a person a job which would enable him to get on to the course of financial independence. **Like the Apostle Paul and Barnabas, every Christian is endowed with the authority to give spiritual deliverance to persons who are affected by problems which may be manifested in natural terms such as poverty, sickness and addictions.**

> **Hospitality to Strangers**
> Hebrews 13:2 states: "Do not neglect to show hospitality to strangers, for in doing that some have entertained angels without knowing it."

Many persons are apprehensive about entertaining strangers in their homes for they fear of possibly being robbed by a crook disguised as a destitute person or by a person who might be a psychopath or a child molester. However, hospitality is not limited to entertaining a stranger at one's home. Visiting the sick in hospital, prisoners, the home of the elderly, where one can carry little gifts to them and/or even share the Word with them, can go a long way in fulfilling this command.

For many persons the habit of giving is a family and even cultural tradition. Even non-Christians have identified the tremendous blessings which occur as a result of giving by individuals, family, business entities, governments and other agencies. Even if they are initially poor, many givers usually receive spiritual, material and other forms of blessing as a direct benefit of giving. Givers can be undertaken in ways such as:

(a) The offer of beverage and/or food items visitors, Providing a regular source of food and other items to homes for spastic children, the elderly and other charitable organizations,

(b) Adopting a destitute child or children, and for the wealthier persons and for those with a higher level of faith; establishing a home for street children, the handicapped or other needy persons in the society to benefit from.

(c) Donating money, clothing, food, books and other items to the poor, charitable organizations, to national and international disaster relief fund and other worthy causes,

(d) Many persons have an elaborate birthday party, thanksgiving and other ceremonies where they invite their relatives, friends and even total strangers to celebrate a special event and to offer thanks to God for the mile stone which was attained. They may also establish important contacts with persons who attended the function, which may serve them well in the future.

(e) It is a practice in many communities that a person donates at least 10% of their first and subsequent salary to their church body, and/or to a charitable organization and/or to purchase items such as sweets, cakes and/or other items and give them to beggars and other poor persons.

(f) Many persons work as volunteers; giving of their time, professional expertise, financial and other resources to charitable organizations, working in impoverished communities in developed countries, developing countries, and for other causes.

It is important that acts of kindness be not extended only as an investment with the express purpose of receiving a blessing or net return. Rather, such acts should be out of a heart of love, where the giver would perform such a service even if there is no reward to be received. It is a fact, however, that every act of kindness will be justly rewarded by the Lord, even if we do not receive even a word of gratitude from the receiver.

The practice of giving has been used by the devil as a counterfeit to produce and maintain material possessions, supernatural powers and for other reasons. Persons would offer up money, food and other items to the devil (in the name of the ancestors and/or others) after which it is distributed to the needy and even friends and loved ones. Some persons offer money, animals or other items, themselves, members of their family and others as a sacrifice so that they can receive material wealth or 'spiritual' endowments. Items offered up as a sacrifice to the devil and distributed to others may have a negative effect on persons who accept them who are not covered under the 'blood of the Lamb'.

There are instances where parents would 'offer a child to the devil' in order to receive prosperity, that their business would progress and to fulfill other desires. That child may become crippled or suffer from some other physical, mental, spiritual or other defects while the family business or other goals are accomplished. Such families usually have to continue to make annual sacrifices and conduct other rituals in order to maintain the activity for which the sacrifice was made. Thankfully, as Christians we do not have to engage in such practices since God has provided us with the only way to lasting material, spiritual and other blessings; the benefits of which may be manifested for generations and which will be pleasing in His sight. The crucifixion of Jesus was the perfect sacrifice which was made for our redemption and continual success in this life and for eternity.

It is important to be selective in our giving, but we should not be always judgmental since our giving is a ministry which the Lord can use to bless others. Matthew 7:6 states: "**⁶Do not give what is holy to dogs; and do not throw your pearls before swine, or they will trample them under foot and turn and maul you.**"

The above passage pertains to some of the issues which Jesus addressed during His encounter with the Gentile woman in Mark 7:26-30, whose daughter was demon possessed and she was entreating Jesus to cast the demon out of her daughter. Verse 27, 28 states: "**²⁷He said to her, "Let the children be fed first, for it is not fair to take the children's food and throw it to the dogs." ²⁸But she answered Him, "Sir, even the dogs under the table eat the children's crumbs."**

Jesus was impressed with the faith of the mother and he cast the demon out of her daughter.

We can conclude that there is a right and a wrong way in giving, so that we can benefit from the blessings of the Lord and that our giving will be a blessing to the receiver. (Some of the attributes of a cheerful giver are discussed in Chapter Four). As we give to others and to the Lord, we will receive bountiful blessings in return).

> God has not promised us a 'bed of roses' in the present life. As a matter of fact, Jesus told His disciplines that His followers must be prepared to suffer afflictions and adversities as a result of following Him. As we choose to shun unscriptural practices such as stealing, and gambling, we will be rewarded on earth and in the life after since we will be enjoying His presence in our life and other spiritual and material benefits.

Many persons enjoy giving to others but they have difficulties to accept items offered by others. They often exhibit a sense of false humility by rejecting gifts which are genuinely offered by others. Even though the Bible identifies that it is better to give than to receive, the Bible also expands on the blessings which are inherent in receiving gifts offered by others. In accepting a genuine gift the receiver releases blessing to the giver. It would therefore hinder the blessing of the giver if the receiver refuses to accept the gift which is being offered. Many persons because of pride, hidden hatred or for other reasons refuse to accept a gift which is offered by another person.

Similar to the experience of the Apostle Paul on his way to Damascus, the Lord may 'put a person's backs to the wall' and instruct another person who one may even despise to offer what he needs. In refusing the gift, the needy person would be rejecting the ultimate source of all good gifts, the Lord, while it leaves an unfulfilled need in his life. If we reflect on the way the Lord used the widow to house and feed the Prophet Elijah, we can identify the importance of persons being good givers and also receivers. If the widow was not an obedient giver and receiver, then she and her sons may not have been able to benefit from the miracle of the Lord through the Prophet Elijah providing the oil, and her sons may have been sold as slaves.

When a person continues to reject the gifts which the Lord is using the giver to provide due to his ingratitude, pride and other sinful reasons, the Lord will eventually cause the 'brook' to become dry. Unless that person repents of his sin of disobedience and accepts the gift, he may be denied other blessing in the future. The potential receiver may suffer for the continual want of that gift or in other areas of his life since he obstructed the fulfillment of the blessings of the giver by rejecting the gift. The giver may be directed to other persons where he can exercise his willingness to give, or at the extreme, he may become barren since there is no source of outlet for his quest to give.

Many pastors and other church officials suffer from physical exertion, financial and other lack because they are reluctant to accept the gifts offered by members of their congregation and other persons. This is very often because they do not want to be perceived as 'parasites'. They may use the example of the apostle Paul who refused to accept the financial support from the churches which he founded, even though he emphasized the principle of the church supporting its minister as a right to which he and other church officials were entitled. There are, however, some 'unruly' members of the congregations who use their 'gifts' and the salary from the tithes and offering of members of the church in an attempt to control the leadership style and even the types of sermons which the pastor preaches. Persons who use money and other methods to manipulate the work of the Lord will face the wrath of God. Many such persons suffer from serious illnesses, poverty and other difficulties as a result of this practice.

Since there is no giver unless there is a receiver, the two practices must work in unison. For this reason the Lord attributes a blessing to both processes, even though giving in the right spirit attracts a larger quantum of blessing.

> Even after a person asked, knocked and sought, he may still be financially poor. The Lord gives to us discernment, wisdom, direction in areas such as our health, spiritual and other attributes. He also provides blessings using methods such as inheritance, promotion on our job and increased profitability of our business.

IS MONEY THE ROOT TO ALL EVIL?

It is common knowledge that nothing in the natural world is inherently free. This statement is presented from a human standpoint that *nothing comes from nothing*. A price has to be paid for the production of goods and for the provision of services, even if the final users do not incur a monetary or other cost in acquiring it. This reality can be identified in several occurrences. Santa Claus, for example, supposedly goes around on the night before Christmas with his bag filled with gifts for the 'good little boys and girls,' whose eyes will be gleaming on Christmas day to see their stockings filled with toys and other gifts.

We are aware that the Santa Claus whom the little boy saw kissing his mommy (as highlighted in the song 'I Saw Mommy Kissing Santa Claus') and he was seriously debating with his friends whether he should tell his daddy, was in fact his father, disguised as Santa Claus. He did not realize that the gifts were in fact given to him by his parents. However, in the supernatural realm, God said, for example, 'let there be light and there was light' Genesis 1:3(b). He spoke the Word, and the world and all that is in it was created.

Parents should not perpetuate a lie such as Santa Claus presenting free gifts to their children. Even at a charitable or other gift distribution program the source of the financing of the gifts should be explained to the child. **The lie of Santa Clause is merely Satan using one of his deceptive ploys in an attempt to detract the center stage of the birth of Jesus. It obviously is no coincidence that the mere movement of the 'N' two places to the left of SATAN we have SANTA.**

Even though the air which we breathe is often propagated as, being free in that we do not have to literally pay to inhale it, we are increasingly being made aware that a very high price tag is attached to ensuring that we breathe clean air. The publicity surrounding issues such as environmental pollution, the continual destruction of the ozone layer and the necessity to alleviate the possibility of a nuclear holocaust, for example, are all topical issues. Increasing emphasis is also being placed on the necessity of decreasing environmental destruction, even as the human race pursues programs in an attempt to eradicate poverty and promote technological advancement. Many of the programs promoted by some governments, national and international agencies are suspect, since there are usually conditionalities which have to be fulfilled before a country qualifies for funding and also how the funds one used, even though the grant or soft loan may not promote the sustainable economic development of the country.

Jesus declared that we will always have poor people among us. However, as Christians we are obligated to focus on reducing the number of poor and also to consistently seek to reduce poverty as we promote the economic, social and spiritual development of our communities and beyond.

Some of the issues from the second part of the above song alluded to earlier, focuses on love. Common questions are important in understanding what love is:

(a) Is it a gift?
(b) Is it a commodity that can be bought and sold?
(c) Can it be earned?

Here again, we may be familiar with the fact that men and women often prostitute their bodies and soul under the guise of **buying and selling 'love'**. Such temporary gratification obviously cannot be pure, unadulterated Agape love. In contrast, Eros or erotic love is such an important aspect of the lives of many persons that they spend a significant amount of time fantasizing about the life one would live "if I were a rich man". Many persons also spend most of their lifetime in pursuit of wealth in order to attain a lavish life style and also in an attempt to attain the power, economic, social and/or political power which wealthy persons often enjoy.

Regardless of how we perceive love, it is one of the strongest emotions on which our lives, society and the world thrive. In the name of love for each other, Romeo and Juliet, for example, were willing to overlook the feud between their relatives and openly confessed their love for each other to the point where they felt that they could not live without each other. It is noted, however, that they defiled one of the primary principles of the Bible as detailed in the Ten Commandments – Exodus 20:13 states: **"You shall not murder."** which include committing suicide. For the love of his country, a soldier is often willing to lay down his or her life. For the love of this sinful world, Jesus gave up His throne in Glory and came to die for our redemption. In each of the examples, we can recognize a common trait; there was a price associated with the demonstration of love, even though the price cannot always be measured in monetary terms. In these three examples, the price was that of human lives.

There are several items which are philosophized as being beyond the purchasing power of money. They include:
(a) A baby's smile,
(b) True happiness and contentment,
(c) The formation of a home where love, peace and joy abound, in contrast to merely living in a house where there is constant disagreement,

If we were to analyze the first example, several interesting observations can be made. The most likely conclusion would be that liquid money (such as notes, coins and checks) would not induce the smile of a baby unless someone playfully dangles it before the child's face, for example. Yet money is an essential requirement to purchase the necessities which will enable the child to be healthy and happy. Inducing a smile from a healthy child is usually easier than from a child who is dehydrated due to sickness or an acute shortage of water due to a drought, or a child crying from hunger or sickness.

The Bible highlights the importance of money in 1 Timothy 6:10, which states: **"¹⁰For the love of money is a root of all kinds of evil, and in their eagerness to be rich, some have wandered away from the faith and pierced themselves with many pains**." – underline, mine

This verse is often misinterpreted to infer that Christians should abandon all desire to accumulate material wealth, since it ultimately leads a person to focus so much on material possessions that it would become an obsession or his god, and he would eventually forsake serving Jehovah. The verse rather decries lusting after it, which will cause persons to sell their very souls, in some instances, in an attempt to acquire it. Christians are not expected to be misers, as is portrayed in the life of the legendary Charles Dickens' character Mr. Scrooge. Neither are we to love money merely for the joy of having it, for the power that can be exerted over others when we have it, nor are we to indulge in sinful acts to acquire it, or to maintain and expand the amount which we have. Jesus admonished us in Matthew 22:21 that we should: *"²¹**Render unto Caesar the things which are Caesar's."***

From this verse we can infer that we should pay our taxes, contribute towards the development of society and be involved in other legitimate activities. Unless we live in a society where barter (the exchange of goods and services without the use of money) is in operation, we need money (notes and coins or at least a replica of money such as checks, credit or debit card) to purchase the necessities of life. We can reflect on the lives of Monks, Yogi and Sages, for example, who often relinquish 'worldly attachments' to live a life of seclusion. However, for most of us, money plays an important part in our lives.

> **Contradicting Concept of Wealth**
> Many unbelievers view wealth as providing power, where one has to be greedy, selfish and indulge in dishonest practices if necessary in order to acquire, maintain and expand it.
> **Christ teaches that wealth comes from God and we must acquire wealth honestly, with the commitment to use it to also be a blessing to those around us and to spread His word by giving, hence, we will receive more than we give so that we can keep on giving.**

Very often we engage in a financial transaction which incurs costs without recognizing it. A typical example is the neglect of attaching a cost to the labour input of the wife and children in a family business. In addition, the domestic services of girls and women often attract little significance since it is propagated that they are conducting duties for which they were created to perform. If we were to attach a cost to many of these activities, our lives will be greatly enriched since we will recognize the significant contributions of others.

> *Greed is desiring to, and keeping all or most of our financial and other resources for ourselves, family and friends without a willingness to give to the Lord, to help the poor and to give to others without a selfish motive.*

There are several reasons why money is held by private individuals. They include:
   (a) Defraying everyday expenditures such as purchasing food and the payment of utility bills (**transactional**),
   (b) Financing emergencies such as sickness and bereavements (**precautionary**),
   (c) Savings for future needs such as the education of children and to purchase a house (**store of value**),
   (d) Engaging in investments that have the potential to increase one's earning power in business ventures and investing on the stock market, for example (**speculation**),
   (e) Conducting spiritual duties such as paying tithes and giving offering and helping the poor ('**Kingdom business**'),

A person who takes out an endowment life insurance policy, for example, may be more interested in catering for the financial needs of his/her family in the event of the serious incapacitation or death of the policyholder. Conversely, an investor on the stock exchange might be more interested in increasing his wealth, although it is often used as a long-term investment. A common practice by many persons is to hold one or more bank accounts and investing in securities while they hold liquid cash, credit cards and/or check book/s, saving accounts to finance their daily expenditure.

> **_An Important Question which Every Christian Must Answer_**
> Why are you following the Lord? Is it only for His benefits or is it because you are willing to give even of your very life in order to serve Him and to proclaim His word? Sadly, many Christians remain at the stage of desiring the 'fish and bread' and to see miracles and the spectacular. As important as these experiences are, our desire should be to know Him on an intimate basis, to make disciples of men and demonstrate other attributes which depicts spiritual maturity. In fulfilling His purposes, we will also receive the benefits of His blessings.

Does the command to 'live by faith' imply that we should leave all financial decisions to God and allow Him to direct our path, so we merely fold our hands and wait on Him? Jehovah has given us wisdom to enable us to be prudent managers of financial and other resources which He places at our disposal. Joseph, for example, used the wisdom of God to enable him to amass much wealth and power (Genesis 41). It is noted that Joseph was chosen by God to go to Egypt for the special purpose of preserving the Israelites in their hour of need.

> Loving money or anything else more than we love Jehovah is idolatry.

A story is told of a woman who was at home alone when she saw three elderly strangers sitting outside of her home. Being a hospitable person, she went outside and invited them into her house so that she could offer them a meal. The men refused, sighting that they will not enter the home of a married woman when she was home alone least it caused contention with her husband and other persons. When her husband returned from work he also invited them in and they refused. Feeling very offended at the refusal of his kindness he inquired from them what was the basis for their refusal. Before giving an explanation, of their action, the men told him that they usually do not enter a home together, and would only do this on the odd circumstance when the occupants of a home make what they have come to recognize is a most unpopular choice.

The visitors told the homeowner that their names were **Love, Wealth;** and **Happiness,** and that all three of them would only enter his home if he first invited the leader among them. Since he was a wise man, the homeowner requested that **Love** should first come into the home. With his choice, all three men got up and went into the home. They explained that persons who choose **Wealth**, then **Love** and **Happiness** would seldom enjoy their lives since such families are usually too engrossed in acquiring wealth to place much emphasis on love and togetherness among members of the family. The men also explained that they did not usually come into the home when the wife or the husband is at home alone, since if one spouse alone acquires wealth, for example, without the other knowing the source of it, or one is selfish and is not willing to share the wealth among loved ones and others, it usually causes enmity in the home and in the community. Similarly, if **Happiness** is selected as the first choice, the other two would not normally enter the house, since in the quest to acquire happiness many persons are led astray by accepting temporary gratification which often leads to further unhappiness and other negative effects such as drug addiction and sexual and transmitted diseases and other misfortunes.

Deuteronomy 8:18 states: "[18]**But remember the Lord your God, for it is He who gives you power to get wealth, so that He may confirm his covenant that He swore to your ancestors, as He is doing today**."

This was an admonishment to the Children of Israel which can also be applied to the lives of individuals today. This scripture confirms that God does not pour wealth into a person's pocket, per se´, rather He empowers His people to acquire wealth. This principle of the wisdom of God empowering persons to become wealthy can be identified in the lives of several persons in the Bible such as Job, David, Solomon, Joseph, Abraham and Jacob. In these examples we are told that they received specific revelations of principles which enabled them to amass much wealth. Even though the methods may differ, the application of His wisdom enabled these men to become wealthy.

The principle of God giving us the power to become wealthy is still applicable today, for there are numerous Christians who are rich materially as well in wisdom, hospitality and other aspects of their lives. Many of these persons are involved in giving in abundance to charities, to various foundations, financing the spreading of the gospel, creating employment opportunities for thousands of persons through their business, ministries and other organizations.

Is the above verse insinuating that all Christians will become materially wealthy since we all have the same Heavenly Father who created the world and everything that is in it? It should be noted that the Bible does not confine the definition of wealth to material possessions but also include:

(a) Our abundance of spiritual authority such as the weapons of our spiritual warfare,
(b) Protection of our health – by His stripes we were healed,
(c) He would not see His children begging bread,
(d) Abundance of blessings in our home, work, for our family,
(e) The blessing of having the Holy Spirit guiding us, the Lord making intercessions for us, angels protecting us and other advantages,
(f) The blessing of the spiritual gifts operating in the church and other forms of support for the individual and to other believers,

(g) The fact that we have an inheritance with the Father, the angels and the other saints when we die,

> Methods of acquiring wealth:
> - Work
> - Inheritance
> - Returns on assets
> - Imputed blessings from the Lord (favor).

ACQUIRING AND MANAGING MATERIAL RESOURCES

There are four basic ways in which a Christian can acquire wealth. They are to:

(a) **Earn it** from his salary, income from a business venture, or from a professional sport (such as professional athletes, cricketers, footballers, baseball and basketball players),

(b) **Receive an inheritance and other forms of blessings** from a relative or some other benevolent person. This is prevalent where the children and other relatives are included in the will of a deceased person,

(c) **Return on assets** – in this mode, a person receives additional wealth from returns from savings, and from personal and/or corporate or business investments,

(d) **Imputed** means such as from the **unmerited blessings from the Lord or favor.** It is true that as heirs and joint heirs with Jesus and the fact that we are in a covenant relationship with the Lord, there are several blessings which are inherent with this relationship. However, the Lord often blesses us merely as a demonstration of His love for us and also to use us to 'show off' His mercies as illustrated in the life of Job. 'We do not deserve it, yet we are blessed.' This is often demonstrated in activities such 'men giving to us,' surprise job promotion, the receipt of a substantial inheritance, the Holy Spirit often births and develops investments and other revelations which enable us to acquire financial and other blessings.

There is hardly a sane adult who would enter a marriage with the preconception that throughout their marriage they will live in abject poverty, with no foreseeable opportunity or plan to significantly improve their standard of living. Even though the initial stage of the marriage may not be as the couple may have desired, the more ambitious couples would consistently work arduously at improving their standard of living. The financial position of the family would improve substantially as the couple prayerfully plan and execute their plans in unison. For this reason many couples are willing to forgo even the high standard of living which they may have been accustomed to prior to their marriage in order to acquire their own material possession as a family unit.

The Christian couple who attend a Pre-marital Counseling program would usually be asked by the Marriage Counselors for them to explain the strategies which they have agreed on to manage the financial responsibilities of marriage. A review may also be made of the assets which they are taking into the marriage. They may include:

(a) The amount of salary earned by one or both of them, and the potential for and efforts which are being made to improve the strength of their material resources. This would include if they are embarking on acquiring other skills to enable them to command a higher salary and/or engage in other activities which have the potential to significantly improve their standard of living.

(b) If they are involved in one or several business ventures, they may be asked whether or not plans are afoot to increase their net income generating capacity of the business by expanding current operations and/or diversifying into a new product range, expanding to other locations and generally to 'grow the business'.

(c) The likelihood of their parents or other relatives leaving an inheritance from them,

The option of winning the pools, national bingo or lottery or other forms of gambling would not be considered as appropriate financial decision for a Christian to pursue. Christians are expected to use their talent to earn as comfortable a standard of living as possible for them and their family. This may include engaging in activities such as establishing a cottage industry, farming, selling of fruits and vegetables, rearing of animals such as poultry, cows, sheep on a commercial level which they can conduct as their sole or primary source of income or at least as an additional source of income. Persons who are so inclined, may engage in income generating activities such as singing professionally, playing a musical instrument, paint and/or engage in the production of craft items or carving, for example.

> The fundamental principle of lasting spiritual and material prosperity and in every aspect of our lives is to give our lives to the Lord. We then have to observe **all** of His commands including giving of our tithes and offering, time, talents and assisting the poor and needy, so that He can give us more than we need personally and to enable us to give to others.

As outlined earlier, it is important that we have a vision in our lives as individuals and also as a family, and in other areas of our lives such as our business activities. The following principles are reiterated in Habakkuk 2:2, 3: "²*Then the Lord answered me and said: Write the vision; make it plain on the tablets, so that a runner who passes may read. ³For there is still a vision for the appointed*

time; it speaks of the end, and does not lie. If it seems to tarry, wait for it, it will surely come, it will not delay."

It is important that Christian parents have a macro broad vision for themselves and the family unit as a guide, and as a source of inspiration and a reminder of what their objectives are. In the same way there can also be micro visions for individual areas of their lives such as what they expect to achieve in a business venture and material possessions which the family is aspiring to acquire over a given time period. The projections are usually based on what the couple brought into the marriage, what is realistically within their ability to achieve, and what they believe God will provide. The projections can be subdivided into short, medium and long term goals. The propriety and composition of such a statement will be based on the projected earning capacity of the family and projected expenditure.

Material security should not be the primary reason for a woman to agree to marry a suitor or *vise versa*. However, it is at least important that a responsible suitor be in a position to show that he will be well able to adequately provide for his family in the near future such as after graduation from an academic or vocational institution. The question which is often asked in this area is what about Christians living in poorer communities or where one is called to serve in such a community. It is noted that the Lord has promised to satisfy all of our needs and not our wants, once we walk in all of His Ways. There are occasions when the Lord, like the good Father that He is, will 'spoil' us and meet even our wants. However, we should be like Job and be prepared to serve Him even if He chooses not to deliver us from a life of material want.

After attaining, by God's grace, a significant target, a couple often reminisces on the struggles which they underwent and how the Lord gave them the inspiration and encouragement, grace and strength to successfully achieve their objectives. As mile stones are achieved, the couple will be challenged to launch out for others. Nevertheless, it is important that the couple should strive to enjoy periods of **rest**, where they can sit back and enjoy the fruits of their labor, not only during their formative years but by going on vocation together, possibility every year or so, and even in other ways on a consistent basis. This does not mean that life loses its meaning after this stage, for there are always targets to be achieved in some area of our lives as individuals and as a family for as long as we live.

During the process of working to achieve important targets, a couple usually has to make strenuous sacrifices. Unless a couple has mastered the process of cleaving, their marriage can be plagued with much tension from attempting to conserve on spending, even in vital areas on some occasions. For this reason it is important that both spouses are fully committed to the plans and it is not merely one spouse superimposing their will on the other. There is also a need to consistently assure each other that they are working for the common good of the family, and that the intensive sacrifices will not be throughout the marriage. It is also vital that such projections take into account the needs for periods of relaxation and review of plans to assess whether or not the sacrifice is having any serious negative effect on any member of the family or other persons. A review should also be made of strategies which can be used to improve the output or return of the project.

There are several philosophies pertaining to the management of materials assets which are important to families. They include:

(a) That the husband is the provider, hence, it is his responsibility to provide assets such as a well furnished house, where possible, some means of transportation, and be in a position to provide entirely for, or at least be the primary bread winner of the family.

(b) A wife who enters marriage with just about all of the materials amenities, (according to the norms of the society), already provided by her husband, would have missed out on the unique opportunity of the couple lovingly planning and implementing their plans over a number of years.

(e) Contrary to the previous point, many couples would be more at peace if they did not have to struggle together to attain 'basic' material resources. Years of struggle to achieve assets such as a house and car, educate the children, for example, can create much tension and dissatisfaction, particularly if the couple have not bonded to a very high degree and they have communication and other serious marital challenges. A wife or husband, in some traditional society, even among Christians, may have to provide a dowry to their partner.

> Many persons can transform some activities which they conduct into an income generating business venture. Even if it is a small project initially, it can mature into a viable small, medium or even large business entity.

When planning financial matters, as in most other areas, it is important that each mature member of the family be conversant with alternative options which are available to them. For example:

(a) If they are credit worthy, they may be able to **secure a mortgage** from financial institutions such as a mortgage company, commercial bank, credit union or building society. Many couples take the option of securing the land initially and building their home in stages using their savings instead of securing a mortgage. Others purchase the house and land as a single unit using mortgage financing. The former method is advantageous for some couples who are desirous of avoiding the usual high interest rate charge of most commercial mortgage agencies. However, this strategy must be weighed carefully against financial considerations such as the opportunity cost (that is the outcome which was possible if an alternate strategy was employed), they would incur if they are renting another house or apartment. In addition, it might not be cost effective to provide adequate security or the unfinished building to incur the additional cost of purchasing building materials and other inputs and pay for labor cost which increases over time.

(b) They may be risk averse, and prefer to save their money in a **financial institution**, invest in financial instruments such as government or municipal treasury bills and debentures,

(c) Invest in their children. This may include purchasing books, computer hard and software, ensuring that they attend the best school that their parents can afford and that they obtain the necessary nutrients, including vitamins and other supplements. It is a fact that many parents do the best they can for their child/ren, yet they do not achieve the level of academic and/or other levels of prominence which their parents envisaged. In such a circumstance the parents should take solace in the fact that at least they did the best they could have done for their children.

It is important that Christian parents assist their children to achieve God's best for them by using methods such as praying with and for them and encouraging them to attend a church where the five-fold ministry and the nine gifts of the Holy Spirit are consistently in operation and other scriptural practices are being observed.

Some Christians indulge in what has been popularized as the **'name and claim theology'**, that is to believe that the Lord will impress it upon the heart of the owner of an asset which they have prayed for and to make it available to believers. They rely on the principle which Jesus highlighted in Matthew 19:18 which states: **"Again, truly I tell you, if two of you agree on earth about anything you ask, it will be done for you by My Father in heaven."**

The practice of 'naming and claiming' is not always successful since Jehovah may desire that they use their wisdom along with His guidance to work to purchasing the asset on their own.

Some families emphasize on **acquisition of one or several properties** and other assets as an investment into the future development of the family. One or more properties can be rented and a consistent stream of rental income will be coming into the family. Conversely, a property can be renovated and sold, and the proceeds deposited as a fixed deposit or another interest-bearing account which they can enjoy as an additional source of income along with their pension. Properties are also assets which can be passed down as an inheritance from one generation to another. In some families, the parents would endeavor to secure and allocate at least one property to each child so that when the child marries, the new couple enjoys the advantage of starting their marriage without a mortgage.

> A famous proverb states that a fool and his money would soon part. This may be due to factors such:
> (a) He would not be able to detect the cunning devices of persons who are merely out to fleece him.
> (b) He spends his money foolishly and before he realizes it, the money is finished.
> (c) He is robbed, since he did not take adequate security measures to protect his wealth.

Wealth can also be stored in the form of jewelry, art pieces, antique items, vintage vehicles, coins and/or other non-monetary assets, providing there is adequate protection and preservation arrangements in place to guarantee its safety, and that its value appreciates over time. Some large private entrepreneurs may have a fire proof safe in their office or/and at home and/or store jewelry and other small valuable items in a safety deposit box at their bank or other financial institution, usually for a small fee.

The execution of a financial plan for the family can be temporarily or permanently interrupted by or they may loss of a significant amount of the value of their assets due to economic downturn, mis-appropriate of funds by one or several family members or other persons, major illness of one or several members of a family or the death of a spouse. Where possible, adequate life, fire and other forms of insurance coverage should be secured by families in order to provide them some degree of financial security. More importantly, we have to consistently rely on the provision of Jehovah for good health, protection from robberies, fire and other incidents which create disaster in our families. In addition, the inevitability of death, unless the Lord returns before we die, cannot be avoided. However, our life span can be extended with healthy living and the grace of God. Even the legendary Biblical character Methuselah who lived 969 years, eventually died.

When contemplating the purchase of expensive furniture, a car and other major assets, many couples choose the option of **hire purchase**, where the item is made available to the customer upon receiving the necessary credit approval, even though they may only have to make a deposit, or even enjoy a no deposit hire purchase arrangement. Payment by hire purchase is usually much more expensive because of factors such as:

    (a)   The store has to add the extra cost of bearing the loss of immediate income since only a small deposit or no down payment is made by customer,

    (b)   An additional amount is charged for the risks of the customer defaulting on the monthly repayment or failing to complete the full payment for the item. The extent of this risk may be reduced to the store if the company purchases adequate insurance coverage against the possibility of default by the customer. This additional cost is passed on the customer.

(c) The customer usually has to pay for the cost of sending a bailiff to repossess the item if the customer defaults on payment and any legal and other costs associated with recovering the outstanding balance,

Hire purchase gives the customer the benefit of using the item with only an initial or a part of the deposit, or no deposit, and making monthly payments for the ownership of the asset, in some stores after a number of months or even years.

Some stores engage in a **lay-away scheme** where persons who cannot afford to pay for an item immediately is afforded the opportunity to make advance deposits to the store for the item. The proprietor agrees to make the item available to the customer when the full or a significant part of the deposit is made by the customer.

Some wealthier persons engage in the practice of purchasing a new motor vehicle every three years or so, trade in the old one and purchase or lease a new vehicle. There are several advantages associated with this practice:

(a) They are afforded the opportunity of always having a trouble free vehicle, since most new motor vehicles will not normally experience major mechanical and other challenges unless they were involved in a major road accident or there was gross negligence in observing the maintenance guidelines pertaining to the vehicle, for example,

(b) They avoid the expense of spending much money on repairs and maintenance due to major wear and tear,

(c) It may be in keeping with the flamboyant lifestyle of the owner who attempts to always be in the fashion.

Unless a person is very wealthy, this option is often not the best, since if he were the owner of the new vehicle, with good care, it may be able to operate for more than five years before major problems such as the need to overall the engine and to re-spray it occurs. Savings from an owner-driven vehicle can be channeled into other areas of the family budget. However, in many instances, a senior executive and persons from other offices enjoy the privilege of a company vehicle being placed at his disposal as a part of his remuneration. This privilege may be extended where he may be chauffeur-driven which adds to the comfort of working smartly at progressing at his career to achieve the highest possible office.

There are several examples in the Bible of believers who held senior public or political office where their decisions were able to influence events which had a positive effect on the economic, political and/or other aspects of the lives of others. Persons such as Kings David and Solomon served Jehovah and ruled righteously for a greater part of their reign. Joseph, Daniel and Queen Ester were also examples of believers who influenced the political system of their day. Abraham and Job were also very wealthy. In the same way, present day Christians should aspire to be the head of corporate, government and other agencies and enjoy the privileges which their offices afford, while at the same time conducting the management, civic, spiritual and other responsibilities of the office to uplift the standard of living of employees and other persons who would benefit from their wise decisions.

It is important for the couple to arrive at a consensus as to how much money they can realistically save in order to attain future goals. However, there may be instances where the family may have to temporarily deviate from this plan due to unplanned urgent expenditure and the availability of lucrative investment opportunities, for example. There may also be instances where the family will be compelled to neglect the less important items in the budget in order to achieve their primary financial and other targets. This must be done very cautiously, ensuring that the sacrifice does not result in more money having to be spent on medical bills, for example, because of not prioritizing what is deemed as necessary, therefore neglecting nutritional, educational, recreational and other needs of the family.

It is remarkable how haphazard family life can be when there is no clearly defined target which they are pursuing. Manifestations of an unmanaged financial budget include:

(a) Items which may not necessarily be important would be purchased and investments which are not lucrative may be undertaken, simply because the couple did not have a specific objective to attain,

(b) There is much duplication in the items which the couple purchases, very often in an attempt to outdo each other in what they purchase, even 'in the name of love,'

(c) They usually save separately and they are very cagy about disclosing their savings and spending,

(d) One spouse may try to persuade the other to take care of the major expenditure of the family which will enable the other to save and invest more,

(e) Major items are purchased in the name of the person who contributed more of the cash or who will be paying the higher purchase account, for example. There may also be much bickering about who owns which item and hence, should have exclusive or more use of it,

(f) The couple lives together for an extended number of years and do not have many material possessions and/or one spouse owning far more than the other and uses their wealth as a way of intimidating the other or boasting about their perceived individual achievement. In such an environment, the couple is living together under a pseudo marital arrangement, while their spirits are operating as single individuals. The disunity in managing their budget will have a negative effect on other areas of their lives also.

There are several important issues which should be considered when formulating personal and corporate or investment goals of the family. They include:

(a) **Knowing God's will for their lives as an individual and as a family and the direction He is leading them.** This is important since it will assist in the prudent allocation of the budget to ensure that the essential expenditures are met,

(b) **Formulating with the guidance of the Holy Spirit, realistic and challenging short, medium and long term goals of the family** and prioritizing these goals,

(c) **Tithes should be allocated in accordance with the prescribed income of the family, one-tenth and offering as the family purposes,**

(d) Provision should be made for the additional blessings and challenges which will be encountered on the road to the fulfilment of the individual and corporate goals of the family.

> According to one preacher, "**Christians should not be the thermometer of society, where we merely test the temperature of morality and godly standards. Rather, we should be the thermostat where we set the temperature of society.**"

Some of the ways by which we are guided on the correct budgetary and other decisions include the presentation of an honest answer to the following questions:

(a) **Is the budgetary item being considered consistent with the will of the Lord at that time?** Very often this is not a lengthy or complicated process, it may merely mean reviewing if one's conscience (which should be in tune with the Holy Spirit) is at peace with the decision. Where there is a negative response, purchasing the items may be discouraged or at least further dialogue among members of the family may be entertained and, if it is necessary, intervention by a competent arbitration may be sought.

(b) **Are the members of the family who are in a position to understand the implications of the budgetary allocations in agreement or at least can appreciate the importance of the decisions?** There may be occasions such as when there is a major budgetary shortfall when non-essential items or those which rank in a lesser order of priority have to be omitted from the budget. Even then, there is a need for persons to effectively communicate or to 'sell' to other members of the family the reason why various items have to be omitted or included.

As far as possible, there should be agreement between the couple, and where applicable, other members of the family, on important budgetary allocations. Where there are major disagreements, care must be taken to ensure that the decision which is being adopted is consistent with the leadership of the Lord for the specific issue. There will be occasions where a decision has to be made by the father or in a single parent home, by the mother, even though other members of the family may not be in agreement with it. Even then, it is important to at least discuss the reason for the implementation of this independent decision.

It is important that a couple '**plan their work and work their plan'** in an effort to ensure that there is a high level of cohesion in their marriage. Failure to do this will result in several major aspects of their lives not operating in unison. Such a couple will be deemed as unfaithful stewards in the management of their financial, spiritual and other resources which the Lord has placed at their disposal.

The process of assessing the areas of success and failure during and after the execution of a budget is very important. **Post budget evaluation** is absolutely necessary at the end of the budget period, in that an objective appraisal can be made of lessons which can be learnt from the last budget and where applicable, strategies which can be implemented in an attempt to prevent the reoccurrence of similar mistakes in the future. A review of possible alternatives to how they managed various aspects of the budget can also contribute to better management of future budgets.

There is a popular maxim which states: "**Show me your check book and I will tell you what your priorities are."** This maxim relates to how a person spends his income and his level of saving and investment. Many persons, even with a well planned budget, would still engage in haphazard and impulsive spending and at the end of the month they may be dissatisfied with the way their money was spent. For this reason we must **prioritize our spending and seek to ensure that as far as possible, we adhere to prudent financial management in vital areas such as in our giving, spending, saving and investment program.**

The way we purchase items also highlight much about our character. Many persons purchase items on impulse, without taking consideration of more important factors since their compulsion to 'spend it all' is overwhelming. This state is often as a result of a person being induced to secure the item as a result of a TV, radio and/or other forms of advertisement, attempting to 'live like the Jones' and/or the person is merely a **compulsive spender.** Other persons spend lavishly when they are angry, happy or they may be persuaded by an influential sales person.

There are also persons who rush to the store and **purchase expensive exercise equipment,** for example, after seeing it advertised by persons who contend that the product contributed significantly to the change of their lives. The well sculptured physique of the model, actor or other persons who appeared in the advertisement are displayed as evidence of the success of the exercise equipment. Little do many such consumers know of the amount of money which the person in the promotion may have been paid to endorse the product, or that the product had made little or no contribution to their beautiful physique or appearance? After purchasing the item, the gullible consumer may only use it on a small number of occasions. He then realizes that in order to achieve the level of success which was advertised, demands a high level of discipline, not only in undertaking a regular exercise routine but other lifestyle changes. These include eating a balanced diet to complement the effectiveness of the exercise program in order to achieve the required results.

When undertaking major expenditure such as purchasing a house, car, heating and air conditioning systems, consumers should secure the unbiased advise of experts in that specific field. It is unwise to invest thousands of dollars to secure a major asset only to find out a short time thereafter that it is defective and/or that it does not provide optimum satisfaction for the purpose for which it was intended, particularly if the contract protects the seller from any liability if the product does not satisfy the requirements of the consumer. Therefore, it is prudent to incur even the cost of obtaining the best possible advice before making a major purchase or investment.

Important steps to take before purchasing major assets include:

(a) **Seek the Lord and ensure that the undertaking is consistent with His will.** Factors to be considered in this area include whether or not the purchase is an attempt to satisfy a need rather than a want which is not very important, at least at that time.

(b) **Avoid making purchases out of a compulsive addiction**, particularly if the prospective purchaser is not versed in the specifics of the item to be purchased. It is prudent to solicit the unbiased expert advice to ensure that the best selection is made.

(c) **Ensure that you have the necessary finance to make the purchase, or are able to negotiate the best repayment package offered by the store or financial institution which one can manage comfortably without having to sacrifice one's spiritual and other important obligations**,

(d) **'Shop around' or engage in window shopping or going from one shop to another**, enquiring from several stores via the telephone and where possible and necessary, via the internet, to ensure that one is in a position to make the best possible selection in areas such as quality, price and where necessary, after sales service of the item,

(e) **Ensuring that the item is exactly, or at least as close as possible to what one wants**,

(f) **Contracts should be carefully reviewed, where possible by a competent attorney in the particular discipline, or at least by someone who is knowledgeable enough to provide competent advice on the protection of the consumer before signing the contract.** Important issues to be reviewed include the provision of an acceptable warranty or at least some recourse that the consumer can take in the event of dissatisfaction over the product and/or the after sale service of the institution.

(g) Where making purchases such as a major electrical appliance or motor vehicle, it is important to ensure that:
  (i) **The agency which sells the item or another agency which is readily accessible, provide competent after sale service**,
  (ii) **Essential spares are reasonably priced and that prompt and efficient after sale service is readily available at a reasonable price**,
  (iii) **An extended warranty of at least between 3 to 5 years is available free or at a reasonable price for the item**,

The warranty should include the replacement of parts and/or labor and other cost associated with ensuring that the item is in perfect working condition. There are several methods which we can use in an attempt to reduce our personal expenditure. They include:

(a) **Taking lunch to work** saves much money as well as it is an impetus to promote the eating of more nutritious diet than consuming fast food. This is of course based on the condition that the person preparing the home cooked meal is observing nutritious principles in the choice, storage and preparation of food items.

(b) **Car pool** is an effective method which relatives and friends who attend the same church, work close to each other or are generally going in the same direction would use. This strategy assists members of the group to save on the cost of petrol and the wear and tear of their motor vehicle. It also provides benefits such as it reduces the traffic congestion and pollution once it is practiced on a large scale.

(c) **Purchasing items from stores which offer discount such as purchasing items packaged by the store or its affiliates.** Very often stores purchase items in bulk from the manufacturers and distributors and package them. The store usually passes on some of the savings to consumers.

(d) **Purchasing when discounts are offered.** Many stores offer sale discounts at the end of a particular season such as the end of winter or the end of the Christmas season, to create space for new stock. The discount may not be only on slightly damaged items but on all items which will not be in demand for the next season, instead of incurring high storage cost, to improve the cash flow and ability to other purchase items which are in immediate demand.

(e) **Purchasing in bulk**, very often stores and suppliers offer lucrative discount to consumers who purchase items in bulk. A group of persons may pool the money and benefit from such discounts.

(f) **Purchasing items which are in season.** This principle is particularly applicable to food items such as fruits and vegetables which are sold much cheaper when they are in-season; hence, the supply is high. Many persons take the opportunity to store some of these items so that they will have a supply when they are out of season and the price is high. Care must be taken that the nutritional and other properties are maintained and adequate cost effective methods are available.

(g) **Purchasing cost effective items** which are within one's budget. This principle is particularly applicable where a person may seek to avoid the purchase of an expensive 'brand name product' when a generic product may be just as attractive, durable and have the other properties as the original product.

(h) **Using energy saving appliances and methods.** By using energy saving bulbs saves much money and energy, even though the initial cost of purchasing and installing them may be higher than that of conventional bulbs. In the long run they are far more cost effective.

(i) **Where possible, use cheaper and 'cleaner' sources of energy such as solar, wind or hydro electrical energy rather than electricity.** Many persons also purchase and use a stove which uses natural gas rather than using an electrical stove since electricity is generally more expensive than natural gas. A caution must be interjected here since the initial cost of accessing alternative sources of energy may be more expensive but is usually more cost effective over the long run.

(J) **As far as possible, avoid panic buying.** Many persons shop excessively when there is a warning of an impending period of adverse weather or other conditions which may restrict their ability to purchase and/or there is an announcement of a possibility of an acute increase in prices. It may be necessary to purchase essential items in preparation for emergencies such as an impending hurricane, severe winter condition, war, the introduction of higher taxes on food and other items. However, many persons shop excessively in preparation for such eventualities and in many instances they are unable to consume much of what they purchase. Therefore, a balanced approach is needed in such circumstances.

(k) **Avoid purchasing excessively before and during festive seasons and other special occasions,**

Marketing agencies take advantage by preying on the gullibility of consumers by launching well targeted campaign on the sentiments of consumers and induce them to purchase excessively during seasons such as Christmas, Thanksgiving and Easter. Consumers have to be able to adapt a sensible approach to balance their desire to participate in these events and maintaining a well managed budget.

We are reminded by Proverbs 13:18 which states: "[18]***Poverty and disgrace are for the one who ignores instruction (discipline), but the one who heeds reproof is honored.***"

The importance of maintaining good financial and other records cannot be overemphasized. Many persons are in the habit of discarding receipts, bills and other documents as soon as the transaction is completed. This may include receipts for the payment of rent, credit card statements, checks and other documents which record the conclusion of particular financial and other transactions. Very often some time after the document was discarded; they realize that they needed it to verify that the transaction occurred. A typical example of this occurrence is if a credit card company is claiming that the value of a particular transaction was much higher than the cardholder is aware of. Since the bill was discarded by the credit card holder and the seller may be reluctant or even unable to produce it, the cardholder may be left in the position where he has to honor the payment since he could not produce the record of the transaction. He may be able to resort to the court to force the seller to produce the record of the transaction; however, the cardholder may be so desperate to use the card in the future that he accepts liability in an attempt to resolve what may be very costly confrontation if the matter goes to court.

In many instances, persons are required to produce their bank statement, receipts or other financial records to verify the authenticity of a transaction for which tax deduction or other means of verification is required. The legal requirement of many countries is that financial and other records should be maintained for up to six years in order to verify particular transactions. It is therefore a healthy practice to retain financial and other important records for at least 3 years after the completion of the transaction. Of course documents such as the title deeds for property, insurance policy certificates and education certificates should be retained permanently.

> **The 10:10:80 Principle of Budgeting**
> - 10% - Tithes
> - 10% - Saving & investment
> - 80% - Family expenditure
>   Among the deficiencies of this principle is that it does not specify the amount of offering which should be given. There are overwhelming spiritual blessings from given an offering to the Lord.

LENDING & BORROWING

In Psalms 37:25, King David related his experience that although he was old, he had never seen the righteous forsaken, or his offspring begging for bread (food). This does not infer that it is legitimate for the righteous to beg for commodities other than the necessities of life. We are reminded that for the forty years that the Children of Israel wandered in the wilderness, Jehovah continually provided for their material needs, including the fact that their shoes grew as the size of their feet increased. This was done although they murmured that the manna did not include the many delicacies that they were accustomed to eating in Egypt. On one occasion when they murmured, Jehovah provided them with quail (a bird) for them to eat. Of course, the Creator of the universe was well able to provide delicacies in greater abundance than they could have imagined. Possibly because He wanted them to focus more on spiritual matters, He did not give them extravagance.

Matthew 7:9-11 states: **"⁹Is there anyone among you who, if your child asks for bread, will give a stone? ¹⁰Or if your child asks for a fish, will give a snake? ¹¹If you then, who are evil, know how to give good gifts to your children, how much more will your Father in Heaven give good things to those who ask Him?"**

A popular interpretation of this scripture passage is that Christians should not be materially poor. A common example used in explaining this characteristic is in the review of the life of the legendary sufferer - Job. It was highlighted that poverty and disaster are curses from the devil (Job 1:12). Because of God's protection over his life and his faithfulness, Job overcame the test and was blessed more abundantly than before.

So what possible explanation can be presented of why so many Christians remain as poor as a 'church mouse' throughout their lives? Possible answers are:

(a) The low level of their faith,
(b) They may consistently ask amiss,
(c) They do not ask (as demonstrated in the life of the brother of the 'Prodigal Son' (Luke Chapter 15),
(d) Some Christians consciously shun material wealth because they fear that they might be distracted from their faith in God if they have to manage much money and other assets.
(e) Some Christians are just too lazy to pursue or prudently manage wealth and/or are not making adequate use of opportunities which will enable us to significantly increase our material and other resources.

For reasons such as the above, many preachers present the pros-and-cons of whether or not Christians should seek to attain material wealth to their congregation and allow each person to decide which path to pursue.

> The embodiment of salvation is a total liberation of our body, soul and spirit. This includes the establishment of a free communication link between us and the Father, through Jesus, healing for our body (by His stripes) and financial and other material blessings. It does not mean however, that we will all be millionaires while we are on earth, even though we have the 'seed' in us which can generate that capacity. Some persons do not know about their financial privilege, others choose not to exercise this right, while others given up this right because of the gospel.

Mark 8:36 states that: **"36For what will it profit them to gain the whole world and forfeit their life?"**

There seems to be no reason why a Christian cannot seek to legitimately acquire material wealth and yet remain focused on serving the Lord. How can Christians assist their neighbours with financial and other material needs, when the Christians themselves do not have money and other material things for themselves? Peter and John, in Acts Chapter 3, demonstrated a classic example of this principle when they were going to the temple to pray. They met a lame man who was begging alms at the gate called Beautiful. Although they did not have money to give him, God, through the disciples, performed a miracle and the blind man received his sight. This no doubt was more important to him than if they had merely satisfied his temporary financial need. Can we give a better gift to this sin-sick world than the love of Christ in its totality, including; healing for the sick, the provision of sound financial advice, rendering assistance to at least significantly reduce poverty and leading them to the path of eternal life?

As we preach the Gospel to the poor, we have to follow the example of Jesus who did not only satisfy the spiritual needs of the people but also provided physical food for the hungry. Financial miracles still occur in the lives of Christians and in communities throughout the world. There is also the need for Christians to provide financial assistance to other Christians and to the unsaved.

In many instances when Christians embark on projects such as the construction of a church, they are unable to raise enough capital though their congregation or other supporting bodies. They often resort to obtaining credit from financial institutions such as a bank or building society. The leaders of some Christian organizations advocate that Christians should not borrow from, or lend money or other commodities to other persons or institutions. This principle largely constitutes the activities of some Christians who believe that they should '**live by faith**.' The Bible advocates that an adult who can be gainfully employed, but who deliberately chooses not to work when he is well and the employment and other facilities are available for him to do so, should not be given any food. (2 Thessalonians 3:10).

Many Christians believe in the principles of trusting God for miracles in healing and other matters. Yet in emergencies and in business ventures, they may resort to borrowing money from relatives, friends, financial institutions and from the church they attend. Several church bodies have emergency and/or contingency funds to help destitute believers. They provide financial support to believers in emergencies; help the poor, widows and orphans in the community, and even capital for enterprising members. These programs often go a long way to enable believers to emerge from poverty by engaging in income-generating activities.

While we are in this world, Christians share most of the basic needs as everyone else. We need items such as food, clothing, housing, a high standard of education and sometimes capital for investment. In many countries

Christians follow several traditions of their communities including the financing of elaborate weddings, birthday celebrations, 'naming' or christening ceremony to celebrate the birth of a baby, and also the financing of funerals. Financing these activities is often beyond the means of the family. Hence, credit has to be secured to meet these expenditures. In weddings, for example, even for Christians, due to their personal desire and/or the pressure from relatives and friends, elaborate wedding receptions are often held. It is sad to observe that many couples start their marriage with a huge debt that stifles their financial progress for many months, if not longer.

> There are several privileges which Christians enjoys from the Lord. They include:
> - Granting an abundant harvest to the sower and persons who tithe and give of their offerings,
> - Whatever we put our hands to do is blessed,
> - Eternal life where we can enjoy the treasures which He has laid up for us,
> - He repays those who 'lend' to Him when we assist the poor and needy,
> - He directs our paths,
> - We have spiritual weapons at our disposal to protect us from the attacks of the devil and for us to be on the offensive to prevent our assets from being devoured by the devil and his cohorts.

CHALLENGES IN OBTAINAING A LOAN

Similar to other members of society, Christians are often unable to satisfy the requirements to secure a loan from commercial financial institution. Therefore, many of us, (particularly in rural areas) would secure credit from traditional or informal financial institutions such as moneylenders and pawnshops.

Among the disadvantages of obtaining credit from these institutions is that they usually demand high interest rates and request valuable collateral such as jewellery, cattle and/or a lien over the transport or lease of property. These items may be seized if repayments are not made as scheduled, even for reasons which are beyond the control of the borrower. Interest rates on credit from moneylenders may be as high as 50%, but in many societies, 100% or more. The question that is often paramount in such circumstances is if the investment would generate enough profits to adequately cover the high cost of the credit facility (commitment or negotiation fees, legal and other expenses in addition to the principal, interest). Activities such as petty trading often generate high level of profit in the short run once it is managed, thereby enabling the borrower to repay the high cost. Very often persons have no other choice than to borrow from moneylenders since the moneylender may be the only source of credit that they can secure.

There are examples, particularly in developing countries, where groups within a congregation, work colleagues, relatives and/or other persons practice a saving technique commonly called **Osusu** (in The Gambia), **Susu** (in Trinidad and Tobago), **Box** (in Guyana) and **Meeting Money** (in Barbados), for example. The basic principle governing this system is that a group of persons decide on a fixed amount of money that each member can realistically contribute to the pool of funds of the group for each period, which they compute in days, weeks or months. The whole pool is given to a pre-selected member on each of the maturity dates and rotated, until each member of the group receives his or her 'share', 'hand' or pool of funds. Some groups use a system where a small amount (usually less than 1% of the principle) is retained in a pool which is kept by the treasurer to increase the capital of the group. The amount retained, along with membership fees and money generated from fund raising activities organized by the group is also used as loans to members and/or donated to worthy causes. This source of funding is integral in several communities where participants use this fund to purchase goods in bulk and benefit from reduced prices and resell the item and generate substantial profit. Some persons participate in several small groups and expand the benefit from such drawings personally and/or as a commercial venture.

> A principle which often comes in handy in finding specific areas which the Lord is leading us is to **obey the general and God will lead us to the specifics**.

Irrespective of how well we plan, very often emergencies arise at a time when we are not in a position to meet such financial demands. Therefore, we may be compelled to seek financial assistance in order to defray these urgent expenses. These may include situations such as:

(a) The Christian entrepreneur may need capital to embark on a business venture or to expand an existing business venture which necessitates that capital be acquired,

(b) A Christian student who is unable to secure a scholarship or whose parents are not in a position to provide adequate financial assistance; often has to borrow money for tuition, books, living and other expenses to attend college, university or vocational training institution.

(c) Many Christians, independently or on entering marriage, secure a mortgage and other forms of credit to finance the purchase or construction of a house, to purchase or lease a car and/or acquire other major assets and for major medical, funereal and other expenses of one or several member/s of the family.

(d) To finance emergency expenses.

The overwhelming rationale seems to be that even though this is not the best option, for the Lord does not desire for us to be the 'slave to the lender', it is legitimate for Christians to borrow sensibly, particularly for major items such as a house and car which may be beyond the ability of the average couple to purchase at the cash price, at least at the initial stage of their marriage. However, care must be taken that unnecessary and excessive credit, particularity for nonessential consumer items, is avoided as much as possible.

Among the things that Jehovah was angry about, as highlighted in Nehemiah Chapter 5, was the practice of paying interest among His people. Jesus also said in Acts 20:35(b) that giving is better than receiving. This admonition is ever present in our lives, for most persons are usually ashamed when they have to ask favours from neighbours, colleagues at work and even to negotiate a loan, particularly to purchase consumer items. We often feel, at least at that particular moment of negotiating the loan, that the appraiser has some degree of power over us, in that he/she or the appraising body can accept or reject the loan application. In addition, one is 'enslaved' (compelled) to meet the monthly loan payment or face consequences such as of having the item repossessed or collateral confiscated and the delinquent customer may be taken to court if he fails to repay the loan as scheduled. This issue was reiterated in Proverbs 22:7(b) which states: "[7(b)]**...and the borrower is the slave of the lender.**"

There are also some unscrupulous, unsaved loans officers who are dishonest and may only recommended or approve a loan application when the applicant agrees to pay a bribe in the form of cash and/or kind. Christians are well aware that we should not accept or pay bribes or indulge in any dishonest transactions.

Ten is the number for redemption. When we give the first tenth of our earning, we redeem the other ninth, or make it holy unto the Lord, who blesses the user and multiplies other returns.

TITHES & OFFERINGS

God introduced tithing and offering in the Old Testament before the laws and commandments were introduced and the principle was continued in the New Testament. The proceeds from the tithes were primarily to support the priests and their families and to finance other activities pertaining to the temple. The offering was presented for reasons such as an appreciation of the loving kindness of God, as atonement for the sins a person, his family and the nation of Israel had committed, and at the end of a period of uncleanness. In Genesis 14: 20, Abram gave one-tenth of his possession to King Melchizedek. After this incident, Abram received the promise of God that his descendants were to be as numerous as the stars. His name was also changed to Abraham and Sarai, his wife to Sarah. Other references of tithing, or first fruit, include Numbers 18:26, 2 Chronicle 31:5-6 and Hebrew 7:4-9.

We, along with everything that we own belong to Jehovah. However, there is a mandatory 10% of our income, and other forms of earning which is classified as the tithe. A person can choose to give more than the mandatory 10% as a tithe. The offering, on the other hand, constitutes amounts above the percentage that is given as the tithe. Common activities to which an offering is given are for the building and expansion of the work of the Lord in the local church and other congregations, as a gift to individual believers, pastors and missionaries, and to help the poor and needy. Much blessing will be received by individuals, families and others who give an offering, particularly, when it is given from a heart of love, and to a worthy cause.

Malachi 3:8 states that a person who does not pay the **full tithes** into the house of God is in fact robbing Him. Hence, tithing is a very important requirement of the believer, so that God can also fulfil His covenant of protection, provision and other blessings to us. Many persons detest using the word 'paying' with reference to the contribution of the tithes and offering, since they are of the opinion that these two contributions should be viewed as love offerings rather than as a person being 'forced to keep this command or face the wrath of God'. In addition, each household of the children of Israel was obligated to present the produce of their first harvest from their farm, and the first born of their cattle and other animals to the priest, which is classified as the **first fruit** and has special significance to the giver to the Lord.

The following are eleven important principles which have to be followed when giving of the tithe and offering:

(a) **As far as possible, the tithe should be the first item which is deducted from our salary.** The word 'tithe' and the phrase 'first fruit' are used interchangeably in several scripture verses. It can be concluded therefore that if the tithe is made after other deductions, then what we are giving to the Lord is an offering from our net income, and not the tithe. It is true that deductions such as income tax, national insurance, group medical insurance and a loan payment, for example, may be deducted before a salary earner receives his **net income** or what is commonly referred to as his 'take-home-pay.' Even so, **the tithe represents one tenth of the gross, or salary payable before any deduction is made.**

(b) **We should give as a sign of worship**; we are merely giving back to Jehovah a percentage of what belongs to Him in thanksgiving for what He has enabled us to achieve. The Apostle Paul stated in 2 Corinthians 8:3, 4: "**3For as I can testify, they voluntarily give according to their means, and even beyond their means, 4begging us earnestly for the privilege of sharing in this ministry to the saints – and this, not merely as we expected they give themselves first to the Lord and, by the will of God, to us..."**

(c) **We should sow cheerfully**; that is, our attitude should not be one where we are only doing it because we are obligated to; for there is an abundance of blessing allocated to a cheerful giver. 2 Corinthians 9:6 states: "**6The point is this: the one who sows sparingly will also reap sparingly, and the one who sows bountifully will also reap bountifully.**"

(d) **The amount that we give as offering is an individual decision, and others should not impose or compel us to give a prescribed amount.** 2 Corinthians 9:7 states: "**7Each of you must give as you have made up your mind, not reluctantly or under compulsion, for God loves a cheerful giver.**

(e) **We must give with the correct attitude;** a popular representation of this truth is the parable of the 'widow's mite'. Among the principles highlighted in this parable is that our hearts should be right with God and we must be humble as we give, or our giving will be like 'sounding brass', where it is a curse rather than a blessing to us.

(f) **Our giving should be generous,** when we reflect on how much He has done for us, no amount should be too much for us to give to Him. Can we measure the goodness of God to us, for example, by the contribution of 20% of our salary to His work, for example?

(g) **If we sow on barren ground our harvest will be minimal, if any at all.** Therefore, it is important that we tithe at a church where the full Gospel of Christ is preached and practiced, where believers are in unity and there is a dynamic evangelism outreach program, for example.

(h) **Claim the promises of God** as found in Malachi 3:10-12, for example, which states that God will bless the produce of our land, and all the blessings that we can conceive as 'overflowing.' This includes good health, financial prosperity and spiritual blessings.

(i) **We should give expectantly**; as alluded to earlier, He is no man's debtor and when we give to the poor, we lend to the Lord,

(j) Similar to the previous point, **our giving should be with the full understanding that we are not giving to a person or organization but to the Lord.** Our giving should not be a means of 'buying favour among the leadership of the church, and we should not stop giving when we cannot have our 'own way', for example.

As far as possible, our giving should be consistent; there must be a commitment and obedience to give our tithes and give offering on a consistent manner every month, in order to enjoy God's full blessing. The devourer (the devil and his cohorts such as sickness, poverty and other hindrances which rob us of progress and peace, for example,) must be stayed on a consistent basis for us to enjoy continuous blessing. Many persons experience some 'good days' but much more 'bad days' because of their inconsistency in giving their all to the Lord each day of their lives.

Unless an individual and/or his family tithe in the correct way, they cannot enjoy the full benefits of the promises covenanted by God to this principle. The tithe is usually given to the church where a believer is a member, or at least where he is comfortable fellowshipping. In a situation where a person resides in a location where there are no bible believing churches in close proximity, some believers pay their tithes to a ministry or an international evangelist that/whom they feel is fulfilling Biblical principles.

A simple example which illustrates the difference between tithes and offering is shown when reference is made to a person dining in a restaurant. The tithe equates to paying for one's meal (one, two or three course), drinks and dessert, where applicable. The payment of the bill goes to the restaurant (the local church). When a person moves to a location where there is no easy access to his local church, the tendency is usually to maintain the relationship with the former church by sending his tithes to the former church. Care should be taken when applying this principle since a person should 'pay where he eats'. The offering in this analogy is viewed as the tip given to the waiter (in appreciation of the courteous service which was extended).

In the same way that a person cannot eat at one restaurant and pay the bill at another, it is unethical to fellowship at one church and tithe at another. A waiter would usually seek to ensure that a good tipper is given the best service. Can we really fathom the outpouring of blessings which we will receive from the hands of the Lord, as we give to His work, to the poor and other areas of the ministry? God is no man's debtor, and He will give out of His abundance, which is far more than we can ever think or imagine.

As we 'cast our bread on the water' it will be returned to us in abundance, passed down, shaken down and running over, will we receive from others. As we bless others, we, the members of our families, our descendants and other persons will receive blessings in abundance in return. God appreciates it more when we give, even when we are in need, rather than when we give merely because we have in abundance. Our giving should be based on factors such as out of a heart of love and gratitude for who He is, what He has done for us, and from our love for others. A typical example of this principle is illustrated in the parable that Jesus related of the widow's mite (Mark 12: 41-44 and Luke 21:1-4).

> When we sow financial seeds by giving to the poor, giving towards evangelism and to support missionaries, for example, we will reap financial, spiritual and other forms of blessings from the Lord directly and also through other persons.

The issue of tithing has received much negative criticism from members of some churches where this system is not emphasized as much as in many Pentecostal and Charismatic churches. The view is often that the leadership of the churches who emphasize tithing do this primarily to 'fill their own pockets'. Many of these church leaders live an affluent lifestyle which some persons will criticize. This may include travelling to international conferences, visiting other countries with an entourage of members, driving fancy motor vehicles, and living in a 'fancy house' in upper-class neighbourhoods. Even though the source of the affluence of senior officials of the church may be from personal investments, they will still be viewed as funding their lifestyle from the financial and other resources of the church.

There are, of course some dishonest church officials, who have brought disrepute to the name of the Lord. However, this practice is not usually wide spread in many countries. Nevertheless, regardless of how the leaders and other members of a church live there will be critics of their lifestyle. Many persons feel more comfortable attending a 'church' where the building is attractive, the pews are comfortable, air conditioned or at least fans and other amenities which project comfort, provided of course, that the Spirit of the Lord is doing mighty things in the lives of believers, sound doctrine is preached, persons are being saved and other scriptural practices are adhered to. In addition, many Christians would invite others to attend a service and other activities at such a church. We have to pray for our leaders and for every person, that they will serve the Lord and not divert their financial and other resources to activities which would not have a positive effect on the world. A leader whose life reflects success in spiritual, material and other areas, is usually better able to challenge, inspire and assist others to improve their lives and standard of development in their community.

> I have found out, from painful personal experiences and that of others who attempt to, figuratively speaking, 'put the cart before the horse' by endeavoring to give the Lord's tithes and offering after fulfilling other obligations. In giving, even out of one's need, the Lord rewards us bountifully for our faithfulness. Giving sparingly does not bring glory to the Lord and we suffer financially and otherwise from this practice.

> What we spend our money on and how we arrive at that decision tell of our spiritual standing.

CHARITY & THE CHRISTIAN FAMILY

Several large charitable organizations are known for their involvement in the distribution of aid and other programs to assist the poor and destitute and other needy groups locally and in several countries. Some of these organizations are the Christian Aid, Save the Children Fund of the UK and USA and the Catholic Relief Service. These agencies provide relief and aid, particularly to developing countries. Some programs that they undertake are the construction and furnishing of schools, providing medical services, the provision of pure water supply and the introduction of new and improved technology in farming and industrial projects. Many of these organizations rely on the generous contribution of individuals, corporate and other agencies and governments to contribute food items.

Voluntary contributions from Christians support many aid organizations and the poor in several countries. Many Churches have a committee involved in raising funds to purchase medical supplies, food items, clothing and other items to contribute to the needy in their community, to disaster relief programs and to provide financial and other forms of assistance to impoverished countries. Such contributions may be over an extended period or when a particular need arises, and/or when enough funds are available.

There are missionaries and Christian volunteers in several countries who are assisting communities in areas such as teaching literacy and numeracy programs, providing health care and other services. A common view in many Christian circles is that we will only make a significant positive impact on the community if our focus is concentrated on preaching the Gospel by word and deeds. We are to be doers of the Word, which implies that as the light of the world, we must be good examples in giving of our time, material assets, professional skills, talents, other attributes in winning the lost to the Lord and generally helping the poor and needy. These principles demonstrate the extent of our love to the Lord and for our fellow man. They are popularly summarized in **the '3-**

T' principle of giving to the Lord, that is of our treasury, time and talent.

> The three principles of giving to God:
> **Treasury** – giving to God His tithes, offering and also adequately supporting our family, giving to the poor and needy and other areas of financing the promotion of the Gospel.
> **Time** - quality time should be spent each day, as far as is possible, studying the Bible, in prayer and praise to God, spreading the gospel and assisting the poor and needy and to promote the economic, social and other aspects of the development of our community.
> **Talent** – most persons have some form of talent which they can use to enhance their standard of living as well as person in their country and further a-field. This include writing and publishing of Christian literature, singing gospel music, teaching literacy and numeracy programs and being kind and loving to others.

Some Christian congregations have extended the strategy of assisting communities beyond preaching, hence, they propagate doctrines such as the **Liberation Theology**. Among the emphases of this doctrine is that the Christians should be actively involved in every aspect of the daily lives of the community where it is located. This principle has been extended to the involvement of some churches, particularity in Latin American countries such as Nicaragua, Argentina and several African and Asian and other countries where persons take up arms and fight against the government or for other causes. Conversely, there is the more conservative view that Christians should not be members of political parties, and be involved in military and other activities which characterize human government. The rationale for this response is usually presented in the 'principle' that we should not love this world or the things which are in it (1 John 2: 15).

Every aspect of our lives should be focused on perpetuating the 'principles of the Bible.' The Jehovah Witnesses are renowned for the dogmatic approach of not voting at regional and national elections and nonparticipation in military activities which they consider as supportive of earthly government. Their focus is on the promotion of the gospel and the government of Jehovah, and the New Jerusalem after the present heaven and earth pass away. The result is that they are ostracized and even banned from operating in several countries.

Some Christians advocate that the best way to evangelize a country is by being involved in politics and other public offices, from which they can effect positive change at the national level and/or internationally. There are examples of born-again Christians who have become rulers in countries and occupy ministerial and other senior offices in government and community leadership. However, there are many examples where 'Christian governments' and Christian government ministers and other senior functionaries make pathetic decisions which are often a source of embarrassment to the Christian faith. The continuous fighting between Catholics and Protestants in Northern Ireland (which thankfully seems to have abated) was a classic example of this unfortunate situation. We should be aware that Christianity is not a religion; rather it is a relationship between an individual and his Creator, Jehovah. Therefore, not everyone who professes to be a follower of Christ is a true believer.

There are many examples where Christian politicians and public officers have compromised their faith in their quest to broker peace between disputing factions of persons and for political, material and other gains. Situations such as these have caused several preachers to discourage their congregation from becoming actively involved in secular politics. The rationale for this is that the pulpit, that is, what we preach and witness by our lifestyle (providing that we are consistently practicing what we preach) should have enough influence on governmental politics and international affairs. In other words, **the pulpit is our political platform**, propagating the politics of **the Kingdom of Heaven**, which entails as far as possible, pursuing attributes such as living peacefully with all men, honesty, integrity and love. We are also reminded that the economic and other national activities will receive the prosperity and other benefits as the people of God humble themselves, seek His face, pray and turn from their wicked ways.

Christians hold the balance of power in the development of the national and international economies if we would only take our authority which is in Christ. Nevertheless, account must be taken of the coming catastrophes which the book of Revelation and other books of the Bible foretold and which must occur before the second coming of Christ.

We are also obligated to execute the Great Commission each day of our lives by going into all the world and making disciples of all men (Matthew 28: 19 to 20). Many Christian organizations are known to lobby against legislations presented for ratification in parliament and otherwise, and internationally, such as the unilateral support of abortion, the legalization of addictive drugs and other issues that contravene Biblical principles. In addition, the effective fervent prayers of saints have gone a long way in securing peace and progress in many nations.

> God often provides through the natural, until our faith rises to the level when we can believe Him for the supernatural.

> Even though some Christians are divinely called by the Lord to leave their secular jobs and pursue a life of '**full-time ministry**' such as being a pastor and/or missionary, the majority of us are also called to serve in '**full-time ministers**' on the secular job as a professional.

LIVING BY FAITH

Habakkuk 2:4(b) states: **"4(b) ....but the righteous shall live by their faith."**

This passage implies that Christians should rely on God to supply their physical, material, spiritual and other needs. This principle is also repeated in Romans 1: 17(b). The Bible has several references where miracles were performed to satisfy a particular need. They include:

(a) The Children of Israel wandered in the wilderness for forty years and God sent them manna (food) which fell from the sky. Water was also provided when Moses struck a rock with his staff.

(b) A prophet had died and his creditors threatened to enslave his sons if his widow did not repay the outstanding balance. She consulted the prophet Elisha who instructed her to borrow oil jars from her neighbours and to fill them with oil from the one jar of oil that she had. She obeyed this instruction, and as she poured the oil into the borrowed jars, the oil from the original jar was continually replenished until all the jars were filled. She sold the oil and accumulated enough money to repay her creditors.

(c) Jesus changed water into wine at the marriage feast in Cana (John 2:1-11),

Jesus prayed and five loaves of bread and two fishes were miraculously multiplied so that there was enough food to feed 4,000 men (the number of women and children were not stated but they were likely to be more than 4,000). There were seven baskets of crumbs collected from the meal (John 6:1-14).

There are also many examples of modern day miracles. Many Christians have taken the Scriptures literally when Jesus instructed his disciples in Luke 9:3 that they should not take anything for their journey when they go to proclaim the Gospel, not even a change of clothes or money. Many believers have also left the secular jobs and careers to purse the 'call' of the Lord on their lives and to enter a life of 'full-time ministry'. These 'full-time' believers usually claim that they have received a personal revelation from God, via methods such as a prophecy, a specific text from the Bible and/or a vision, confirming that God has called them into a life set apart for His service.

There is some controversy among many believers on the concept of 'full-time ministry'. Many persons feel that each Christian is in fact engaged in a life of full-time ministry, in that our lives should reflect the goodness, authority, love and other attributes of Jesus wherever we are. However, similar to Apostle Paul and Barnabas, many Christians stated that they have received a special call from the Lord to dedicate their lives exclusively to serving in specific areas of the ministry.

When a person receives the 'call of the Lord to full-time ministry', it is often associated with several piercing questions. The first of which is usually on the issue of financial support, particularly if he has a family. An answer to this question is found in Philippians 4:19 which states: **"¹⁹And my God will fully satisfy every need of yours according to His riches in Christ Jesus."**

The second question is usually whether he will be accepted in the specific area of the ministry to which one has been called? For most persons, the answer to this question is usually revealed over a period of time.

There are several examples where the spouse of a person who enters into 'full-time ministry' still maintains a secular job and can provide the financial support to the family while the other partner fulfil their calling. Several conflicts can result from this arrangement unless the couple is fully conversant with and accept the demands that this practice would make on their personal lives and that of the family. This is another example that emphasizes the importance of being and staying 'equally yoked', since major disagreements in such areas have resulted in divorce of couples or a believer being unable to fulfil his/her calling.

There was, for example, a wonderful missionary from Jamaica whom I knew, whose wife was initially content to continue working to support their two children while he went around the world preaching. They also travelled with him occasionally. It was evident that there were difficult moments for them, but the important factor was that they recognized and accepted that fulfilling the calling of the Lord on the life of a person was the most important reasons for living. This does not mean that the wife was playing a subservient role, for her ministry, as the 'caretaker of the children' must have received special grace and blessing. Sadly, after over twenty years of marriage the couple was recently divorced. Possibly because of the grief of separation, he died shortly after the divorce.

Some Christians who feel this special call of the Lord on their lives to serve as a missionaries and in other capacities in full time ministry, may obtain financial assistance from their local church and/or be sponsored by individual, national and/or international sources. It is usually easier if one is serving under the administration of his local church or other bodies since some established churches provide their full-time workers with amenities such as a salary and allowances, a furnished house, some means of transportation and other material benefits. There are, however, some persons who are called into serving in a particular geographical location or area of the ministry that their local church may not be willing to, or cannot provide the necessary financial and other forms of support. Even in such circumstances, it is important that such persons be supervised, or are 'covered' by some ministry, if not from the inception, as early as possible. This is because Christians should not operate as 'headless bodies.' Very often a person who chooses to be 'nonaligned' eventually forms or joins a cult and/or preaches false doctrines.

> Many Christians prefer to sacrifice earthly wealth in order to enjoy the riches of our heavenly kingdom. Sadly, many unsaved persons prefer to enjoy the wealth of this world to the detriment of the eternal wealth. Christians, on the other hand, can choose to enjoy the best of both worlds.

> After we have asked, knocked, and sought, we may still be financially poor. We must have the discernment, capacity and wisdom to use wisely what the Lord gives to us through others and directly in terms of our health, material and other blessings in order to maximize our effectiveness as Christians.

TIME MANAGEMENT & THE CHRISTIAN FAMILY

Since important aspects of time management are presented in several sections of this book, only brief mention is made of this important issue in this section. There is a famous maxim which states that '**time is money**'. The rationale for this is that the time it takes to produce a particular item or to provide a given service, is often one of the most important factors in determining its value and price. Advertisement during prime time on the radio or television, for example, is usually more expensive than during off-peak periods. Similarly, the way we spend our time often has positive or negative financial implications on our lives and that of others on whom our lives have a direct impact.

As it is in the physical, even so importance is attributed to time management in the spiritual realm, but there are usually some profound differences operating in the two realms. The way we manage our time on earth determines the level of spiritual rewards which we will receive while on earth and also in the life hereafter. However, the 'treasures' in eternal life cannot be measured in earthly financial terms. We cannot, for example, affix a financial value to eternal life, the crown of glory or being with the Lord forever and ever. However, while we are on earth, the Bible exhorts us to make good use of every moment. Our time should be prudently apportioned to ensure that maximum use is made of this most valuable asset which is at our disposal. Many references are made in the Bible to the need for us to ensure that we are not slothful, lazy or manifest other traits which portray inefficient and ineffective time management principles.

Effective time management can be measured from the perspective of what we achieve over a given time-frame, given factors such as our age, maturity, academic, vocational and other qualification, financial resources and spiritual maturity. The amount of time which is spent by a person to achieve a particular objective would have a profound impact on his ability to succeed in his career and other endeavours. Many persons who attempt to take shortcuts by not investing the necessary time and resources to acquire succeed,

often end up:
- (a) Having to accept mediocre jobs,
- (b) Remaining unemployed oven an extended period,
- (c) Engaging in dishonest practices to acquire finance or gain a promotion, for example,

As beggars, homeless and living in poverty even in an affluent society since they did not acquire a job, or at least one with the required benefit, the person did not save and invest prudently and/or they experienced significant disasters personally, with family members and even nationally.

It is particularly important for persons who live in societies where there is a high unemployment rate to observe prudent time management principles in order to emerge from poverty. Even though it is a general principle that we reap what we sow, it does not necessarily mean that the product of what we reap would be the same as the 'seed' which was sown. There are also thieves such as sickness, natural and man-made disasters such as war, drought, inflation and other adverse circumstances which hamper persons from acquiring the full potential of the return from their investments. On the other hand, persons often benefit from investments made by others such as the receipt of inheritance, which may not be as a direct benefit of what the receiver 'sowed'.

Time management is also important in identifying how well we apportion our time during the day, for the results will be manifested in what we have achieved in various aspects of our lives at the end of the day and future investments to be made. Many persons have a well organized system of planning and recording at least the major activities which they have to embark on for the day, very early in the morning and work assiduously to achieve at least the very important aspects of the plan.

No one can accurately determine the exact way events of the day will unfold. The closest one may be to achieving this feat is if one is possibly confined to a prison or operates in other environments where a rigid system is maintained. Even in such circumstances, there are often variations from the normal routine. At the same time it would be unrealistic if one attempts to rigidly follow a diary of events which are planned for the day, when as situations of the day unfold, there is a need to make major adjustments to the time table. The Lord expects us to plan effectively in our pursuit to do His will. However, there must be versatility in our plan to cater for the inclusion of unplanned important events which may occur during the day.

It would be interesting to analyze how we spend an average day in an attempt to determine how effective we are in managing our time. The average person sleeps at least eight hours per day even though many situations such as demands of work or studies cause many persons to live for extended periods on a dramatically reduced period of sleep. At the other end of the spectrum we have babies and smaller children, the elderly and persons who are ill who sleep for longer hours. There are also lazy persons who sleep their lives away, very often contributing to, or further worsening their state of obesity, poverty and/or other undesirable states. It is important that we have enough sleep each day to give the organs and other parts of our body a rest and to allow the rejuvenation of new cells, for example.

Other ways in which we can misuse time include:

(a) **Spending much time on activities which does not contribute very much to our academic development, improve our reading skill or creativity,**

(b) **Looking at soap operas and other television programs for extended periods which are not** *in keeping with our personal development and which do not inspire us to live very productive lives.* In many instances we admire the success stories of others, without seriously endeavouring to improve our own lives, even by becoming actors, writers and/or pursue other careers.

(c) **Gossiping**, instead of trying to use our time to upgrade our lives and that of others,

(d) Worrying, instead of seeking positive solutions from the Lord, and from other sources,

(e) **Constantly changing one's career path**, resulting in much time, energy and money being wasted on moving from one career path to another. Younger people are particularly susceptible to such actions. To assist in this process they need the assistance of prudent parental guidance, the assistance of qualified counsellors and of course they should learn to know and rely on the direction of the Holy Spirit in every aspect of their lives.

Having analyzed the above factors, we can observe what many persons who have achieved prominence in their career, business and in other secular and religious activities have done with their time. Very few persons have achieved outstanding feats without a period of intensive training, and working smartly and making full use of opportunities presented or which he can create. Of course there must be room for the moving of the Holy Spirit in our lives, since we will not achieve lasting success and fulfil the full purpose of the Lord in our lives in our own strength or wisdom.

The Apostle Paul did not achieve instantaneous transformation from Saul, the prosecutor of Christians, to the very successful 'father of the modern day church', Apostle Paul. Galatians Chapters One and Two identifies that the process of preparation occurred over a period of more than fourteen years and even while he had achieved international prominence he still receive a new spiritual, managerial and other revelations. Even Jesus underwent a period of preparation before He launched His ministry when He was thirty years old. Several prominent ministers of the gospel today attend seminary and/or other programs of training.

The salary of a person is often influenced by factors such as his profession, how he is able to market himself based on his performance on the Job. In the heavy weight boxing arena, for example, boxers such as Mike Tyson earned over US$10 million for knocking out an opponent in a matter of minutes after the commencement of the first round. Prominent personalities are also paid handsomely for public appearances and other activities which are determined by the amount of time they have to expend preparing and making such presentations. Many persons are not paid a large salary for the job which they perform, and they may not have the necessary qualifications and other requirements to secure another job which will pay them a higher wage. Nevertheless, it is at least important, where possible and necessary, to seek avenues to earn additional income.

There are several things which we can do to maximize the way in which we use our time. This includes:

(a) **Know the perfect will of God for your life and continually stay on that course**,

(b) **Live each day of our lives as if it is our last one**. Jesus reiterated that we should work diligently since we do not know the time or the hour when He will return (Matthew 24:19). This is not only a spiritual principle, but it also has material implication.

(c) **Delegate responsibilities** to other members of the family and to colleagues at work, so that you can be released into areas where you can be most effective and successful. The

Medianite Priest, for example, encouraged Moses to institute this principle since Moses was tiring himself out judging all cases of the Children of Israel when they were in the Wilderness.

(d) **Count the cost**, and embark only as activities which can be realistically accomplished in the most cost effective and efficient way, of course taking cognizance of spiritual and other implications of such decisions,

(e) **Engage in leisure**; our day should be so well structured that we have time to relax and engage in other activities which would enable us to recuperate from a hectic lifestyle and plan effectively for the future.

> Do not live a life of fear and failure, depending on your limited ability? Instead, enjoy a life of success – harnessing His unlimited favor, maximizing the utilization the resources which He places at our disposal and persons for council, guidance, assistance and/or other forms of support.

CHRISTIANS BENEFIT FROM THE TREASURES OF THE UNRIGHTEOUS

God has given each person a measure of wisdom at birth. This ability can be increased as one embarks on following after His ways, for the fear of God is the beginning of wisdom. Many persons, even though they are born into a materially poor family, are still able to achieve significant academic, financial and other forms of success. Other persons are born into a wealthy family and are able to use this foundation to expand their personal wealth independently or that of the family and benefit from the corporate affluence. Conversely, there are some persons who would squander the wealth of their family and die in abject poverty.

There are several factors which determine the level of fame, wealth and other forms of success which a person will achieve in this life. These include the standard of guidance and council which he is exposed to and how well he utilizes business and other opportunities at his disposal and which he uses to his advantage. These will, to a large extent, determine the level of success. For the Christian, there is the additional benefit of the unmerited favour and grace which God provides to His children.

Several scripture passages admonish us that a person who reaps what he did not sow is a thief. Nevertheless, widows, orphans and other needy persons were allowed to glean the field and take the produce which the reapers do not want or which they find in the field after the reappears would have left. Similarly, there is provision in the Bible for the righteous to receive as a part of their inheritance, the treasures of the unrighteous. As alluded to earlier, many Christians who felt that they had enough faith (the so called 'name and claim theology'), laid their hands on other person's cars, walked around a building and other items and claimed that a miracle will occur and they will receive the item. Sadly, many such persons prayed and fasted, and possible had persons backing them in prayer, yet they did not receive 'the desires of their hearts.'

There are several instances in the Old Testament where Jehovah allowed the Children of Israel to plunder the property of the heathen nations after a victory in battle. There are also several examples where heathen nations merely surrendered their sovereignty, which included their possessions of animals, crops and precious metals to the Israelites. Conversely, when the children of Israel were leaving Egypt, Jehovah instructed them to ask the Egyptians for jewellery and other items and they were given these items in abundance.

A very interesting concept is highlighted in Psalm 49:10: **"¹⁰When we look at the wise, they die; fool and dolt perish together and leave their wealth to others."** Christians fall into the category of the wise and are therefore expected to benefit from the wealth of the unrighteous. How are we to derive this special grace from the Lord? This could take several forms such as:

(a) A person who is terminally ill may bequeath (leave) a percentage of their assets to their Christian relative, friend, doctor, nurse or other persons,

(b) Christians are offered lucrative business opportunities by associates and other persons who may be impressed with the management style of the believer,

(c) Christians being offered significant discounts when purchasing items,

(d) Christians experiencing miraculous debt write-off from agencies with whom they are indebted,

(e) Christians being promoted to very senior positions in organizations not only because of their outstanding performance but primarily because of the special grace which is on our lives as a result of our walk with the Lord. We are a chosen people, a royal priesthood.

(f) Special favours being received by the children and other relatives of Christians because persons in the society recognize the exemplary lives which their Christian parents lived and their contribution in tangible ways to society,

Jesus identified in Luke 16 some very important reasons why many Christians have not been successful in acquiring material wealth. In this parable Jesus related that the servant had squandered the property of his master and the master had called him to give an account of his stewardship. Fearing that he would be fired, he went to his creditors and agreed with them to reduce the amount which they owed his master. He did this in anticipation that if he was fired he would possibly be hired by them. Luke 16:8-12 states: **"8And the master commended the dishonest manager because he had acted shrewdly; for the children of this age are more shrewd in dealing with their own generation than are the children of the light. 9And I tell you, make friends for yourselves by means of dishonest wealth so that when it is gone, they may welcome you into the eternal home. 10Whoever is faithful in a very little is faithful also in much; and whoever is dishonest in a very little is dishonest in much. 11If you have not been faithful with the dishonest wealth, who will entrust you with true riches? 12And if you have not been faithful with what belongs to another, who will give you what is your own?"**

This is a very serious passage since at face value a person may arrive at misconceptions such as:

(a) It is okay to be dishonest, once it is for the purpose of 'saving his skin',
(b) It is permissible to conduct business deals with dishonest persons,
(c) The accumulation of wealth by dishonest practices is scriptural,
(d) When you lose your wealth which was acquired by dishonest practices, you will still have friends among the rogues whom you befriended during the dishonest deals which you conducted,
(e) Even if you accumulate wealth due to dishonest practices, you also have to take good care of it,

The following statements are presented to address

the above misconceptions:

(a) In the first instance God never expects us to indulge in any sinful act, even if our ultimate intention is to create a positive outcome. God expects one hundred percent honesty in all of our activities and we are not to seek to 'assist Him' by committing a sin even in an attempt to lead someone to Christ. We should not feel, for example, that by over-exaggerating a testimony, it would enhance the chances of a person being converted. If the testimony is what He is directing us to give to lead that person to Him, we can be assured that there is something about our true experience that would lead that person to Him.

There are many testimonies of people in the Bible and also among modern day Christians who chose the extreme of death rather than to renounce their faith. These experiences have resulted in the conversion of millions of persons who in cowardice renounced their faith. The martyrs preferred the reward in the Lord rather than nailing Him to the cross once again in denying Him. It should be recalled, however, that Peter thrice denied that he knew Christ, as Jesus foretold that He would have done before the cock crowed. However, Peter repented and he served the Lord faithfully thereafter.

(b) Christians should not indulge in, or encourage non-Christians to engage in a sinful lifestyle. Jesus, for example, as highlighted in Luke Chapter 19, dined with Zacchaeus who was the Chief Tax Collector, a profession which was classified as being very corrupt. However, there are several scriptures which rule against Christians being yoked to unbelievers.

(c) Using the example of Zacchaeus, again, we see that when he came to Christ, he was prepared to give half of his possessions to the poor and also make restitution of four times the value of whatever he had taken fraudulently from anyone. He also expressed the commitment to live a life of honesty. This is a demonstration that genuine repentance entails the six following stage; recognizing his sins, confessing them to the Lord, repenting of the sins, accepting the forgiveness of the Lord, turning from his former sinful ways, and follow the Lord faithfully.

(d) Even though we are still in the world, we are not of the world. This implies that as far as possible, we should not disassociate ourselves from non-Christians who may have been our friends before we were Christians. However, our relationship with them is expected to be different. Many persons, upon becoming a Christian, relinquish a close business association with persons who are not Christians. This is so because their business ethics may now be vastly different.

Jesus was not condoning unrighteousness; rather, He was possibly lamenting the fact that as Christians we very often do not tap into the wisdom and other gifts which He has vested in us. Rather, we are often willing to give up when we are confronted with challenges. An illustration of this attitude was displayed by the Prophet Elisha who, after he was mightily used by the Jehovah to perform extraordinary miracles, went and hid himself under a juniper tree in fear because of threats on his life made by Jezebel, the wicket queen. It was very likely that he could have called the fire of God's wrath down from Heaven to consumer her. Instead he hid from her. In the same way we are often willing to accept poverty, rather than find useful things to do and see God use our obedience to provide business concepts which we should invest in, or the right type of job which we should apply for and accept. When we are in difficult situations and/or need advice on a particular issue, we have recourse to seek council from persons with any of the five fold ministries operating in their lives.

Some of our methods will be unorthodox and contrary to the understanding and practice of the world, yet we have the necessary tools which are needed to succeed in all of our undertakings. There are two scripture verses which are often viewed as contradictory. Exodus 22:8 states: ***"⁸You shall take no bribe, for a bribe blinds the officials, and subverts the cause of justice"***

This scripture clearly outlaws a person presenting a gift to another with the deliberate intentions of perpetuating a dishonest deed. Yet Proverbs 18:16 states: ***"¹⁶A gift opens doors: it gives access to the great."***

This scripture is very dear to a very good friend who is a businessman. He has a principle of bringing gifts from overseas for persons who assisted him to facilitate the successful completion of a business deal. His rationale is that he is genuinely showing appreciation for favors granted to him, even if it was within the terms of reference of a person's job for which he is being paid. He ensures that the gift is given in secret and he does not leave without informing the recipient that the gift is a genuine show of his appreciation and he does not expect any special favors from the person in the future.

There are many employees who would refuse to accept a gift from a client particularly if they may have to interact with that person in their professional capacity in the future. This is so because there may be a feeling by the employee that he would be expected to extend favors in the future even at the expense of other customers who possibly should have been given preference. A person may also be afraid that it would be circulated that he is on the 'payroll' of the giver, which could result in disciplinary actions from the management of the organization.

It is important to be able to differentiate between a bribe and a genuine gift. A bribe is offered with an ulterior motive such as the subversion of justice or the anticipation of the return of some favour. A gift on the

other hand is usually extended in appreciation of a kind gesture which one received, in appreciation of someone and in commemoration of a special event. Even though some of the same sentiments may be presented by the person offering the bribe, the ultimate objective is to subvert justice and/or fair play. The difference between a gift and a bribe can be illustrated in the action of a husband presenting his wife with a bouquet of flowers as an expression of his love for her, and she may be appreciative of the gesture. However, his motive may be questioned by her if shortly after he presents the flowers he begins to make what she may deem as unrealistic demands which he is aware that she would not be normally disposed to concede to.

The above focus is but one of several interpretations of Proverbs 18:16. Another principle which is identified in this verse is the fact that each of us is endowed with gifts or talents, which if they are carefully nurtured and developed can open doors for us which we may not have imagined could have become a reality. For this reason it is important that a person learns from an early age and early in his Christian life, what is God's specific calling on his life. Knowing this and being able to consistently 'tap' into the resources which He has placed at our disposal to facilitate the fulfilment of that calling is integral in ensuring that we are successful in God's agenda. It should be recognized that the 'door' may not always be the way to enormous material wealth. Christians should also recognize that financial and other blessings are not to be used for selfish or sinful purposes, but for the furtherance of the Gospel.

It is important that a person seeks to attain the necessary qualification to enable him to be admitted to an educational or another institution, or to secure a job. However, a person should not be boastful and convey the impression that the achievements were as a result of his superior ability. We must give honour to God for what He has imputed in us for all glory and honour belongs to Him. It is true that we should thank others for their input into our achievements and also recognize that it was our sacrifice, ingenuity and other positive inputs which contributed to our success. Nevertheless, we should never forget that our existence is dependent on the protection and other blessings which come from the Lord.

Every Christian should be resolute in his pursuit of the Lord for his life with a sense of urgency and commitment to fulfil it. The importance of this thrust is confirmed by numerous scripture verses which condemn slothfulness, double mindedness and other unscriptural practices. On the other hand, many persons make very bad decisions; destroy their lives and that of others because of their pursuit of aspirations which are inconsistent with the will of the Lord for their life. This may be because of selfish aspirations and by using misguided methods in an attempt to acquire and maintain material wealth and even in other aspects of their lives such as their spiritual vocation. The disobedience of Jonah, for example, caused disaster to befall the sailors and the vessel when he chose to sail to Tarshish rather than Nineveh.

There are many wealthy persons whose lives are filled with much misery, and they are living at enmity with relatives, neighbours, their employees and other persons. Of course there are also persons who are poor and who experience bad relationship with others. Even though being a Christian does not guarantee material wealth, it does enable a true believer to be content with whatever material possessions he has, while being challenged to significantly improve his status in life. Christians are not expected to be lazy but should be challenged to significantly improve their standard of living, knowing that the Lord has promised to bless the thing which we put our hand to do, guide our paths, and to protect us. In Deuteronomy 8:17-18 God identified the source of lasting wealth which will be a blessing to the person/s who accumulated it and also to others. "**[17]Do not say to yourself, "My power and the might of my own hand have gotten me this wealth. [18]But remember the Lord your God, for it is He who gives you power to get wealth, so that you may confirm His covenant that He swore to your ancestors, as He is doing today."**

It is interesting to observe the method which God used when dealing with the generation of the children of Israel under Moses and Joshua. Under Moses, God opened the Red Sea for them, manna fell from heaven and other miracles were performed. Under Joshua, it was a different relationship in many respects. The people had to work very hard to provide for themselves, they had to dig wells to obtain water and fight to expel hostile nations. There is reason to believe that even though God has already provided us with the means to improve our material resources and other aspects of our lives, we must use the tools which He has placed at our disposal to enable us to achieve success. These include:

    (a)   His untenable favour, which is given freely to each Christian. Very often we experience opportunities being presented to us that we have no other choice but to recognize that it must have been the Lord who provided the avenue for us to improve our financial and other resources. This does not infer that every opportunity comes from the Lord, for we must be discerning in differentiating what is a blessing from the Lord as against a deception by the devil.

    (b)   The word of wisdom, discernment and other spiritual gifts which may be manifest in our lives or in others, from whom we may seek godly council and direction,

(c) The weapons of our warfare, many of which we can apply to the management of a business, on the job or whatever method we are using to increase our financial resources and other areas of our lives,

It is a fact that God often opens an avenue for us to acquire material wealth and enjoy other blessings without our having to work excessively hard to acquire. This is usually in response to principles such as:

(a) Granting us the increase from investments which we have made such as sowing 'financial seeds' to help the poor and needy,

(b) The blessing of receiving an 'inheritance' from our parents, grand-parents and/or other persons,

(c) We do not incur high medical and other expenses; we enjoy protection from burglars and other catastrophes because of His grace, mercies, favours and other blessings which He extends towards us directly and through others,

The Lord would not expose His children to situations which are beyond the grace which he gives us to endure and/or our ability to manage. This principle is illustrated in the life of Job, Daniel and Joseph, for example. However, there are many occasions when we have to 'work smart' in order to ensure that continued success is achieved and maintained.

GAMBLING

The issue of whether or not Christian should be involved in gambling has split many congregations, families and persons in the wider community. Nevertheless, many governments have legislated gambling. There are established horse racing dens, casinos, national lotteries, bingo and other betting houses and other facilities in most countries. In addition, there are several sporting and other activities where betting and other forms of gambling play an essential part. They include horseracing, football and boxing. Several church organizations would also host bingo lottery and other forms of gambling as a part of their annual fair and other fundraising activities. This causes dissatisfaction with members who do not agree with these practices.

There are several references in the Bible of persons 'casting lots' in order to arrive at a crucial decision. This includes incidents such as the sailors who cast lots in an attempt to find out whose sin was causing the ship to experience the turbulence. The lot fell on Jonah. Secondly, after Judas committed suicide, the disciples met with the intention of selecting a successor for him. In the latter example it was stated that the disciples prayed before the names of the persons whom they had identified as suitable candidates for the position were placed in a container. A member of the group placed his hand in the container and randomly selected the name of the candidate. Even though there was no 'scientific' method of selection to determine the candidate, the fact that prayers were offered before the selection, the process was seen as being directed by God. If, on the other hand, the process is not preceded by prayer and other measures which involve the direction of the Lord, then it is tantamount to gambling or using some method which is not scriptural. However, the practice of praying that one wins the lottery, or for a special revelation of the 'lucky' number/s' is not supported by scripture.

There are several issues surrounding the act of gambling which render it unscriptural. These include:

(a) **Gambling on games such as bingo and lottery does not usually entail having to use a high level of intelligence or personal ingenuity in order to be able to win.** It is primarily dependent on 'luck and chance,' which is not consistent with Biblical principles. It is noted, however, that persons who gamble by playing games such as poker and horseracing may require some level of skill, research and the application of knowledge in order to win on a consistent basis.

(b) **A very high percentage of persons who engage in gambling become addicted to gambling,** even though they may not be willing to admit it, or may not have even recognized it. Stopping the practice is very often very difficult. Many persons continue to play with the hope that the next game will be the 'big one,' where they will become rich whenever they are 'bated' by several small wins, they continue to realize a net loss from gambling.

(c) **Gambling fuels greed,** in that as a person endeavors to acquire more than he would normally be able to earn. After not being able to achieve this goal, many gamblers indulge in criminal activities in an attempt to achieve this elusive dream.

(d) **A large percentage of gamblers engage in stealing, lying and other sinful acts in order to finance this addiction.** Persons who live with a compulsive gambler can relate to the dramatic mood swings which the gambler experiences as he is propelled to take 'a final chance' in an attempt to regain his/her loss or to win 'the big one'. Such persons are usually abusive to those around them as they attempt to secure the money to gamble. Many gamblers end up selling all of their assets, their bodies and any other item they can get their hands on in an attempt to gratify their addiction. Many such persons have to undergo therapy, prayer and deliverance in order to be freed from this demon.

(e) Once a person is willing to deal with 'lucky numbers' and other issues of 'chance', the devil and his advisers are in the background to lure them further and further into demonic deception. **Many governments, church officials and other persons support gambling even though they condemn the use of narcotic drugs, since they fail to recognize that the same devil controls both addictions.**

(f) **Gambling lures persons into a false sense of security** as they fantasize on what they would do 'when they win'. This deception often causes such persons to spend lavishly and make financial and other decisions which they perceive will reflect their lifestyle 'when they win'. Sadly, for most gamblers, this is never a reality, at least not to the extent which would make their 'dreams come true.'

(g) **Many persons consult fortune tellers, witches and other mediums for their 'lucky' numbers and other directions**. Therefore, the money which is paid out is 'tainted'. It is true that the same criticism can be leveled at the managers of some businesses and other institutions and persons who sell themselves and their activities to the devil in order to derive financial and other forms of 'successes'.

(h) Persons who indulge in this practice are often possessed, or at least influenced by demons. A topical question which is frequently asked on this issue is whether or not it is scriptural for a church organization to accept a financial or other gift offered by persons who win from gambling, the sale of illegal drugs and indulge in other sinful practices. Many preachers categorically reject offerings from such persons while others would accept it providing they are reassured that their action does not contravene laws such as being an accessory to a crime, for example, since 'the unrighteous

will give into the bosom of the righteous.'
- (i) **The average gambler is never satisfied** and he endeavors to win higher stakes,
- (j) **The lives of most gamblers have becomes more unhappy after the win.** Many persons who have won large amounts on bingo and lotteries, for example, often confessed that they found themselves surrounded by relatives and friends whose loyalty and affection may not be genuine and is only extended with the aim of receiving a monetary gift or other favors. A person may be robbed and/ killed by an intruder.
- (k) **Gambling contradicts the very basis of our relying on the principles of God's provision** since it takes our reliance away from God, as the gambler seeks to invoke demonic forces in their quest for a win. The same analogy does not normally apply to us working to earn a living, unless a person is also indulging in dishonest working and other ethical practices.
- (l) After the fall of man in the Garden of Eden, God decreed to men in Genesis 3:19 as follows: "[19]**By the sweat of your face you shall eat bread until you return to the ground, for out of it you were taken; you are dust.**"

Over the years, women have also joined the work force, which is also extended to non manual labor. **The primary principle of work is that it entails the use of a person's intellect, physical strength, skills, the application of knowledge, experience, training and other faculties to generate a desired output.** Usually the element of 'luck and chance' does not enter the main stream of what is classified as work. It is true that factors other than market forces often influence the salary of a person or the level of returns on investment, for example. For the Christian this is not dependent on 'luck and chance'. A farmer, for example, may decide to plant a crop outside of the normal planting season and harvest it outside of the normal reaping season and therefore generate a high return as a result of the demand for the product since there is a shortage in supply. This breaking away from the tradition may have entailed that he would have had to be more attentive to the crop and possibly use more fertilizer and apply water and more care and attention to sustain the plant through the adverse weather condition. However, the outcome was not a result of 'luck or chance' but may be because of the use of his wisdom and knowledge of farming and market forces.

> Since the 'flesh' will never be satisfied continually, many persons are hooked on lust, gambling, greed and other sinful activities. A person will only find continual satisfaction when he is living for Christ and consistently give Him pre-eminence over every area of his life.

CONCLUSION

This chapter reviewed several aspects of financial management from a macro and micro perspective as it relates to the family. It reiterates that many persons have to overcome misconceptions such as that Christianity is synonymous with poverty. It is therefore important that we manage our financial and other material resources so that there is enough remaining to enable us to contribute towards the spreading of the gospel to this world which is dying from unethical business and other practices. For this principle to become effective, it is important that Christians be aware that financial management is not merely a textbook or academic vocation.

Although some readers may have found some issues discussed in this chapter a bit 'over their heads' the intention is to challenge our awareness that Christianity is not only shouting 'glory hallelujah,' although this is a very important aspect of worship. It also entails taking the scriptures literally and allowing the Holy Spirit to guide us into managing our finances, investing prudently and reaping a harvest of abundance in every aspect of our lives, to the glory of Jehovah.

It was highlighted that money is not the answer to true happiness; this only comes from a consistent relationship with the Lord. Very often persons who are rich are more miserable than the poor. This may be due to the fear of theft and of persons who only display affection and loyalty merely because of their quest to be handsomely compensated financially or otherwise. Even though many persons prefer to be rich and miserable rather than to be poor and happy, Christians can enjoy the best of both worlds by being rich and happy, even though our riches are not only found in material assets. This is so because we are indeed true royalties; for we are the children of the Most High God, the King of Kings and Lord of Lords. Therefore, the quest to achieve financial security is important for a family, and Christians should endeavour to achieve the best for their family and still have excess to assist the poor and needy and also to contribute towards the financing of the spreading of the gospel.

The mismanagement of financial resources is one of the primary reasons for millions of divorces, underachievement by persons and a major contribution to financial and other major challenges in families and the wider community. **Christians should be happy budgeting, investing prudently and generating substantial returns from business ventures and/or enjoying promotions on their job. We should not be a people who are merely surviving from one pay check or payday to another on a meagre wage, on welfare, on a meagre pension, or even begging for assistance, when God has made the provision that while we are on this** earth to enjoy material and other blessings. Instead of living in poverty, we should be helping the poor, going on vacations, and attending conventions in various countries and be able to cater to our personal, material and other needs, that our loved ones, other believers and the wider community have.

No Christian family should be living continuously in abject poverty (unless one takes such a vow as the late Mother Theresa of Calcutta did), when the Lord has promised us abundance even while we are on earth. As a meek people, we were promised that we will inherit the earth (Matthew 5:5). In addition, Jehovah has promised to meet all of our needs according to His riches in Glory (Philippians 4:19).

The Money (Currency) Paradigm		
1. Money (currency)	=	Current (free flowing water).
2. Stagnant water	=	Sickness & death.
3. No giving, excessive spending, unwise saving & investment (squandering).	=	Stagnation or little material growth and adversely affect the spiritual and other aspects of our lives.
4. Free & wise giving, prudent saving and investment	=	Replenishment and addition from the Lord and men.

Notes

Chapter 2
CHILDREN – A WISE FINANCIAL INVESTMENT

INTRODUCTION

As alluded to in Chapter One, nothing in this life is inherently free, even though the final user may not have to pay a monetary price for it. Salvation, for example is a free gift which God has offered us. However, Jesus paid for our salvation by dying on Calvary for our sins. Even so, we should not expect to enjoy the pleasures of having loving, god-fearing children who are fulfilling the calling of the Lord on their lives, unless we are prepared to pay the price by meeting the financial, spiritual, emotional and other demands of good parenting.

Some couples choose to, or because of medical or other reasons, remain childless all the days of their marriage. Couples who choose to do so when they are able to parent children may pursue this course of action on the basis that they feel that they are unable to adequately parent children. This may be because of financial and other reasons which they feel would render them incompetent to adequately rear children with excellent values. The sad thing is that most couples who embark on such a course of action may be financially better off than many couples who choose to have a large family. This certainly is a contradiction, which infers that for most couples who have a large family, the immediate financial position of the family is often not the most important consideration.

Parenting is very demanding on our time, finances, patience and other aspects of our lives. Fortunately, it is not only about giving, for parents are blessed from the time the child is conceived. Once we do our part and allow the Holy Spirit to do His in the rearing of our children, we will have the ultimate pleasure of parenting men and women who have learnt what it is to fulfil the calling of the Lord on their lives and to make a valuable contribution to the development of society. If we are so blessed, we will also live to see our children and even future generation/s being a blessing to our children also.

It should be noted that the returns from investing in the lives of children should not be for selfish reasons on the part of parents where the children would be obligated to care for their parents if/when they are elderly. Instead, investment in this context should be viewed as parents sowing godly principles, our time, love, finance and other resources into the lives of their children so that they can be the best persons God desires them to be. The returns which godly parents desire are to know that our child/children mature into adults who are walking in the way of the Lord. This pathway also credits responsible citizens capable of loving and caring his family, qualified professional in his area of specialization.

Some persons would prefer to say that parents are merely fulfilling an obligation of being the best parents they possibly can be when they undertake the responsibility of parenting. There are too many parents who have not been successful in this vital role because:

(a) They have not committed their lives to the Lord, and therefore, have not allowed the Creator of the universe to direct their lives and that of their children,

(b) They are often too consumed with their personal problems, poverty and marital difficulties to be able to devote the necessary time, finances and other requirements essential to being good parents,

(c) Children are often rebellious and reject the godly teachings and examples of their parents,

The following sections review important financial issues which are relevant in the upbringing of God fearing children.

THE PRE-NATAL PERIOD

The span of time between the conception and delivery of a baby is the pre-natal period. The reaction of the couple to the confirmation and announcement of a pregnancy is primarily dependent on whether or not the couple was desirous of having a baby or not at that particular time. Some of the reactions are:

(a) A couple may have been married for a number of years but for medical or other reasons the wife was unable to conceive, this could be welcome news,

(b) The wife may have suffered one or several miscarriage/s. This experience may cause much anxiety as the couple consults their physician for advice on how another miscarriage can be avoided. There may be financial demands such as having to pay for the services of a maid to attend to the mother to be since she may be confined to bed-rest by her physician. This may be because if she is very active she may experience a miscarriage.

(c) For an unmarried couple who may have indulged in sexual intercourse without using a suitable contraceptive to prevent the ensuing pregnancy, a pregnancy is not welcome news. This may also be the response of a couple who have more than four children and were not desirous of having an additional child, but their contraceptive did not prevent the pregnancy. Even though a couple should not indulge in sexual intercourse unless they are married, many couples contravene this command of the Lord. The consequence is often that the mother may be saddled with the responsibility of having to rear her child as a single parent since her partner abandons her. Securing the assistance of the court or welfare system may only result in the father having to make a minimal monthly contribution to the upkeep of the child. There are also numerous 'dead-beat dads' who abandon even this responsibility and keep eluding law enforcement agencies.

The pre-natal period is usually one of the most expensive times in the lives of many couples. Some of the major issues to be addressed are:

(a) **The diet of the mother.** Some mothers undergo dramatic changes in their preference of food type from day to day or shorter periods. Many women would have a craving from exotic food items to outrageous items such as sour or bitter fruits or other items such as chalk or charcoal.

(b) **Visits to the gynaecologist, family planning clinic and/or other medical facilities.** Payment may have to be made for expenses such as for consultations, medication and the ultrasound. Some mothers also attend special exercise programs to assist in the delivery of the baby.

(c) **The preparations for the baby.** These may range from the design and decoration of a special nursery for the baby, to simply purchasing or securing a crib from a relative or friend. In poorer families, the baby may have to share the bed with the mother and eventually with both parents. This obviously is not a healthy practice, since it exposes the baby to infections particularly if the bed linen is not hygienic and contagious diseases can be easily transmitted from the parents to the child. In addition, someone may accidentally lay on the baby.

(d) **The purchase of special clothing and other items for the baby:** These may include a stroller, toys, pampers and/or napkins. There may also be special gadgets such as a communication system where a mini amplifier is placed in the baby's crib, bed or wherever the baby is and speakers placed at strategic rooms such as the kitchen, and bathroom, where the mother can hear the baby's breathing and crying. In the event that the baby is in distress, assistance can be granted promptly.

(d) **Care must be taken to ensure that the mother is as comfortable as possible during her pregnancy so that she has the best opportunity of delivering a healthy baby.** Some families make major renovations to the house to ensure that the mother is protected from the possibility of falling down a steep stairway or bumping into objects, thus a room is renovated on the lower flat to prevent her from having to climb the stairways.

The importance of ensuring that the mother uses a balanced diet, has adequate amount of rest and exercise and be in an environment which is stress free as far as possible, cannot be overemphasized. It is a fact that many of the conditions which affect the mother can have an adverse effect on the baby. In addition, it is possible for addictive chemicals such as caffeine which is added to some brands of coffee, tea and coke, nicotine in cigarettes, cocaine and marijuana to penetrate the protection of the placenta and can cause the baby to develop addictions to such substances but also in many instances could cause permanent damage to the child. Physical injuries to the mother, particularly in the region of her stomach can also damage the frail body of the foetus.

A healthy spiritual atmosphere in the home and comfortable environment where there is much love and understanding between the couple and other persons with whom she comes into contact on a regular basis and other aspects of a healthy life style go a long way towards enabling the baby to experience a comfortable period of growth and development in its mother's womb. There is no financial tag attached to many issues which are important to see a mother successfully through to a successful delivery of a healthy baby, where she does not suffer post-natal depression and other negative side effects as a result of the delivery. Many women suffer an extended period of post-natal depression and/or other symptoms and may have to undergo spiritual, medical, and other forms of treatment to enable them to overcome the ailment. Successful prenatal care and deliver but there may be post natal considerations and negative effects of the delivery. Treatment of the latter may incur some expenses.

EARLY CHILDHOOD

The joy of the delivery of a newborn baby into the world can be overshadowed by severe pains as her body heals particularly after a caesarian section. Fortunately, if she and her husband are employed and/or they are financially secure, then they will not have to be unduly worried by the financial strain of the delivery at a private hospital or clinic. The public hospitals of many developing countries, in particular, experience a high rate of post-natal mortality and other problems, as alluded to earlier. Therefore, most women who can afford it would prefer to deliver their baby in an environment which is safe for her and also for the baby.

Many women who have private or group medical insurance, which covers the expenses of a delivery, deliver their baby at a private clinic. Their medical insurance scheme may cover a significant amount of the cost of the pre- and post-natal expenses, which are very significant in most countries. For women who are employed outside of the home, the National Insurance Scheme and their employers usually pay their salaries; (in some countries as many as three months after the delivery). During this period she is expected to have weaned the baby and be physically and mentally prepared to return to work. Some mothers suffer from post-natal depression which may be so severe that they have to be hospitalized. In extreme cases, the mother may completely reject the baby, resulting in her having to seek psychological and other forms of treatment and an attendant may also have to be hired to care for her and the baby.

Incidents of **cot-death** are prevalent in many countries. As a result there are a number of theories on how babies and infants should sleep and the care to prevent our precious jewels from dying before they have a chance to grow and develop into the gems whom God created them to be. Every care must be taken to ensure that the environment in which the baby grows is as accident free as possible. Some of the important considerations which are necessary for the healthy growth and development of a child include:

(a) **Providing a proper diet for the baby.** This must be appropriate to their nutrimental needs. This includes breast feeding for at least the first few months of the life of the baby. Some babies have the privilege of being breast fed for over two years. This feature is common in mothers who remain at home with the baby. A mother who works outside of the home may secure a breast pump to extract milk which is then stored in a sterilized container in a refrigerator and fed to the baby at the prescribed feeding time.

(b) **Adding supplementary food to the milk that the baby is taking.** Supplemental foods to the breast-feeding are introduced to the diet of the baby during the weaning stage. This may include the use of power or liquid milk specially formulated for children in various age ranges, Soya and other non-animal based milk for babies who are allergic to animal-based milk, packaged and bottled baby foods, cereals, fresh fruits, cooked vegetables, eggs and other appropriate food products to the baby's age and needs.

(c) **Making sure that the baby has appropriate clothing.** The baby's clothing can be very expensive particularly for families living in a country where there are several widely varying climatic seasons. There is, for example, the need to purchase winter and summer clothing, clothing to be worn at home and also clothing for special occasions such as church and visits to the post-natal clinic.

(d) **Having adequate amount of money to cover medical expenses and other necessities.** Some parents have the undesirable experience of having to spend much time and money on medical expenses on the baby. This may be as a result of birth defects which affect the child, the ingestion of harmful substances, injuries sustained in and around the home or on the playing field, and also common infections such as influenza and gastro-enteritis. Many parents rely on a combination of prayer and medical advice and treatment to enable the child to overcome such ailments.

(e) **Having the basic necessities to care for the baby.** Depending on the financial strength of the parents, this may include the purchase of a crib, stroller, play pen, toys, napkins, baby oils, shampoos, powder, towels, bath tub and other items needed to ensure that the baby grows healthily.

(f) **Making sure that the child is safe.** If a family has a car or other motor vehicles, there will be the need to purchase a car seat for the baby where the child can be strapped with a seatbelt. This is a legal requirement in an increasing number of countries. This important feature can be extended to include the installation of gates at the top of the stairs to protect the child from falling down steps, the installation of protection for electrical sockets, locks for cupboard and other features to protect the child from being injured, ingesting harmful substances and from being harmed in other ways.

(g) **Getting additional help for the mother.** As the child grows, some parents opt to have a day-helper to care for the baby and to assist the mother in washing the clothing of the baby feeding him, cooking and other responsibilities. Other parents opt to leave the child at a day care and the child is collected after the parents return from work. This is often a difficult decision since the child is exposed to contagious diseases which affect children even in the best day care centres.

(h) Caring for a child demands commitment of parents since it entails them having to sacrifice much of their time, finances and other resources to ensure that the child grows in the desired way of the parents and the Lord. It is often said that the greatest gift that parents can offer to their children is that of their time.

There is much merit in this statement, even though it must be viewed in its correct context.

Parents giving of their time from a Christian perspective include features such as:

(a) **Spending quality time in devotion with the family, attending church and engaging in other spiritual activities together as a family**,

(b) **Dedicating themselves to seek to understand what the needs of their children are and, as far as possible, attempt to meet those needs**,

(c) **Being around with their family as much as possible** so that the child can observe the good leadership and other positive qualities in the lives of their parents so that leadership is by precept,

(d) **Paying careful attention to situations when the child is experiencing discomfort** and seeks to remedy the problems, where possible, and prevent a recurrence,

(e) **Knowing the importance of, and implementing the art of cuddling, particularly for smaller children** (by ensuring that they do not experience discomfort due to over exposure to the elements). Acts such as cuddling the child and providing reassurance that the child is loved, are also important.

(f) **Spending time reading stories to them, and when they are learning to read listen to them reading.** Quality time must be taken to listen to them read, review their performance at pre-school and also monitor and assist them to complete their school and other assignments,

(g) **Playing indoor and outdoor games and enjoying other leisure activities with the child**,

(h) **Spending quality time giving guidance to the young adult** on important decisions such as their career path, dating and managing finance,

Rearing a child is often fraught with many financially demanding situations. They include:

(a) **Coping with medical conditions** such as measles, influenza, dysentery, diarrhoea, gastro-enteritis and other ailments are quite traumatic for parents and children as they ravish the little bodies of our children,

(b) **Children grow so quickly that caution must be taken that exact size clothing and footwear are not bought**, since in a matter of days they can be outgrown. New clothing usually shrinks after washing. Hence, a slightly larger size should be bought which will accommodate the projected growth of the child over the anticipated life span of the item. It must also be taken into consideration that an excessively large size makes the child uncomfortable and should be avoided. (Some families with children of the same sex, close relatives or friends who out grew their clothing may be able to use some of the clothing and other items from the older siblings or others. Poorer families may receive some support from relatives and friends, their church, charitable organizations, and the government in the more affluent societies).

(c) **The financing of the education of their children is expensive for most families**. This is particularly evident where parents opt to send their children to a private institution which may offer a higher standard of education and a better disciplined and well rounded student. There is usually tighter control and protection from gangs, illicit drugs and other undesirable practices.

Early childhood is an expensive period for most parents. The beautiful thing is that, for most parents, it is a joy to watch the baby grow, take the first step, and utter the first and subsequent words. The sad thing is that regardless of how rich and generous parents are, there always will be additional things which they would have liked to purchase and to do for their children. The important thing is for us to be able to differentiate between the wants and needs of the child and endeavour to meet at least the needs. Failure to satisfy the needs demand that parents examine issues such as:

    (a)   Is there a system of allocating the budget of the family? This would ascertain if there are items which can be omitted or at least deferred in order to satisfy the needs of the child or children.

    (b)   Is there an adequate amount of money coming into the family? If the answer is no, then parents can examine ways of generating additional amounts of income.

    (c)   Should external financial and/or other forms of assistance be sought from relatives, friends, the church, government and non-governmental agencies, where possible?

> Encouraging their children to save in a 'piggy-bank,' taking them to a commercial bank to open their own bank account and giving them small amounts to bank on the account, are great starters to encourage thriftiness in children. Similarly, encouraging little entrepreneurial ventures are incentives to promote the investment desire of the child. Above all, teaching the child Godly principles on prudent financial management principles and leading by being a good example will leave an indelible mark which will only auger well in the child's future.

THE MATURING CHILD

As the child grows older, the demands and expenses usually increase. Some of the important areas of spending are:

    (a)   **Food, clothing, shelter, educational, and other essential items,**

(b) **Extra curriculum activities**. These can also be an expensive expenditure depending on the financial status of the parents and the aptitude of the child. Some children indulge in sporting and other activities such as acting, lawn tennis, golfing, musical or other activities which are usually very expensive to finance. In many examples, parents are willing to take a second mortgage on their home, secure an additional job, relocate to another part of the country, or even immigrate to another country, to ensure that a child receives the best coaching and other facilities which will equip the child to excel at that activity. This decision has proven successful for a number of families, hence, the emergence of child prodigies, outstanding young athletes and academics.

(c) **Vacationing and camping expeditions, exchange programs**, particularly to other countries can be a very expensive exercise

> Children from richer families are usually offered a higher standard of education and more access to educational materials such as computers than children from poorer families. Adequate nutritious foods and other amenities are also provided. The result is that richer children are often two years ahead of their poorer counterparts in their educational attainment and other achievements. However, this does not mean that children from richer families will necessarily be outstanding achievers academically and otherwise while children from poorer families turn out to be social outcasts. Persons born in poverty are often challenged to significantly improve their standard of living, while those born in wealthy families are often not challenged to achieve much on their own. It is therefore important that parents and other influential persons instill financial discipline, the quest to achieve excellence and other positive influence in them and support them to achieve God's best for their lives.

Many children and young adults have gained national and/or international acclamation. Some of them have been able to translate their fame into generating substantial amounts of money for themselves and family. In many such instances, a family member would manage, or at least oversee the spending of the money generated as a result of the activities of the child.

There are instances where experienced business promoters and even family members and other close relatives exploit these young achievers, and they receive little financial and other returns for their success. Thankfully, some of these young people are securing adequate professional guidance on the management of their career and deriving most of the benefits for themselves and with whomever they desire to share it. Some prudent financial advisors make a generous amount available to the child and its parents, while the major part of the returns are placed in a trust which is administered by the parents and/or other reliable persons. In some instances this implies taking away the management of the affairs of the child or young adult from their parents.

As the young adult, or even adult contemplates furthering his/her education, the big question is how to raise the finances to cover this major expenditure which may include expenses such as the following items:

(a) **The cost of tuition** is usually the largest component of financing the education of most students,

(b) **The cost of boarding and lodging.** This can be very expensive particularly if the student is living in a dorm and boarding at the facility or other eating houses. It is often cheaper in accommodation where the student can cook, do their own laundry and perform other services for him/her self. However, this cost must be weighed against factors such as the time one would have to spend performing such duties, versus the time spent studying or engaging in sporting or other activities.

(c) **The cost of books.** The cost of books increases each year and most students, particularly those who attend higher institutions of learning, find it necessary to secure at least the core books for the subjects or courses being pursued. Some students take the option of purchasing used book where they may be able to benefit from notes or at least highlights from the previous reader. However, they can be distracted if such notes are misleading.

(d) **Clothing** is usually a major expense particularly for younger students who are caught up in wearing 'brand-name' clothing and keeping up with current trends. The result is that this constitutes a major expense for the students/and or their parents.

(e) **Computer facilities and accessories.** The use of the computer has become popular in educational institutions, in offices and at home. The use of the internet to access educational material, as a fast method of communications and for other purposes. There is thus a cost securing one or several computers, printers, the payment of internet fees and the purchase of accessories where more than one child is being educated.

(f) **Travel and transportation.** This can vary depending on one's proximity to the educational facilities, and whether or not one is desirous of using public or private transportation.

(g) **Student guild and student union dues, and fees for sporting and other activities**,

The life of a student is usually an exciting period for most persons. It is the period when many persons feel particularly blessed to be in an atmosphere where one is challenged to absorb the various concepts being taught and to make the best possible representation in examination or whatever form of assessment used. Some students, because of their academic, or sporting activities are able to secure a full or partial scholarship from their employers, the educational institution which they attend and/or will be attending, from their or a foreign government, an international institution or another agency to pursue their course of study. Others are able to work part time or full-time to finance their course of study, thus dramatically reducing the dependence on their parents or personal finance to pay for their studies.

Students who immigrate to another country to study, often have to pay more than twice the amount of the fees as local students. The rationale for this is often that the taxpayers of the country may be subsidizing the cost of tuition for the local students. In addition, the fact is that the local students are far more likely to remain in their country so that society will benefit from the training which they receive. The foreign student may also be at the disadvantage of having to purchase special clothing to suit the local climate, learning the local language, adjusting to the food and culture and making other adjustments as befitting the new environment. Fortunately, many foreign students are able to secure a scholarship from their government and/or international agencies to pursue their course of study. Of course, there are instances where students from third world countries are able to comfortably finance their studies from their own resources or from that of relatives and friends at home or in the country where they are studying.

Families living in the US, UK, Canada, France and other developed countries are often willing to finance at least the first year of the studies of their relatives in developing countries who are desirous of pursuing studies in these countries. Thereafter, the students may be expected to secure a scholarship and/or work part time to pay for their tuition and upkeep. After the student receives a formal acceptance letter from the education institution, the relative in the developed country would usually send a bank statement, a job letter and other supporting documents to the person who is desirous of studying in the developed country. These documents are submitted to the relevant immigration authority during an interview with a consulate officer where it will be determined if that person is eligible to be granted a student visa.

An essential role of parents is that of **teaching their children Biblical principles of financial management**. They will learn about many of these principles as they study the word and from the teachings at Sunday school, church, youth group and other forums. However, the best example is usually the parents who lead by godly example. Important training techniques include:

(a) **Teach them to observe that everything which we have belongs to God**. Therefore, we are accountable to Him for all of our actions, including how we earn and spend money.

(b) **Once they are old enough, allow them to participate in the process of preparing the family budget**. When they understand the direction in which the Lord is leading the family, there are usually less demands for items which could disrupt the achievement of their goals.

(c) **Encourage them to tithe and give their offering, donate to the poor and other worthy causes**,

(d) **Inform them of financial goals which the family is endeavouring to achieve for them**. This may include a savings program for their higher education or an endowment insurance policy.

(e) **Encourage them to save from their allowance and increase their saving when additional funds are available**,

(f) **Encourage them to spend their money wisely**. It is remarkable how the taste of the child can be moderated when he has to spend his own money to purchase an item, as against his lavish taste when the money is coming from his parents.

(g) **Avoid giving the child a large allowance if he is using it to purchase non-essential items.** Parents who are lavish spenders often pass this trait on to their children. There are also parents who, even though they are now financially secure, were very poor when they were children. Hence, they allow their children to spend lavishly, possibly as a deliberate or even subconscious way of enabling their offspring to enjoy the lifestyle which the parents were deprived of when they were younger.

(h) **Avoid giving monetary and other gifts as the only or main way of expressing love** for our children. Many parents are too busy to spend quality time with their children, so they shower them with gifts in an attempt to make up for this deficiency. Even though the gift may be appreciated, it is better if parents are able to devote more personal care and attention to their children.

(i) **Avoid using money or any other item to create friction in the home.** This may be done when one child is always showered with the best gifts while another is neglected. Even though it is wise to use a reward system for children who complete their chores and achieve excellence at school, care must be taken that material things are not the only things used to reward and/or punish children.

(j) **When children see their parents achieve financial and other goals, they are often encouraged to set and to achieve themselves**,

(k) **Children should not be denied essential items which their parents can comfortably afford merely for the parents to show 'who is the boss' or for other selfish reasons,**

Some parents experience that by giving an allowance which is not based on the performance of duties or other standards which reflect the achievement of goals, that it did not adequately prepare a child for the world of work where it is common that a person is only paid for duties performed, and the higher the standard of performance the greater the reward will be.

Many of our offspring, even after they are married, experience difficulty in managing their finance and other aspects of their lives. On impulse, many parents may reach out and offer financial and other forms of assistance. This may be a continuation of a trend which was perpetuated as the child grew and, because of his inability to manage money and other facets. **There is a stage when we have to say that 'enough is enough' and the adults have to master the principle of managing their financial and other responsibility with little or no input from parents and other persons.**

One of the serious mistakes which many parents make is to continue financing the education and other ventures if the child does not have an aptitude, discipline and other positive attributes and ability to succeed in. A typical example is where a student continues to change majors at college or other institution over several years when their parents are financing the program. A better approach is often to advise the students to attend the institution on a part-time basis while working and paying their own fees. Some students also attend a junior college at the initial stage of their education where the fees are cheap and transfer their credits to a senior college or university which has a higher accreditation. During the early stages of their studies, they will be afforded the opportunity of assessing what they would like to major in and also the career path to pursue.

> Many persons attempt to 'box God in,' in that they expect Him to operate in a stereo-type way. There are a number of things which often move God. They include:
> - *His Word; He never deviates from the principles outlined in His the Bible.*
> - *To bring glory to Himself (which is also in accordance with His word)*
> - *His specific plan for that person's life and those persons whom his life would impact.*
> - *Persons who walk in obedience to His word and act in faith.*
>
> For this reason we should not think it strange when one person receives an abundance of blessings while another may just be able to 'keep his head above the water' or even sink. Since Cain did not appreciate this principle, he killed his brother Abel in a state of jealousy. Some Christians seem to be working hard all the days of their lives and never seem be able to 'make ends meet,' while other persons may seem to be 'taking things lightly,' yet abundance follow their lives. The difference may be as a result of the relationship with Him, our confession and the extent to which we are able to apply His promises in our lives.

HEALTH ISSUES

The Bible places a high premium on the importance of caring for our bodies, the temple of flesh which houses our soul and spirit. God expects us to take good care of our bodies. For this reason He instituted several health laws which are designed to ensure that we are healthy in body, soul and spirit. Some of these principles are identified in the condemnation of activities such as gluttony and the mutilation of our bodies.

It is scriptural that we should consciously seeking to avoid worrying and other conditions which cause mental agony and prevent the healing of our body, soul and spirit. However, only brief mention will be made of health issues since several Christian medical doctors and other persons have elaborated on this topic. However, it is noted that the observance of God's health and other laws has financial implications in that they save us having to pay for medical services, and promote a healthy lifestyle throughout our lives. We are also able to study and absorb what we study, be more productive in our jobs and perform better in just about every area of our lives when we are physically healthy.

The importance of managing our intake of food cannot be over emphasized. Many persons literally eat themselves to death by not eating the correct types of food and also by eating too much or too little of the important food groups which are essential for our sustenance and health. Common problems which arise associated with eating include:

(a) **Anorexia and bulimia, which are two eating disorders**. Many persons who suffer from these sicknesses have to undergo spiritual deliverance, psychotherapy and other forms of treatment,

(b) **Irregular metabolism**. This is associated with the malfunctioning of the thyroid glands, liver, pancreas and other organs. The malfunctioning of the digestive system and other areas of the body results in its inability to absorb the nutrients. The result is that there are millions of persons who are seriously overweight or underweight and as a result suffer from other digestive related ailments. There are millions of persons who are obese because they overeat, do not follow a disciplined exercise program, and so experience sleeping disorders and other physiologically related problems. However, there are a significant number of persons who suffer from this condition because of the malfunctioning of organs of their bodies. Many such persons have to undergo surgical and other medical programs in order to correct or at least control these problems.

(c) **Gluttony** which is the sinful act of overeating. Most persons can recognize when they have had enough food to satisfy themselves. However, many persons when experiencing psychological and other problems deliberately overeat. This leads to overweight with all of its associated problems. There are several financial and other negative consequences of overeating. They include:

(i) A high food bill since one or several members of the family may have a craving for particular types of food. These are usually foods which are high in fat and carbohydrate contents. Foods improperly cooked by methods such as deep frying also contribute to this state.

(ii) The difficulty in obtaining ready-made clothing to fix extremely obese persons often means that they have to secure a tailor or seamstress to make clothing for them. They may be very expensive,

(iii) Because of the pressure of the excessive fat in their bodies, many obese persons experience heart and other physical problems,

(iv) There is also the psychological problem of being taunted by associates and even scoffed at by strangers because of one's size. Many such persons have to undergo medical treatment in an attempt to manage the adverse effect of the fat on their bodies.

We should not scoff at persons who are obese but instead we should express understanding and where possible, offer to assist in whatever way we can. Ways in which we can assist include being a good friend who would encourage such persons to eat sensibly, assisting in an exercise program and encouraging them to substitute eating with other activities such as being involved in sports. Since many persons are obese because of hormonal imbalance and other medical reasons, we have to be very sensitive to their self-consciousness and show love and understanding instead of shunning or taunting them.

Many younger women in particular feel pressured into achieving a figure which is seen as attractive. This enabled many models, singers, actors and actresses, beauty queens and other persons to achieve much fame and fortune. As a result, many other persons attempt to achieve these goals which demand a regular exercise program, possibly with a personal trainer at home or at a gym, and adhering to a disciplined lifestyle. Most of these activities have a high price tag and persons who pursue them are not guaranteed the success which could bring them national and international acclimation and the concomitant financial and other rewards. There are so many 'rags to riches' stories in Hollywood, in the music, sporting and other industries, that many persons are willing to dedicate much of their youthful life into pursuing such dreams. Thankfully, many of these persons who are in pursuit of their dreams in glamour and fame have seen the importance of having at least a college education. The rationale is having a 'fall-back' position to which they can resort in the event that their dreams do not materialize.

The Bible refers to several types of fasting and there are specific instructions which have to be adhered to when fasting. Spiritual fasting should be complemented with consistent prayer and constant communion with the Lord. Many poor persons undergo periods of compulsory fasting since they do not have money to purchase food. Other persons practice fasting purely for the health benefits of detoxifying the body from impure substances which accumulate in our bodies from the foods we eat, inadequate amount of exercise and other unhealthy life style choices which we make. Some persons use the principle in 1 Corinthians 7:5 which relates to abstaining from sexual intercourse while devoting themselves to prayer during the period of fasting also. The importance of fasting, should not be under emphasized as an important spiritual as well as physical discipline.

Biblical fasting is a primary way of 'mortifying the flesh' and a sure way of getting closer to the Lord where

He can instill His purpose and direction in our lives. (Jesus, for example demonstrated the spiritual strength which can be derived when He fasted for forty days and forty nights). It is also an important way of maintaining a healthy body and active mind. Many persons undergo a period of detoxifying the body where one gradually reduces the intake of solid foods, use purifying medications including herbs and other natural materials to prepare the body for the extended period of decrease in the normal food intake. It is also important to gradually attune the body back to the normal eating habit at the end of the fast by using liquids and softer foods initially to prevent damage to the digestive system.

There are several types of fasts which can be practiced. They include:

(a) Total abstention from food and water over a period. Jesus practiced this type of fast when he secluded himself in the wilderness for forty days and nights. This is a very demanding exercise where the body after being deprived of nutrients from food, would engage in internal cannibalization by absorbs nutrients from internal tissues in order to survive. It is therefore necessary for persons who are desirous in engaging in an extended period of fasting, should be supervised by a qualified medical practitioner or nutritionist if it is being undertaken over an extended period.

(b) Total abstention from food while taking water and fruit, eggs and/or vegetable juices,

(c) Abstention from eating meat in general or certain types of meats and other types of food items,

A large number of families have the additional responsibility of caring for a member of the family who suffers from some form of challenge. This ranges from blindness, deafness, muscular dystrophy, heart problems, persons suffering from Down Syndrome, polio and other forms of illnesses. There are also persons who have lost one or several limbs as a result of motor and other forms of accidents and persons suffering from wounds inflicted during a military and other forms of combats. This is often an extra responsibility which parents and other relatives have to shoulder very often with little assistance from the church and the state. Thankfully, many countries are increasing the emphasis or making these persons as comfortable as possible by providing financial, medical and other forms of assistance for them and persons who care for them. There are also special provisions such as making public and commercial buildings accessible to persons using wheel chairs and are otherwise challenged.

There are special schools which cater for the special needs of persons who are physically and/or mentally challenged or who have special needs which have to be addressed. Persons who are bind are taught to read using Braille while sign language is taught to the deaf. There are also special facilities such as physiotherapy for persons with walking and other physical challenges. Many churches have also employed the services of persons to communicate with the deaf by using sign language and providing special access to church for persons using wheel chair. However, there is still a need for more to be done to assist persons who are challenged in one form or another to be fully integrated into the community.

More financial and other forms of assistance should also be provided to parents and other persons who care for the physically challenged. The cost of medical insurance coverage and other expenses for such persons are usually very high and their relatives often have to bear most of the expenses once the elderly did not make adequate financial provision for such eventualities. In addition, the children and other relatives of the elderly usually have to dedicate much time and patience attending to their needs. The Lord still heals and many persons are healed from their challenges. However, the Lord often gives us the grace to provide loving care to these persons who are a special blessing to their families.

> **Our attitude** in terms of savings, investments and our general financial discipline, **determines our altitude** in terms of our progress in academics, savings and investments, spiritual and other areas of our lives.

CAREER GUIDANCE AND PERSONAL DEVELOPMENT

There are several implications in choosing a career path. There are usually financial implications in choosing a career since the process of training adequately to maximize one's return from the career usually involves the investment of finance, time and other valuable resources. The irony is that some parents choose the career path which they want their children to pursue even before they are born. As a matter of fact, they often act as God, who knew us before we were born as highlighted in Jeremiah 1:5: "⁵**Before I formed you in the womb I knew you, and before you were born I consecrated you. I appointed you a prophet to the nations.**"

There are several factors which may lead to a person pursuing a particular career path. They include:

(a) **Being 'pushed' into it by parents and other family members**. This may be because the family has a history in a particular area such as farming, medicine, law or business. Predecessors may have the necessary books, influence in society and other attributes which are admirable to younger generations who seek to emulate elders. Conversely, parents and other members of the family may coerce younger ones into accepting a particular path since it would be an asset to the family business.

(b) **Possessing a 'natural' aptitude for a particular career.** Some persons have an innate liking for a particular career. It is not uncommon to find a person who may be struggling to attain academic pursuits, while if that person is placed in a kitchen, even without any formal training, that person has a glow about experimenting with various dishes and is an excellent chef or caterer. Even though a person may not be 'born as a genius,' some persons seem to have an innate ability to excel in particular endeavours. It is not uncommon to find a child from an early age declaring that he wants to pursue a particular career and despite numerous changes by others is consistent in his choice. Such an occurrence is usually appreciated by parents, which contrasts with other persons whose parents may be spending an enormous amount of money on them since they choose to change career paths when they may be near to the completion of the training for a previous choice.

A person may decide to become a lawyer, early in life since one likes debating and also admires the command which the lawyers seen on television, have over the courtroom and also their assisting in determining the fate of persons accused of committing various crimes. A child may desire to become a doctor, since he is desirous of caring for the medical needs of his parents and others who he has seen suffering from some ailment. Of course it is normal for a person to change his preference of a career several times as his perception of life changes. This may be due to financial and other considerations and of course when one identifies the specific calling on one's life which may be different from one's personal choice. For this reason children and youth should learn what it is to hear from the Lord for His direction in vital areas such as their career.

(c) **Expecting lucrative financial returns**. This may include careers such as professional acting, modelling, sporting activities, computer science, medical science, and business executives, of course for persons who have achieved the zenith of these professions.

(d) **'By accident.'** This phrase is highlighted since nothing happens by accident or by chance to a Christian who is consistently in **fellowship** with the Lord. However, it is the experience of some persons that 'an opportunity appeared' and they took advantage of it, the result being that they are/were able to pursue a career is/was financially rewarding and/or provided them with much job satisfaction.

(e) **There is no authorized retirement age in that career path.** They can continue to perform their duties for as long as they live, or are able to continue to function in that office. There may also be spiritual considerations such as how long the Lord wants them to function in that office. Of course they may have to be cognizant of the need to familiarize themselves with new developments in that and related areas and the need to keep abreast of recent technology and other features which are introduced into the practice. This would include careers such as farming, engineering, teaching, nursing, law, and medicine.

Even if such persons retire from the public service, they may continue to work with a private institution or provide consultancy service, for example. Many such persons function in the office of a Justice of Peace, and may be able to earn an income from this vocation. Even so, a person must recognize that there is a period of rest which the Lord expects each person to enjoy. For this reason we are instructed to '**work while it is day'** not only from the perspective a twenty-four hours day, but primarily when we are physically and mentally able to do so.

'**Old age**' or the more matured aspect of our lives should be primarily focused on relaxation and to guide the younger generation to take over and expand the dream which the Lord has so graciously allowed us to establish or continue from the inputs of persons from previous generations. It is also a period for enjoying the fruits of our labour, which should include our well-placed children and their offspring.

(f) **Fulfilling the calling of the Lord on one's life**. Some persons are pursuing spiritual offices or a secular career since they have received a personal revelation of a specific calling on their lives to pursue a particular career or vocation. A person who pursues a career as a medical doctor, for example, may be specially called by God to minister to the many terminally ill patients whose last source of being ministered to and for them to have the opportunity to accept Him as their Saviour is at the hospital. One may also serve as a missionary and render medical attention as an avenue to minister the gospel to the community in which one is serving.

We are admonished in 2 Timothy 2:15 as follows: "**¹⁵Do your best to present yourself to God as one approved by Him, a worker who has no need to be ashamed, rightly explaining the word of truth**."

The importance of adopting the correct attitude in order to excel in academic pursuits, maturing in the things of Christ and which constitutes a well-rounded personality, cannot be over emphasized. For this reason, parents have to begin planning for the upbringing of their children. Important considerations when bringing up our children include:

(a) Providing a stable home environment where the presence of the Lord dwells continually, and where the spiritual, material and other aspects of family life are adequately managed,

(b) Providing the child with toys, books and other items which would stimulate the spiritual and intellectual development of the child,

(c) Increased emphasis is being placed on phonics and other principles which would challenge the child to learn to read. The importance of the maxim which encourages the principle of '**learning to read so that one can read to learn**' cannot be over-emphasized.

> If only our young people in particular could conceptualize the importance of **studying and achieving excellence** in their academic, spiritual and other pursuits. If they could only shut themselves away from the distractions which would prevent them from achieving their goals, then their future can be dramatically transformed into that of great success. As we make the effort, the Lord will grant us the desires of our heart.

Knowing God's will for one's life is of primary importance to Christians. It should be explained that there are two aspects of the will of God. There is the **permissible will**, where every Christian is instructed to do good deeds, make converts of men, carry out the mandates of the great commission. However, as explained in the above scripture verse, there are duties which each of us was specifically created and saved to perform and thus, walk in His **perfect will**. Failure to perform that specific function would prevent us from saying like the apostle Paul that we have fought the great fight and kept the faith. The latter concept is the most important consideration for a Christian since only things which are done in conformity to the will of God have eternal significance. Our primary purpose as Christians should therefore be to fulfil the purpose of God for our lives and to walk in His perfect will. Choosing a career path merely because it offers high financial reward should not be the primary choice of Christians.

Most parents hope that their children would pursue financially rewarding careers that they would be successful in their careers and will be financially independent as early as possible. This would enable the parents to utilize their money to finance the education and other requirements of other siblings. In addition, more money would be available for them to go on a vacation, to invest and to save for their old age.

It is common to find parents who desire that their offspring become a medical doctor, lawyer, pilot, university professor, computer technician and other careers which generate lucrative financial returns and have some degree of respectability in the community, country and internationally – **white collar jobs**. On the other hand, many parents discourage their children from pursuing careers such as mechanical engineering, farming and jobs where their clothing and skin are likely to be dirty, or at least untidy – **blue collar jobs**. Thankfully, this stigma is quickly losing its influence and most jobs are classified as important to the development of society

Every legitimate job has its place of importance. The services of persons who were previously classified as lower cases, second class citizens or by other derogatory terms because of their jobs, colour of their skin, sex and other superficial stigmatization are now being recognized. The failure to do this in the past has resulted in chaos in many societies. (A person's sexual orientation which is not consistent to Biblical principles cannot be included in this class since the Bible only concedes to sexual intercourse between a husband and a wife, and does not condone homosexuality, lesbianism and other perverted sexual practices. Even though Jehovah hates the sin, He loves the sinner, and Jesus died so that everyone could be saved, if we confess our sins, repent, accept His forgiveness and turn from our wicked ways, and receive Him as our Lord and Saviour).

There are several methods which God may use to reveal His perfect will to a Christian. They include:

(a) Being in a close relationship with the Lord where one can **hear His voice** and consistently commune with Him. Biblical examples of persons who experienced this relationship include Adam and Eve, Moses, Samuel, Samson, Mary Magdalene and the Apostle Paul.

(b) **Divine revelation** personally and/or through one or more Christians. Examples of this occurrence are the revelation of the part of the future life of David through Samuel and the disciples through Jesus. Jesus instructed his disciples to leave their secular occupations and to follow Him to be 'fishers of men.'

(c) **Being placed in a situation** where one realizes that this is the exact situation which one's training and aptitude were designed to fulfil. Examples include Gideon and Moses in leading the children of Israel where he applied many of the principles of leadership which he learnt when he was in Pharaoh's household. Nevertheless, he had to rely more on the Lord, who brought assistance such as the Medianite Priest to guide him in other systems of administration.

(d) **One's innate or 'natural' ability.** For example, Queen Esther's beauty in securing her the position of queen was an opportunity which was used to save her people from annihilation by the plot of Haman.

Some of the important issues which should be considered when choosing a career path include:

(a) **Being in the perfect will of the Lord, as alluded to earlier,**

(b) **Studying and undergoing other forms of training to be well equipped to maximize one's competence to perform one's duties with excellence,**

(c) **'Selling oneself'** by seeking to convince the prospective employers at the job interviews and other forums which are used to recruit employees, that one is the best person for the job.

Many Christians are in organizations where they are not receiving any or substantial promotions. Some factors which can contribute to their stagnation in a low paying position or job are:

(a) **They are not paying their tithes and giving their offerings consistent with Biblical principles,**

(b) **They may not be displaying the correct attitudes which are consistent with the culture of the organization.** This may include:

 (i) The fact that they are not adequately qualified or are not applying themselves to perform their duties at the required high standard which is expected,

 (ii) They may not be consistently punctual, constantly ill, not a conscientious worker and may disregard the dress code of the organization,

(iii) They may have poor attitude towards fellow employees and/or their customers. This may include an attitude of disdain towards others who are not Christians, not being a good witness in essential areas such as showing love and kindness.

(iv) They may not be willing to 'work beyond the call of duty' when this is demanded. There is usually an unspecified clause in the job description where it is stated 'any other duties' as designated by one's supervisor or management. This clause is usually applied in a reasonable way to balance the smooth operation of the organization and job related and other activities of the employee. When this clause is applied to the detriment of the employee, there is usually a need to attempt to resolve the disagreement with management.

Failure of management to arrive at a speedy amicable solution in a dispute on the job may result in the employee consulting with the Shop-Stewart or Union Representative, in an unionized workforce. For a non-unionized workforce, the employee would have to weigh the severity of the dispute verses considerations such as their ability to secure another job.

There are many organizations which are not owned by or managed by Christians where there is a deliberate policy to employ a large number of Christians. This may be because it is felt that Christians are honest, conscientious workers and/or that they are less likely to be rebellious and stage industrial actions. They may also be perceived as persons who are more likely to promote love and harmony among fellow employees. When a Christian employee does something which disrupts the functioning of the organization, the employer may contact the pastor or other senior members of the church, who may intervene in an attempt to amicably resolve the conflict.

Many persons who have the prerequisite qualifications and working experience are unable to secure the job of their dream primarily because they are unable to get past the preliminary stage of being selected for an interview. This is so because they were unable to 'sell' themselves to the selection panel since their résumé or curriculum vitae was not impressive enough to convince the management of the organization that the applicant warranted being short-listed. This is an unfortunate occurrence since the application is a simple process.

Most organization would request **a formal letter of application** and an attached résumé. The formal letter of application gives one the opportunity to sell one's self to the organization in a few paragraphs. It would include one's full home or contact address, the name and address of the person (usually the Administrative Manager) who is representing the organization which is advertising the position, the body of the letter, the salutation and signature of the applicant.

Some organizations prefer if the email address of the applicant is included in both the cover letter and the résumé. Care must be taken that one's presentation is clear and concise and highlights one's eligibility for the position and commitment to give of one's best to the organization. Some organizations request a hand written application since they will have a handwriting expert attempt to analyze the character of the applicant as depicted by their handwriting. In this scenario the applicant must be patient and form their letters correctly and write as neatly as they possibly can.

The curriculum vita is usually structured in the following segments:

(a) **Personal details** such as name, address, email address, contact telephone number/s, where applicable. Many specialists in this area advise that details such as marital status, ethnic origin and age should be omitted until the interview or unless the perspective employee specifically requests them.

(b) **Academic qualifications**; special training which one may have undergone and certificates, degrees and other qualifications which one has acquired which are relevant to the position for which one's is applying (listing the name of the respective institutions, their address, the year the certificate was awarded and grade awarded). Depending on the position, it may also be useful to list the major courses which constituted the program of training.

(c) **A summary of one's area of specialization** which makes one suitable for the position. This may include factors such as one's experience in a similar position.

(d) From the more senior applicants:

　(i) **A list of the relevant positions at various organizations where one worked**, providing a brief outline of one's job description, one's major achievements in the position, and one's reason for leaving the organization,

　(ii) **A list of the papers, publications, books and other documents which highlight one's achievements in one's field of specialization.** For some positions, applicants are requested to include a copy of a recent publication as a testimonial of one's ability to present

written reports and conduct independent research.
(e) **Other related skills** which would enhance the applicant's suitability for the new job. This could include computer skills, the mastery of a second language and one's hobbies.
(f) **The testimonial of two or three referee testimonials (as requested) or the name, address, telephone, fax number and email address of the referees,** as detailed in the job advertisement. Care must be taken to select as one's referee, persons of high repute in society and persons who are well renowned. This is because when a person writes a referee report for someone else, the writer is placing their professional integrity on the line in making such a recommendation. It is important that the referee agrees to submit the report on one's behalf.

Getting past the selection panellist and being called for an interview is a very big step towards being employed for the job which one is pursuing. This is so since there may be many applicants for the job to whom the organization may not have replied because they were ruled out. Usually, organizations do not shortlist a placebo, (a person in this instant, who is used as a control mechanism, but is not considered as a suitable prospect for the position) unless they are conducting a survey. Therefore, it is important that if one is truly desirous of accepting the job that one is well prepared for the interview. Some of the important aspects of the preparation for a successful interview include:
(a) It is important that one is conversant of what the organization or department does, who are some of the key managers of the organization, what one's general function would be and how the organization would benefit from the specific skills which one has to offer. It may

also be important that one is aware of the salary scale of the position, so one may be able to negotiate for the highest possible salary scale for the position without jeopardizing one's possibility of being selected. In addition, some prospective employers attempt to have the applicant agree to enter the organization at the starting stage of the grade, where if one was better informed, one may have been able to negotiate a better employment package which may include wage and fringe benefits.

(b) Some persons attempt to anticipate some of the likely questions which one would be asked at the interview and rehearse an impressive answer. Even though this may work in some instances, the important principle is to be as knowledgeable as possible of what the requirements of the position are and ensure that one is well equipped to present appropriate responses with an air of confidence.

(c) The importance of dressing well for an interview cannot be over emphasized. In this regard, it is useful to know the dress code of the organization and dress accordingly. It may be self-defeating to be overdressed and feel uncomfortable at the interview. It may be easy for persons on the interviewing panel to recognize that you are not comfortable, and may perceive that you may not be comfortable working in an environment in which you are not accustomed to. Similarly, if one is underdressed, it may convey the impression that one is rebellious and not the team player that they are looking for.

(d) It is important that one speaks clearly and confidently, and ensures that one is understood, and that one completely answers the specifics of each question. Even if one does not know everything which is being asked, one should make a credible attempt to provide the best possible answer. However, it may be necessary to say that one cannot answer a particular question rather than to give an unfounded answer. It is important to realize that apart from attempting to assess the ability of the perspective employee to perform creditably at the position for which they are being interviewed, the panellist may also be trying to assess one's character traits such as honesty, friendliness and one's ability to make competent decisions when one is working under undue pressure.

(e) As a Christians, one must recognize that the forces of darkness are unleashed in an attempt to frustrate us,

(f) When we are consistently not being called for interviews and are turned down from job applications which one felt confident of acquiring it is very frustrating. This is a sure way where some Christians turn away from serving God since they feel that He is not concerned about them and that He is not working on their behalf. It is thus important that we learn to take authority over the forces of darkness and see God work on our behalf.

Christians can walk into an interview room with the foreknowledge and conformation from the Word and/or a specific prophecy, that God has already selected us for the job. However, we still have the responsibility of studying and showing ourselves approved and of convincing the interviewing panellist that we indeed have the correct aptitude and prerequisite skills and are the best person for the position. When a Christian is selected for an appointment, he has the obligation to confirm by his dedication, hard work, commitment and other positive attributes that he was indeed the best person to have been selected. With consistency in our outstanding performance, good stewardship and the manifestation of the Excellent Spirit which dwells in us, as was present in the life of Daniel, Jehovah will guarantee a promotion to a senior position within that organization or to another.

Some persons directly or indirectly contact members of the interviewing panel before the interviews and try to find out what are some of the issues which will be highlighted at the interview. This is not a very good approach and an applicant may be disqualified from the interview if he is found to be soliciting undue support particularly from members of the prospective interviewing panel. There may be no harm in finding out specifics such as the salary range of the position.

However, care must be taken that undue assistance and overtures are not made to representatives of the organization.

There are several ways a person may learn of a vacancy which exists in an organization, such as:

    (a)   A number of organizations publish vacancies in popular newspapers, magazines, on radio programs and television channels and other news media. There are also several magazines which specialize in publishing vacancies. Persons who are desirous of securing local or international jobs can subscribe to such publications and have them. The Financial Times, Wall Street Journal and News Week are popular publications where several local and international appointments are advertised.

        It is a law in some countries that senior positions in government corporations and publicly quoted organizations must be published in popular newspapers and the best candidate is hired from the applications. Very often, even though this requirement is satisfied, the management of the organization formulates the requirements in such a way that they give a distinct advantage to a person who is identified internally for the position. This may include the years of experience, qualification and other prerequisites. Of course this is not always the case since an external applicant may be better suited for the job, to the frustration of the person who was previously identified for the position.

(b) The internet has become a popular medium for publishing vacancies. Vacancies are usually advertised on the website of the organization. There are also several websites which specialize in making such vacancies available to persons who subscribe to the organization or the list of vacancies is advertised as a free service. A popular website is www.devjobs.com. Increasingly, applicants are invited to email their applications for positions which have been advertised. The web page of some organizations has a blank application form which applicants are invited to fill and email the organization. For some appointments the applicant may have to submit additional data such as a copy of academic and other certificates and recent testimonials, police clearance and other documents.

(c) Referees' reports – usually from two or three referees,

(d) A person may have been informed by someone who is working in an organization of a vacancy,

(e) Some persons send applications to a number of organizations which may have a specific position within the organization or an enquiry is made about possible vacancies which may exist that are commensurate with one's qualification and work experience as highlighted in one's résumé.

(f) There are private and government employment agencies in several countries where persons can obtain information on vacancies, and secure an appointment for interaction with prospective employers. There is often a cost involved, particularly with private job placement agencies. This may include a flat application fee or in some instances as much as ten percent or even more of the first year salary of the successful applicant. These contracts are usually binding and persons who attempt to contravene them may be fired by their employer or be confronted with a lawsuit from the job placement agency.

In some instances, persons find that contracting the services of legitimate job placement agencies secures a faster appointment than if one approached a prospective employer independently. This is so because the job placement agency may have several years of experience of forging a relationship with prospective employers in that particular geographic location and one's related profession. There are, however, several unscrupulous confidence tricksters who play on the gullibility and desperation of job seekers and do not genuinely offer a job placement service.

There are established companies, the military and other agencies in many countries who target prospective graduates at colleges, universities and other institutions and attempt to entice the best graduates to join their organizations. Forums such as job fairs and special relations with the job placement agencies and career guidance centers of these organizations facilitate this interaction. Some agencies also offer scholarships to outstanding students, with the objective of offering them employment under a contractual obligation which is commensurate with the number of years of the program and the cost of the program.

There are agencies which hire persons on a permanent or temporary basis and contract their services to other organizations. These include agencies which offer cleaning, security, medical and other services.

(g) Some organizations offer students the opportunity of working on an attachment program where they are paid a stipend for their services. Outstanding persons may be offered a permanent assignment with the organization.

(h) Usually for positions such as a nanny, maid, security and secretarial services or nursing, there are agencies in several countries where persons can be registered for temporary or permanent placement.

(i) Some established organizations request that suitably qualified professionals submit their résumés which are included on the Roster of Consultants of the organization. The organization would usually submit bids for various contracts and include the résumés of persons who are listed on their roster as resource personnel. This system is used extensively by professionals such as Accountants, Project Managers, Financial Consultants, Architects, System Analysts, Anthropologists, and other professionals who are seeking part-time or permanent employment.

Many professionals who have retired and who are not desirous of continuing a full-time appointment would remain active in their profession by **registering with a voluntary organization.** Other persons established commercial or charitable organizations or

work as a consultant on selected projects and/or programs. Many professionals who enjoy traveling and living in other countries would also take up such appointments in other countries. One may also enjoy benefits such as free accommodation, the payment of utility bills, free medical treatment and transportation facilities and also an allowance for one's spouse and children who accompany the consultant to the duty station.

In many instances a professional takes the option of working as a consultant since he earns far more working as a consultant on a small number projects per year where a high consultancy fee is charged. There are also organizations which actively pursue persons who are distinguished in a specialized field and offer them an attractive package in an attempt to entice them to join the organization. In such instances one is usually able to secure a salary and fringe benefits which would enable one to live as comfortable as one desires. These offers should not be taken lightly, for even if one is in the helm of the organization and can dictate one's terms and conditions of service, the new organization would obviously demand their 'pound of flesh.' In most working environment if an employee does fails to perform at a level which is commensurate with one's salary, he will be fired. This practice is also popular among professional sports personalities and senior executives of established companies. It is therefore necessary that all contracts offered by prospective employees be thoroughly scrutinized, and it is often better to seek the advice of a legal practitioner.

The detailed format of the application submitted in response to a published advertisement is primarily dependent on the request of the prospective employer.

Some organizations request a one-page résumé while others request detailed curriculum vitae. The difference is that some organizations often receive so many applications that the administration department may not be staffed with enough employees to go through all the curriculum vitae and select the best applicants to attend an interview. The result is that a 'summarized curriculum vitae' (résumé), possibly on one page, is requested. They might then request a detailed curriculum vitae for applicants who are short-listed, while some organizations would employ the short-listed candidates based on the résumé. In the latter example much more is usually dependent on the ability of the applicant to orally convince the interviewing panel that one is the most suitable candidate for the job. This system is often used for positions such as Sales Representatives, Broadcasters and TV Presenters and other positions which demand that one has to be convincing and articulate in one's oral presentation.

The issue of children being a wise financial investment is identified from several perspectives. Very often the satisfaction of knowing that the children of the loins and womb have achieved significant success is very rewarding to their parents even if that child never assists the parents financially in a large measure. The joy of knowing that one's labour was not in vain is often satisfaction enough for the parents. The satisfaction of knowing that the sacrifices which they made for their children paid off and their children are well on their way to achieving their career goals is a primary source of pride and joy for most parents. Many parents do not live long enough to see their children achieve their zenith in life. There is however, a special blessing which the parents will receive in the life hereafter for generating high returns for the gems which God placed in their hands.

THE CHILD AND FINANCIAL MANAGEMENT

Children are often better judges of character than parents realize or are willing to give them credit for. This feature is highlighted in the popular song '**Skip-a-Rope**'. We are admonished to listen to the songs which our children sing and the games they play, for they are often reproducing their impressions of their parents and other persons and events in and around their society. Parents are thus instructed to be leaders, not only by words, but more importantly, by their actions. The importance of parents being prudent financial managers cannot be overemphasized. Leadership by both precepts and example would have a more profound, positive effect than leadership by mere precepts.

Parents demonstrate financial management practices each day of their lives since most activities which are conducted have financial implications. They include:

(a) The rating of financial and other considerations versus spiritual matters,

(b) The type of jobs they have and the standard of living which their earnings afford the family. Account will be taken of how prudent parents are, the types of investment and other decisions which they make and the level of returns which they derive. Children living in a poor society and off of welfare benefits are often at a disadvantage to wealthier children in several areas such as the affordability of adequate food, health, educational facilities. Even so, parents from impoverished communities often challenge their children to do better that the parents did, which often result in the next generation enjoying a far higher standard of living than their parents.

(c) For the older siblings, the inheritance which their parents will be leaving or have left for their offspring,

Some of the areas where children and other onlookers can observe where a family is not enjoying much success in the management of their financial and other resources include:

(a) Poor allocation of budget, particularly, if the basic needs such as an adequate amount of food, clothing, shelter, educational and other basic needs cannot be met, or are consistently being neglected by parents,

(b) Poor saving and investments habits,

(c) Concentration on short-term consumption rather than consistently practicing long term planning and executions of the plans,

(d) Not paying their tithes and giving to the Lord, thus, they do not enjoy many financial and other blessings,

(e) Parents are not providing adequately for their old age, thus, they have to depend on the state and/or children or other loved ones to take care of them,

It is common to see children become rebellious, as they begin to socialize and recognize the financial inadequacies of their parents. Poorer children are often taunted by children from wealthier parents since the poorer children are not able to live up to the lifestyles of the wealthier ones. This is often a delicate situation since the poorer child may be outperforming the richer one in academic and other spheres of their lives. The resentment may be intensified when the poorer child is a Christian while the members of the 'in-crowd' are not. It is necessary that parents spend much quality time teaching and showing their children how to manage wealth or lack of it as an individual, as a family and as Christians.

There are several methods which parents use to guide their children to financial independence. The following are two such methods. Firstly, there is the method of **allocating an allowance to the child** which the parents feel is adequate to cover the transportation, snacks at school and other expenditure of the child on a daily, weekly or monthly basis. The parents may have also opened a bank account in the name of the child where they are committed to making monthly deposits as their budget allows, or they may have a structured saving scheme. This may include banking a fixed amount each month towards the college fund and other expenditure of the child, for example. In this system, the child may be expected to perform various chores which may not necessarily be related to the allowance.

Failure to complete tasks may result in some form of punishment such as grounding (debarring the child from engaging in activities which the child enjoys such as watching television, for a number of days). Some parents apply a few strokes with a belt should the parents be practicing corporal punishment – in conformity to the principle of not sparing the rod and spoiling the child. Many Christians do not agree with the practice of corporal punishment and the law of several countries actually prohibits this practice. In this system the completion of tasks is not related to the allocation of the allowance.

The second form of **allocating of an allowance to a child is on the basis of the completion or otherwise, of various tasks.** In this format a merit system is established where a roster is formulated which consists of do's and don'ts and other factors. A list similar to that as recorded in the song '**No Charge**' is highlighted below.

The list includes items such as mowing the lawn which would not have to be completed each day, thus there is no penalty attached to it not being done each day. There are also items such as lying, cheating and other sinful acts which the child is not expected to practice, therefore, only a penalty is allocated if they occur. Parents who use this method would still expect the child to perform other duties such as cleaning their room, for which no monetary reward is offered. This system demands a high level of discipline and understanding for it to be successful. Very often 'gray' areas may arise where the parents still have to exercise their authority and ensure that the child is not deliberately attempting to 'beat' the system and/or that the child is unfairly treated. (It would be a useful exercise if parents and even children can formulate a similar chart which is applicable to their situation. Once there is agreement between the parents and child, it can be implemented. However, care must be taken to avoid the possible negative side effects of this system).

Tem	Value($)	Mon.	Tue.	Wed.	Thu.	Fri.	Sat.	Sun.	Total
Rewards									
Mowing the lawn	10								
Opening & closing windows	10								
Getting up at 6 a.m.	10								
Washing the car	10								
Sweeping the floor	5								
Washing the dishes	2								
Sweeping the yard	10								
Watering the plants	10								
Good conduct	10								
Total	77								
Penalties									
Fighting	-15								
Incomplete homework	-10								
Arguing	-5								
Teasing others	-5								
Lying, cheating etc.	-10								
Messy bedroom	-10								
Untidy clothing	-5								
Being rude	-5								
Total	-65								

Table 2.1. Hypothetical Roster of Activities, Rewards and Punishments

This is not a popular method of allocating allowance since many parents voice disagreements such as:

    (a)   They feel that children should see the necessity of performing duties as an essential part of what constitutes being a part of the family and they should not feel that they are doing others a favor by performing chores.

    (b)   Paying children for chores is tantamount to child labor,

(c) This system often causes siblings to compete against each other and the true nature of family life is stifled. They are thus merely performing duties to satisfy their 'employers.'
(d) If the parents, for some reason, are unable to pay the child as scheduled, he may refuse to comply with the regulations, or may do so reluctantly,
(e) It causes children to become 'too competitive' and they may ill-treat others who cause them to lose money,
(f) It is often difficult to pronounce penalties for situations where a parent was not present and there is a possibility that the child may be misrepresenting the situation so that he is not penalized while another benefits,

Parents who use this system have attested to positive attributes such as:

(a) It teaches children that positive attitudes are socially acceptable,
(b) The child becomes competitive and with proper guidance, will begin to save and invest the money he earns which is above his immediate requirements,
(c) The children learn that with discipline and hard work they can increase their financial earnings,
(d) It reduces the need to impose other forms of discipline such as corporal punishment,

Parents who have used either system have contended that they have achieved the best results which they could have expected from their children. Even though the latter system is generally more controversial, some parents prefer if their children grow up in a competitive environment at home. This, they feel, enables the child to excel at school and in the wider community since most of our activities in the secular world involve a high sense of competition. It is a fact that in every walk of life rewards are usually offered when duties are performed to the satisfaction of the person who is assessing the activity. They include activities at school, where outstanding students are admitted to various sporting and other teams and in the working environment, where outstanding employees are rewarded with a promotion and other rewards. Outstanding persons in church are also promoted to leadership roles.

The amount of allowance which is given to a child is often subject to dissatisfaction as the child grows and the parents may not be in a position to increase the allowance proportionately to the increasing financial demands of the child. In such circumstances care must be taken to ensure that the allocation to the child is consistent with the general budget discipline of the family. Care must be taken that additional funds are given to the child to cater for important financial demands which may arise periodically. Some children supplement their allowance by taking on part-time jobs such as selling newspapers, working for a few hours before or after school and doing odd jobs for neighbors. These activities must be managed to ensure that the academics and other important areas of the life of the child do not suffer merely to satisfy his personal finances, particularly if his parents can afford to comfortably meet those demands.

Children from poorer homes who do not receive an allowance, or at least not on a continuous basis, may engage in income-generating activities as a way of supplementing the income of their parents and meet their personal financial needs. The extreme of this analogy includes children engaging in begging, child prostitution, young drug addicts, street children and other groups who may be exploited because of destitution. It is sad to see that there are also children and adults who are still held in the bondage of slavery in several countries where it is practiced openly or in secret. There are also overwhelming instances of children who are drug addicts, many of whom are controlled by unscrupulous pimps and gang leaders. There are also children who are mentally and/or physically challenged, children who are born with, or contract deadly diseases such as AIDS, and who may need special care and attention in order for them to survive.

FINANCIAL RESPONSIBILITY OF CHILDREN TO THEIR PARENTS

A child does not ask his parents to be brought into this world and no child comes into this world by accident. God has a plan for each person who is born. As a matter of fact, there are several scripture passages which reiterate the fact that God knew us even before we were born. Regardless of how a child is conceived, God still has a purpose to fulfill in that child's life, for **we were all fearfully and wonderfully made by the Lord**. Of course, God detests the act of adultery, fornication, homosexuality and other forms of sins, yet His love extends beyond our sins. Even though he hates the act of conceiving a child during a sexual sin, yet he loves the child.

It is the responsibility of each parent to cater to the material and other needs such as to provide food, clothing, housing and educational, health and other facilities for their children to the best of their ability. Unfortunately, many children are brought into this world by parents who are unable to satisfy their own financial and other needs and, therefore, the children are not adequately provided for even before they were born. In such cases, children are often born undernourished, thus starting their life at a disadvantage. Such children are susceptible to diseases and they may suffer malfunctioning of various organs of their bodies, and in extreme instances, they die before or shortly after delivery.

Many governments and donor agencies have programs to assist pregnant and lactating mothers by providing them with free medication including vitamin supplements and other forms of nutrients. This is in an attempt to enable the pregnant and lactating mother to have the necessary nutrients in her body which she is able to pass on to her baby. It is sad to see that many women do not take advantage of such facilities because they may live too far from the health clinic, they may not be educated as to the benefits of such facilities. As a result, there are high incidents of miscarriage, still births and infant mortality among women in poorer communities in most countries, and particularly in developing countries.

The question which is frequently asked is why is it that persons who cannot adequately meet their basic needs such as food, clothing, housing, educational, medical and other facilities still proceed to have children. Some of the reasons are:

(a) Children are often viewed as a source of hope that determines the future,

(b) Some women, particularly in welfare societies, often become pregnant to secure the public assistance of the state. This may include having a furnished apartment and monthly financial assistance along with benefits such as the wavering of tuition fees for them to further their education.

(c) Children are often viewed as valuable assets who can be used to provide cheap labor to the farm, trade, business or other economic activities in which the family is involved.

Parents are not only obligated to provide for the material needs of their children, but also to provide an atmosphere conducive to the child's grow in reverence to the Lord, to be well educated, and to become a productive individual capable of making a valuable contribution to society. Very often in order to provide those amenities for the children, parents have to sacrifice their personal development and satisfy the needs of their children's.

Even though the children may not necessarily be asking their parents to go the extra mile for them, most conscientious parents feel a sense of obligation to ensure that their children are able to enjoy facilities which they were unable to enjoy. This quest could prove to be disadvantageous where parents push children into careers and to be involved in activities primarily because the parents were unable to participate or even if they did, for the child to follow in their footstep.

The wise thing to do is for the parents and the child to seek the face of the Lord for direction on what career path each child should pursue. It may be the will of the Lord for the children to pursue a similar career path as a parent. However, this should not be taken for granted, for the child may be frustrated merely living in the shadow of a parent if it is not the will of the Lord.

(d) A question which is frequently asked by many persons is if children are obligated to compensate their parents financially if their parents were conscientious and spent a large percent of their adult years attempting to ensure that they have the best that they can offer, and the child/children are successful in their respective careers? In many instances parents offer support to their children in the form of baby sitting and providing other services for their children. Even though, this has proven to be successful in a large percentage of families, it still does not justify poorer families in particular having a large number of children.

Poorer parents are often unaware of, or unwilling to use 'safe' contraceptives. Some poorer parents also make the conscious decision of having a large number of children, to provide 'free labor' for the farm and/or other family business. Some parents also hope that one of more of their offspring appreciation the sacrifices which their parents made for them, and seek to make

their parents as comfortable as possible during their old age. This may include:
  (a) Paying them regular visits if they live in close proximity, making regular phone calls and maintaining constant communication to ensure that they are well catered for and do not feel lonely,
  (b) Taking their elderly parents to live with them in their matrimonial home or moving in with their parents. This could be as a means of reducing housing cost and/or providing security and protection and also to care for their parent/s. This option is usually taken with careful consideration since living with in-laws and particularly elderly relatives could be very demanding and stressful, particularly as they become less able to care for themselves.

Providing transportation to a senior citizen's daycare centre or nursing home during the day and they are returned in the afternoon, or the parent is kept permanently in a nursing home where the child pays the upkeep for the parent or at least visit regularly. This decision for a parent to stay permanently in a nursing home may be at the request of the parent who does not want to be seen as imposing on the lives of their children.

The Bible advocates that children have an obligation to care, as much as they possibly can, for their elderly parents. 1 Timothy 5:8 states: "[8]**And whoever does not provide for relatives, and especially for family members, has denied the faith and is worse than an unbeliever**."

Many persons would be disgruntled over a child having to care for a parent who might have been neglectful. The other issue is what happens in circumstances where the child is also saddled with the responsibilities of parenting their own family and is unable to afford the extra finance, time and other resources that are needed by the parent/s. Even so, a child has the responsibility to assist in caring for an elderly parent and/or other relatives. The church also has a responsibility to assist the needy among us. The responsibility is the child's to assist in caring for an elderly parent or relative.

CONCLUSION

The 'innocence' of childhood must be balanced with the necessity of instilling important Godly principles in the lives of these precious little gems whom Jesus instructed His disciples not to prevent from coming to Him. Parents have to ensure that they are laying the best foundation by being living examples of financial and other principles which they would be proud to see their children apply to their lives. If parents fail to do their part and, God forbid, their children grow to be delinquent, even if the parents are Christians, the blood of their children will be on their heads. The promise that if parents teach their children the ways of the Lord then when they are old, they would not depart from it, is God's prescription to protect and preserve our offspring. Once we do our part, He will never dishonor His word.

Parents must exercise wisdom in every aspect of the training of their children. Our best investment in the lives of our children is to lead them to the place where they can hear from God themselves, and to walk in His perfect will for their lives. Regardless of our vocations in life, it is important that we learn to be good stewards of God's finances, children, ministry and other resources which He has placed at our disposal. It is important to have a good balance between the spiritual and the natural. Both have their places of importance, even though preeminence is given to the spiritual. However, mismanagement of financial and other material resources has caused individual Christians and ministries to 'fall from grace', since they were not good stewards of God's assets which He placed at their disposal. The impact is that it affected their spiritual standing in their home, church, community and even in some instances internationally.

NOTES

****

Chapter 3 *INVESTMENT OPPORTUNITIES AND THE FAMILY*

INTRODUCTION

Investment is an essential aspect of life. As a matter of fact, virtually everything which a person does entails investment in one way or another. The investments which we engage in usually have implications for now and eternally. Each person has been created to perform special tasks. Jesus, for example told the parable of the master who gave different quantity of talents to his servants, most likely in accordance with his assessment of their respective abilities to generate returns from their investment of his money. In the same way, God expect us to maximize on the things which He has placed at our disposal in keeping with His will for our lives.

It is often philosophized that there are three aspects of our lives in which we can invest in order to generate the desired level of return. That is our time, talent and treasury. We can invest our time in doing good and/or evil and in productive or destructive activities for which we will receive our just reward. Time can also be invested to acquire the necessary qualifications which will enable us to secure the type of job to earn the level of salary which will enable us to adequately cater to the financial needs of our present and/or future family. Some persons use the talent which they have acquired to bless others and help the poor, make enough money to support their family, while others use their talent to destroy their lives and that of others. Finally, the wise person uses his resources to spread the Gospel, make his family comfortable and engage in other activities to enhance the development of our societies. Conversely, many persons squander their financial resources to destroy their own lives. Therefore, the onus is on the Christian to ensure that every aspect of his/her life is wisely invested to perpetuate the principles of the Bible in their homes, in the wider society and internationally.

BANKING AND THE CHRISTIAN FAMILY

This section reviews several aspects of banking activities which are very important to the lives of individuals, families and the Body of Christ. Banking activities are commonly practiced by Christian and non-Christians throughout the world. There are several different types of banks including commercial, central, investment, offshore and development banks. A brief description of the activities of commercial banks will be presented.

There are two broad types of commercial banks; retail and wholesale commercial banks. Wholesale commercial banks deal only with very large financial transactions (usually in millions of dollars) and they engage in maturity matching of loans with deposits. That is, a loan for six months is usually given against a fixed deposit of the same principal amount for six months. Retail commercial banks, on the other hand, accept small deposits and withdrawals which can usually be conducted without prior notification to the bank. Some common transactions conducted in retail commercial banks include:

(a) The operation of savings accounts on which interest is paid. In several banks, interest is not paid at all (or at a minimal level) on a direct debit or checking accounts,

(b) Customers are usually able to negotiate personal and/or business (corporate) credit facilities from them,

Many Christians have an aversion to using some facilities of retail commercial banks and other financial institutions. Several Christians view some financial innovations of electronic banking, with a high level of suspicion. Electronic banking has advanced to the point where the need to hold a large sum of notes and coins is rapidly fading in the more developed countries. Nevertheless, the uneducated poor, in particular, often feel that the banking environment is too sophisticated and formal for them. Therefore, they are often alienated from the world of the established financial system.

> We have an obligation to use a combination of savings and returns from prudent investment programs when planning for retirement. Savings as an accumulation of wealth, to meet needs which may arise, and prudent investment programs to generate returns beyond the low level of returns from savings are important.

The arrival of advanced financial instruments such as checks, debit and credit cards, Automated Teller Machines (ATM), and telephone and electronic transfer systems has rapidly revolutionized the world of finance. It is common for persons to present a plastic debit or credit card to the cashier to pay for items purchased. Transfer of the cost of the purchase can be made from the bank or Credit Card Company to the supermarket. Individuals and companies also transfer millions of dollars and other currencies daily between international money and capital markets.

Several analysts have found that many of these financial innovations are subject to possible frauds and errors which often result in the loss of large amounts of money and embarrassment to the financial institutions and customers. There are also many reports of teenaged and older computer 'hackers' gaining illegal access into the computer system of financial institutions and destroying important data and/or defrauding them. Problems of this nature have led scientists to experiment with techniques such as using fingerprints and scanning an eye of customers in order to grant them access to their bank account, and other relevant information.

There have also been experiments to engrave the accounts code on the body of customers which will be electronically identified when that part of the body is scanned by the decoding device at the financial institution. Many Christians believe this innovation is too similar, for comfort, to the 'mark of the beast' as highlighted in Revelation 13:16-18. Persons who are found to have the mark of the beast would not be joining Christ in His second return but instead are doomed for hell. There is an overwhelming amount of evidence in the validity of this prophecy for Christians to sit idly by and accept every financial and other innovations, particularly if they are contrary to the Word of God

The Internet, E-mail and World Wide Webb (WWW) are also viewed as major source of unifying world financial and information systems, as predicted before the second coming of Christ. Although they offer many significant benefits, there are also many negative consequences such as easy access to pornography by children, stalking and the promotion of homosexuality, cults and other undesirable elements on the Internet.

Some Christians, because of their educational background, financial position, sociological upbringing, for example, may prefer not to deal with commercial banks and other formal financial institutions. Instead, they save their money under their mattress, in a hole in the ground or with traditional savings institutions. Although saving small amounts of money at home is usually legal, one would forego the interest, if it is not saved on an interest-bearing account. This practice is similar to that of the foolish servant who buried his talent (Luke 19:11-27) and was sternly rebuked by his master since he did not invest or save the money which was entrusted to him. If money is not saved or invested in an account or activity which at least generates interest or other returns to cover the rate of inflation in that economy, the real value of the money will be decreased by inflation. Believers will obviously not be expected to use devious measures such as concealing correct accounting data in an attempt to defraud the Inland Revenue, or be involved in money laundering or illegal drug trafficking.

Disastrous circumstances such as theft and the destruction of the home by fire are enough reasons for individuals and institutions to deposit their money with banks or other financial institution. There is also the disadvantage of the loss of interest that accrues on a saving account. In addition, if a person is seeking a large credit facility, there is a record with the financial institution on how the customer was managing his cash flow as reflected by the balances of his account. This record may be crucial in verifying the history of one's capacity to save and/or returns from a business venture. For these and other reasons, Christians are encouraged to operate an account with an established financial institution or to save at a secure and trustworthy traditional financial institution if formal financial institutions are absent in their community.

Christians have more of a serious obligation to, as far as is possible, to earn a decent standard of living than other members of society, for we are the salt of the earth and light of the world. It is recognized that salt heals, cures, irritates, flavours and preserves, for example. Light also has characteristics such as dispelling darkness, thus illuminating a given area as it exposes things that were previously hidden by darkness. Light also exposes sin and leads us along the right track. These principles should be evident in the lives of believers. We have the extra impetus in the Person of the Holy Spirit, prayer, the Bible, and the church to guide us in financial and other undertakings. In addition, we have the responsibility of being honest, hard working and displaying all the other positive attributes which are inherent in our new nature. So there is no reason why our businesses should fail because of poor management practices, lack of capital or improper use of the available resources.

Deuteronomy 28:1-4 relates some blessings which we inherit as we keep our side of the covenant to uphold the principles of the Bible. Hence, the onus is on us to secure competent financial advisors, accountants and other persons who can assist and represent us, where necessary, when negotiating with a bank and/or other financial institutions to secure a credit and other financial assistance.

Christian entrepreneurs have several advantages in their favour. These include:

(a) The wisdom of God to direct us,
(b) The favour of God,
(c) The prayer, financial and other forms of support from a spouse, children and/or the congregation,
(d) A peaceful home in which to pray, relax and plan effectively for the advancement of the business venture,

Does the above list seem too theoretical? If one has any doubt of the validity of any of these statements, one can spend half an hour each day and prayerfully meditate on the promises of God and exercise one's authority as a believer. Church counselors and other competent personnel should assist believers to manage their financial resources when they are experiencing financial difficulties or are seeking to expand their investments. In the 'body-ministry' which churches are increasingly implementing, many congregations have believers who have a wide range of academic and vocational skills who share their knowledge and experiences with others. This is tantamount to the principles of the early church where believers shared their resources.

Some believers receive prophetic pronouncement, the guidance of the word of wisdom and other spiritual directives which have been received by various members of the congregation. Some Christian entrepreneurs solicit a special person or group of believers dedicated to consistently 'intercede' for the business. Some businesses provide some form of material support for their intercessors. The Board of Directors is made up of prayerful Christians who have the gifts of the Spirit operating in their lives.

The time is well overdue for churches to use the

talents and assets at their disposal and assist others in areas where they are experiencing difficulties. It is commendable when symposiums, seminars and training programs are held for believers in areas such as financial management and the development of entrepreneurial skills. The body of Christ is also the best forum to forge allegiance with established business personnel who can assist budding businessmen and women.

If we are to experience the overthrow of secret societies such as lodges and the world of the occult in a greater measure, we must establish a superior network to help each other to develop and expand in every area of our lives that are beneficial to the Kingdom of God. This includes being spiritually equipped to withstand the fiery darts of the enemy and to make disciples of men. We are also to fulfil our vocation in the secular world such as our employment and also to bring up our children in the fear of the Lord.

Do commercial banks really need our savings?
Many commercial bank have excess liquidity since for every $1 saved, the commercial bank can lend at least $10, depending on the liquidity requirement of the central bank or other regulatory authority. (This process is known as the Multiplying Effect of Money). For this reason most commercial banks pay savers very low interest rates on the savings and charge high interest rates on credit facilities, thus, contributing to their high net income.

INSURANCE COVERAGE

Proverbs 13:22(a) state: "*22(a)The good leave an inheritance to their children's children.*"

Since Christian parents should be categorized as 'good' we have an obligation to leave an inheritance for our grandchildren. The inheritance must be durable enough that our children can, with proper care, deliver it to the true inheritors when they are old enough to enjoy and/or manage it. This creates a precedent where each generation is a custodian of the assets for the next generation. This principle is inherent in several successful family businesses and even professions. Inheritance can take several forms, including:

(a) Property, business, liquid cash, money held in trust, and other forms of assets, willed to hairs,

(b) Secular or religious titles, goodwill or other intangible assets can be inherited from predecessors,

(c) Spiritual titles such as High Priest (the Levites, for example) are handed down from one generation to the other. Some types of spiritual anointing or blessings and also curses can also be inherited,

Insurance coverage can be classified as a form of inheritance. Some types of coverage are primarily designed to compensate the beneficiary in the event of serious illness, loss of life and/or property of the insured. Insurance companies may specialize in providing a single service, or the more customary practice of providing a range of services to clients.

Insurance policies are generally divided into life and non-life policies. Among the common features of these two types of coverage is that the higher the probability of the insurance company being exposed to liability as a result of a claim, the higher the cost of the policy. A summary of some non-life policies are:

(a) **Marine insurance** policies offer insurance

coverage for the motor vessel, crew and/or cargo of the marine vessel in the event of extensive damage or the sinking of the vessel.

(b) **Property insurance** of homes and other buildings, goods in trade and household effects. Property insurance pays the sum insured or a specified percentage, on successful claim for businesses and private dwelling houses, partially or completely destroyed or damaged in a fire or the loss or damage of such assets by theft or other means. Some fire policies would not pay claims on buildings destroyed in a riot or for natural disaster.

(c) **Motor insurance** is compulsory coverage by the law of most countries for motor vehicles used on public roads. There are several types of motor insurance coverage, including:

  (i) **Motor fire insurance**, which compensates the owner of the motor vehicle in the event of the motor vehicle being partially or fully destroyed by fire (that was not an act of arson during a riot, for example). If it is found that arson was conducted, the onus may be on the owner to pursue private litigation for compensation for the act.

  (ii) **Insurance against theft**, which compensates the owner of the motor vehicle in the event that the motor vehicle is stolen or damaged as a result of theft,

  (iii) Some **third-party policies** only cover the medical expenses and/or repairs to the vehicles of the other party when the driver who is insured by their company was responsible for causing the road accident,

  (iv) **Comprehensive insurance policies** usually provide benefits such as repairs to, or replacement (if it is damaged beyond repairs, or stolen, for example) of a motor vehicle. Both parties involved in an accident are usually compensated once the court and/or the insurance company conclude that the insured person was responsible for causing the accident. A full comprehensive insurance policy usually includes coverage for fire and theft. Hence, the policy is usually the most expensive since it offers the most extensive coverage. Some insurance companies have strict guidelines that the vehicle should not be more than 10 years and in excellent condition before the policy is granted.

There are several insurance policies which provide coverage for people. They include:

(a) **Medical insurance** which includes features such as the payment of medical consultation fees, the cost of medication, outpatient and/or hospitalization expenses. Employees of established institutions are usually compelled by law to have adequate medical, and in some instances, on and off-the-job accident insurance coverage. Private medical insurance policies can also be purchased.

(b) **Whole of life insurance policies** are designed to provide the beneficiary/ies with the face value, and sometimes an additional sum, in the event of the death or incapacitation of the insured person,

(c) **Endowment insurance policies** are primarily designed for persons who are interested in compulsory savings, while at the same time enjoying insurance coverage. These policies usually stipulate that the beneficiaries will receive the face value of the policy in the event of the death or incapacitation of the insured person.

Examples of Insurance Policies	
Life Policies:	**Non-Life Policies:**
- Whole of Life	- Motor insurance
- Endowment	- Property – fire, theft and/or damage
- Medical	- Marine, air and other cargo

Medical insurance; a sad reality for many persons who do not have medical insurance is that statistically they are more likely not to undergo even routine annual medical examinations which may identify potential complications which they may develop later in life. Therefore, when they contract some form of illness, it may be very expensive to treat it or it may be too advanced to save their lives. For this reason persons are encouraged to secure some form of medical insurance which affords them access to sound preventative medical examination and secure advice and treatment which will enhance their standard of living and quality of life.

(a) **Term Insurance** – this is very often one of the cheapest types of insurance and it can usually be bought for a fixed period of time. Term insurance is usually purchased to cover the life of the borrower over the duration of the mortgage or loan. This policy is usually assigned to the financial institution issuing the credit, so that in the event that the person dies before the loan is repaid, the insurance company will pay the financial institution the outstanding balance owed on the loan. If there is a remainder it will be paid to the beneficiaries of the deceased.

(b) **Care Insurance** – in the US and several other countries, when a person needs special care as during their elderly age, the state may supplement a part of the cost, but the patient or their relatives may have to contribute towards a part of the cost. This may even entail the sale of the home and other assets of the patient. Even though the spouse would be entitled to withhold a part of the assets of the family, this is usually a devastating experience. For this reason, the elderly particularly of richer families are encouraged to secure care insurance with a large base to cover such an eventuality. If a person does not have a large estate from which the state can draw funding from, the state is usually obligated to carry the cost. The important criterion is often the standard of the health care which the hospital or nursing home provides rather than the ability of the patient to carry the cost.

(c) **Liability Insurance** - many insurance companies sell liability insurance for medical expenses and other costs associated with a road or other types of accidents for which the insured person is liable. This is a necessity particularly in countries with high medical expenses and where a large financial settlement is usually granted to persons who sustain injuries as a result of an accident, malpractice and other liabilities.

A scripture verse which can be used in support of insurance coverage is Proverbs 22:3 which states: "[3]**The clever see danger and hide; but the simple go on, and suffer from it**." It is important that drivers ensure that they have some form of medical and hospitalization insurance if their motor insurance policy does not cover these eventualities.

Group insurance coverage, which may cover medical expenses, disability and other forms of coverage to the employee and any dependant/s. This type of insurance cover is usually provided by employers other agencies is usually cheaper, and offers superior benefits than the unit cost of individual coverage. Whatever the type of life insurance coverage desired, it should be a healthy balanced between security and affordability.

Many Christians do not purchase life insurance policies since they are of the opinion that they are 'richer than a king' since their 'Heavenly Father has everything, and He has a million mansions in the sky.' Then again, since He provides adequately for the needs of the birds and the bees, surely He will cater much more for His children. There are many instances where Christian parents can hardly provide the basic necessities such as food, clothing and an acceptable standard of education for their families, to even seriously consider securing facilities such as insurance coverage for them. In reflecting on this predicament, reference can be made to the incident recorded in 2 King 4, when a prophet died and his children were saved from being enslaved by his creditor by a miracle performed through the prophet Elisha. It should be noted that the accumulation of material and other assets often serve some functions of an insurance policy.

A serious thought of the inevitability of death should challenge Christian parents to seek to adequately provide for their family. This should go a long way in reducing the financial difficulties of the family in the event of the death or serious incapacitation of one or both parents. An unrighteous man may contend that if he dies before his wife, she may marry another man who will have to take care of her and his children. If she is not already a salary earner, she may also become more industrious and secure a secular job. On the other hand, if he has an insurance policy and he dies, then another man may marry her and enjoy the money that he sweated for and may have even died in attempting to adequately provide for his family. We also hear of instances where the beneficiary of an insurance policy kills the insured person in order to collect the proceeds from the insurance policy. Such abnormalities are not consistent with Christian principles since we are more caring and loving and the fear of the Lord is in us.

For many persons, securing medical and life insurance policies is categorized as satisfying a basic need. Medical insurance is often a blessing in emergencies when the financial resources may not be available. Very often, we can pay very low medical insurance premiums that provide us with coverage of high value should a situation demanding medical attention occur. Once it can be afforded, parent/s, in particular the breadwinner of the family, should secure adequate insurance cover for the entire family, if possible. This facility at least provides the family with some form of financial security in the event of serious incapacitation or death of the insured person.

Many parents enjoy the privilege of living for at least three score and ten (seventy) years. (This is not always so, since even Jesus died when He was only thirty-three years old). The result is that if the breadwinner dies, the children may have to shorten their education while the family undergoes financial difficulties. This situation could have at least been less severe if the parents were prudent enough and financially able to purchase and consistently pay for adequate insurance coverage.

An endowment insurance policy is an investment that Christian parents who are financially secure should be encouraged to purchase for their children at an early age. Some insurance companies would not insure children who are under two years old because of the high incidents of infant mortality and serious illness among infants under that age, especially in developing countries.

Many parents believe that if they insure a child and, God forbid, the child dies, then they would have received payments on the deceased child's insurance. Some persons deem this as 'blood-money.' Of course, this should not be a deterrent for embarking on such an important act, for if the child lives, the payment from the insurance policy would at least provide a good start to one's financial endeavour. If on the other hand, the child dies, if the parents so desire, the proceeds from the insurance policy could be used to establish a trust for the child or it can be given to a worthy charity from which others can benefit.

An endowment policy that matures when the young person is about eighteen years old and is about to enter university, embark on marriage, secure a mortgage to purchase or build his/her home, or enter business, for example, will be of significant benefit. A friend once related that the reason he struggled to complete his secondary and tertiary education was that his father, although he secured a whole-of-life insurance policy, failed to pay the premiums, and his policy lapsed shortly before his unfortunate death. The result was that the insurance company could not honour the claim presented by his mother. We should learn from occurrences such as this to be loving parents in every respect.

Many children are thankful that their parents were thoughtful, and financially secure enough to purchase adequate insurance coverage so that they could benefit from the proceeds in later years. Of course we have to consider the adverse effect of inflation and devaluation, for example, on the sum insured, for what is a substantial sum today, might become a pittance in fifteen years, for example. Despite this, it is a worthwhile investment, especially if one can increase the sum insured over time to cushion the adverse effect of inflation, devaluation and other factors that may reduce the real value of the policy.

In many respects it is better if parents secure an insurance policy rather than to hold a large deposit on a bank account for a child, if a primary focus is on long term funding. This is so because it is obligatory to pay the premium, monthly, half-yearly or annually, as agreed. Once the correct insurance policy is selected, the child can benefit from payment, or the settlement of medical bills that may result from a serious accident. Should the parents who pay the policy die or becomes financially incapacitated, that may not jeopardize the insurance coverage of the child.

There are usually clauses in some insurance policies where, if the person contributing to the scheme for a dependant dies, then the insurance coverage of the beneficiary will continue until the policy matures. A disadvantage of having an insurance policy versus a bank account for the child, is that even in an emergency the parents/guardians of the child may only be able to withdraw the cash surrender value on the premium, which is usually minimal in the early years of the policy. However, when a cash surrender value accumulates on the policy it may be as collateral for a credit facility. Savings from a bank account, on the other hand can be withdrawn at anytime of the day if the account holder has an appropriate bank card (debit, credit and/or credit card).

It is advisable that every Christian adult who can afford to, and where this opportunity exists, should purchase an adequate amount of insurance coverage for himself, where applicable and possible, and for the members of his family. At least the breadwinners of the family should be insured in order to avoid a major catastrophe for the family in the event of the death or serious incapacitation of the breadwinner/s. A good starting point is an endowment policy with a face value of at least four times the annual salary of each breadwinner. Therefore, in the event of a tragedy, the family has some financial support to rely on, which with careful budgeting would tide them through a number of years, by which time they should be able to better their circumstances. It is advisable to shop around and seek honest advice to ensure that the policy purchased is best suited for their insurance requirements and that the premium can realistically be maintained comfortably.

CAPITAL MARKETS

The following are some methods which entrepreneurs use to secure capital for investment activities:

(a) Using their own savings or borrowing from relatives and friends,
(b) Forming a partnership and pooling their individual financial and other resources.
(c) Utilizing funds from retained earnings (profit from the business which is not distributed to shareholders, that is, the owners of the business),
(d) Securing capital from a bank and/or other financial institutions,
(e) Privately offering their stocks and/or shares or floating the share publicly (publicly inviting investors to purchase shares of the company) on the stock exchange,

It might be relatively easy for small entrepreneurs to use their own capital to finance business ventures. There are also many small and medium size businesses which have operated successfully without financial assistance from external agencies. This feature becomes less exclusive on an extensive scale for large businesses.

It may be relatively easy for a small company, particularly if it is not well known, to secure capital from a bank, rather than to successfully float its securities on the stock exchange. In developing countries, in particular, a company which floats its securities on the stock exchange is usually able to raise a large amount of capital easily, depending on the price of its shares and the attractiveness of the impending returns from the shares to prospective shareholders.

The price of the shares of a company is dependent on factors such as:

(a) The demand for the products of the company

locally and internationally, thus, it's selling price,
(b) The profitability of the company, hence, the amount of dividends management can pay shareholders,
(c) The success of economic policies of the country and the effect of the political and other activities on the economy,

The stock market of most countries has been exposed to several scandals which led to the closure of trading and/or the rapid decline of the prices of securities and hence frantic efforts by shareholders to sell their shares. Companies with securities on the stock exchange and investors holding securities will suffer from the sudden depreciation of the value of the securities that they hold. The Big Bang was the name given to the 1985 collapse of the London Stock Exchange that resulted in the loss of millions of pounds sterling by companies with shares in the stock exchange and companies and individuals who trade in securities. Adverse publicity in the early 1990's also affected the Indian Stock Exchange when several racketeers were accused of insider trading and other malpractices.

Investment in government securities such as debentures and treasury bills are classified as 'risk-free investment.' This is so because the government of the country concerned usually guarantees the payment of the specified interest rate upon the maturity of the certificate. This agreement is usually honoured unless there are extreme circumstances such as a military coup or the government is bankrupt.

Investment on the stock market has a propensity to generate a higher rate of return than investing in the banking and non-banking system. This is so because a correspondingly high level of return usually compensates a high level of risk of possible loss; *inter alia* (all things being equal). In other words, since there is a high probability that investors will lose a part of or their entire investment on the stock market, the company issuing the security has to offer a lucrative incentive in an attempt to attract investors.

Many investors on the stock market do not have the time or knowledge of how to optimize their returns from direct investment (that is, trading through brokers and dealers who invest for clients) and would thus indulge in indirect investment instead. This is done by investing through intermediaries such as trust funds and investment companies.

Church officials usually do not have objections to Christians investing on the stock market, although some financial analysts contend that trading on the stock exchange is tantamount to gambling. It is true that **naïve traders** engage in gambling since they do not use scientific methods such as Fundamental and Technical Analysis (two methods of financial analysis) when deciding whether or not to purchase or sell securities. However, the average trader on the stock exchange would carefully analyze market trends of the commodity, dividend reports and other issues which influence the movement of the price of the shares of a company before investing in the company. (A counter argument is often levelled at 'professional' gamblers on horseracing, for example. They would carefully study the ancestry of horses and their history of winning, and also the history of success of the trainers and riders, and other relevant factors before placing a bet. Yet horseracing is classified as gambling by most churches).

Stock markets such as those in Japan, the USA and the UK are classified as 'efficient capital market.' These markets are supposed to be endowed with efficient methods of communicating the prices of securities, takeovers, mergers, the selling and bankruptcy of companies, for example, to players in the market without giving an unfair advantage to one or a few investors over others. In addition, private knowledge of such information by an individual or restricted group of investors should not put other investors at a serious advantage over others. Of course, Christians are characterized by their honesty as they are supposed to be law abiding and therefore, will not be involved in insider trading and other fraudulent activities.

Many companies offer their employees stocks of the company in lieu of a bonus. There may also be offers such as special credit arrangements to purchase the shares of a company which is going public, or expand their capital base. These are often golden opportunities for employees to have part ownership of the company for which they are working. However, investing much money in one company, even if you are employed by the company, must be done after much prayer and advice from competent financial planners. The principle of not 'carry all of our eggs in one basket,' also applies to making prudent investment decisions.

The choice of a broker, financial planner or other investment advisor should be determined by reviewing the track record of the individual/s and the institution which they represent. It is also recommended that such issues are discussed, even though the exact details do not necessarily have to be revealed, with other relatives, close friends and members of the church who may be knowledgeable in these areas. For this reason a potential investor must shop around until the best person or agency is secured to provide sound possible financial advice.

A stockbroker once told me that he would ask a potential client how much he could lose without losing a night's sleep before deciding how much to invest for the client. He would use that as the threshold of how much to advise his client to invest. If the portfolio were even to fall to that level he would advise the client to discontinue the investment scheme. As the portfolio grew he would advise on alternative investment or to place the profit in a less risky investment. Even though this is not a universal strategy, it highlights the fact that persons can lose a significant amount of their capital when they engage in a high risk investments; hence, a fundamental principle of investment is **the higher the risk, the higher the potential for high returns**.

OTHER INTERNATIONAL FINANCIAL OPPORTUNITIES

With the increased prominence given to globalization, several international financial centers have been adopting similar principles governing their operations. Many governments have also implemented economic and other policies in an attempt to attract more local and foreign investors. This phenomenon is becoming popular in both developed and developing countries.

Several catastrophes have recently affected international financial centers. The notorious **Third World Debt Crisis** and **the Asian Economic Crisis** are examples of how phony investors and bad business decisions are plaguing national and international financial centers. The Third World Debt Crisis was caused when governments and private investors (many of whom were guaranteed by their respective governments) sought to invest in the industrialization trust of their economies. Some large debtor nations including Brazil, Argentina, Kenya and Tanzania still owe billions of dollars to banks in the US, UK and other European countries. A greater part of their capital was mismanaged and many projects failed. The result is that the governments of these countries are saddled with the Herculean task of servicing debt in the wake of serious global, national economic and other problems which affect their economies. Fortunately, several of these loans have been written off by creditors and softer terms such as a moratorium and debt/equity swaps have been applied to many of them.

Traditionally, the movement of money in international financial centres has been characterized by **transnational companies** that operate in developing countries using transfer payment, and laundering of money from these countries to their parent companies in the developed world. Although this trend has decreased because of stricter governmental control in several countries, many of these companies have developed other devious methods to repatriate their profits with the host country deriving a disproportionately smaller benefit from the operations of foreign companies.

It is a common practice for well-established **drug traffickers** to launder the proceeds from their corrupt dealings through the official financial system in an attempt to cloud their activities. Offshore banks are often used in an attempt to hide the illicit transactions of dishonest managers of companies, government officials and other individuals. Fortunately, Interpol and other policing agencies are apprehending many racketeers. Several governments have also established legislation to impose harsh penalties and confiscate assets of persons convicted of such illicit activities.

Some persons and institutions invest in securities (that is, shares, treasury bills and debentures, for example) in several international financial centres. This is often viewed as a prudent method of **diversifying their investment risk** of possible default or failure which investors would be exposed to when investing in a single financial centre or in one line of product. However, financial theory advocates that this principle becomes less efficient as the portfolio is diversified beyond a certain point, called beta (β). After this point the returns as a percentage of the investment declines and eventually becomes negative (diminishing marginal returns).

The internet has opened a new world of communication, research materials, commercial activities, photography and other features at our disposal 'at the touch of a key.' There are so many activities which we can conduct from our computer terminal that it has dramatically reduced the distance between the supplier and the consumer. In many countries we can now access our bank account online, engage in the purchase and sale of items online where payments can be made by deducting the credit card of the purchaser or via other methods. Trading of stocks, the securing of credit facilities and other banking transactions are increasing being conducted online. Even though these transactions are becoming increasingly popular, many persons are still maintaining their relationship with financial and other institutions since they prefer the personal contact of a person whom they can see rather than communicating with a person merely with an internet address. For this reason many institutions are using digital cameras where customers with this facility can see the persons with whom they are communicating and *vise versa*.

The popularization of the use of the internet has resulted in the loss of thousands of jobs in several traditional areas of customer service, wholesale and retail outlets, the postal service and telemarketing agencies. However, new jobs are created to support many of the services provided by the internet businesses.

Trading in stocks, for example, reduces the need for the customer to interact with a physical broker. However, there is still the need for financial advisors to conduct market analysis and make recommendations on the best options available to customers.

CHRISTIANS AND BUSINESS

There is often a debate about whether it is easier to become wealthy by being honest or dishonest. The argument that is often used to support the latter claim is that persons, who indulge in drug trafficking, smuggling of commodities, prostitution, gambling, and other illicit activities, once they are not caught by law enforcement agencies or killed by rival gangs, would usually become materially rich in a very short time. This reality sometimes acts as a disincentive to persons pursuing legitimate careers or business, when they see the wealth and affluence of their peers mushrooming overnight; where they are driving the latest model of luxury motor vehicles and living a lavish lifestyle which often characterizes persons who do not earn money legitimately.

Christians should be aware that dishonest gain lasts only for a season. Even while on earth, persons who are involved in illicit transactions would have the discomfort of living with the knowledge that their activities are destroying the lives of others. There is also the fear of being caught one day and disgraced in public and imprisoned for their activities. Such activities also disrupt the unity of the family, since the presence of the Lord cannot dwell where unrighteousness exists.

Several principles are necessary for the success of any business operation. They include factors such as the management of **Financial Management, Human**

Resource Management, Marketing and Sales, Maximization of Production. These can be detailed as follows:

(a) The business must have a well-defined mission statement and vision of the organization, which all staff should be knowledgeable of and committed to work earnestly to enable the organization to achieve,

(b) A strong Management Team (Board of Directors, Senior and Junior Managers and Supervisors – depending on the complexity of the business), which is prepared, as far as possible to keep abreast with the latest development in areas that affect their operations and implement strategies to use them to their advantage,

(c) Management must consist of prudent business decision makers who can secure the necessary capital at the best terms and conditions and manage this primary resource,

(d) Suitably qualified staff must be recruited, trained and maintained to ensure that the necessary skills to man the operations are readily available at a realistic employment package, to ensure, as far as possible, the continual and increased profitability and expansion of the business. Employees must be committed to execute their tasks with maximum efficiency, and where possible, surpassing their production and other targets.

(e) Adequately rewarding staff for the service which they provide and generally maintaining a healthy working environment where workers are comfortable with the physical environment (including working under the best possible health and environmental considerations) and relationship with management and other staff members.

(f) Producing goods and/or services which are in high demand,

(g) Consistent implementation of the correct and aggressive marketing strategy in order to surpass the sales target that is budgeted,

(h) Maximization of the use of the factors of production (land, labour, capital and entrepreneurship) to their advantage,

(i) Employing the best possible technology which is within the financial capability of the business. Important factors to consider in this area include efficiency in the production process, operating with the lowest possible cost of production and, consistently producing high quality output,

(j) As far as possible, secure access to the best source of long term capital to finance the operation of the business. Failure to achieve this results in management's having to accept inadequate and/or too expensive capital, or they may not be able to access adequate capital which is one of the primary reasons for the failure of many businesses.

(k) Implementation of an aggressive marketing strategy, in order to surpass the sales target that is budgeted in the most cost effective way possible, given the financial and other constraints of the organization,

(l) As far as possible, maintain an excellent relationship with suppliers, customers and other persons and agencies who/which are important to the success of the business,

(m) Operate within the confines of the law such as the payment of income taxes and National Insurance Scheme payment of workers and to the relevant authority,

Many of these principles are applicable to a small or medium sized family business and also for a large corporate organization.

The principle that Christians should not be unequally yoked to unbelievers, is applicable not only in a

marriage relationship but also to business and other activities. The foundation of a business owned and managed by Christians must be governed by Biblical principles such as honesty, dedication and foresight. For these reasons, Christians cannot function efficiently in an environment where the *modus operandi* of the business contravenes Biblical principles. It is difficult to conceive a company that produces alcoholic beverages or manufactures cigarettes, for example, being owned and/or managed by a born again believer. This is because such a company will be perpetuating the destruction of the body, soul and spirit by marketing such items. Persons who contravene such principles will contribute to a negative impact of their lives as individuals, their family and Christendom.

Some Christians correctly extend the principles of not being unequally yoked to not purchasing shares and other securities of companies which manufacture commodities or engage in activities which are inconsistent with their faith. The outcry during the latter part of the 1980s and early 1990s regarding the boycott on purchasing shares or conducting business or purchasing commodities produced by companies which invest in South Africa was supported by many Christians who felt that these institutions were perpetuating apartheid.

In the same way, some Christian entrepreneurs do not enter a partnership, or have a minor share over a business transaction or operation, with unbelievers. This is usually in an attempt to avoid unnecessary conflicts that would arise when the unsaved partner may want to engage in unscriptural practices such as bribing officials in an attempt to secure a contract or duty waiver, and deliberately understating the profit on income tax returns. This is not always an ideal situation, since it is sometimes difficult to obtain Christian partners for specific ventures. There is usually some consolation where a Christian is a major shareholder, since the business can be managed consistently with the principles of one's faith.

There are several examples of the way God-fearing men in the Bible conducted business activities. A prominent example is the way Joseph conducted his business activities when he was in Egypt. As a result of the ability which God gave him to interpret Pharaoh's dream, Pharaoh appointed Joseph as his deputy, as governor over Egypt. Joseph's prudent management of the grains and other food items during the years of abundance enabled Pharaoh to amass much wealth during the extended famine. This was because the Egyptians and surrounding nations were forced to sell and subsequently barter their cattle, and eventually their labour power in exchange for food.

Several commentators criticize Joseph's bartering system of governance, claiming that Joseph used his monopoly power to exploit the people instead of being compassionate and provide charity, in view of the natural disaster that affected the region. In fact, this is an illustration that God sometimes uses the natural elements to punish persons who do not keep His commandments. It can be recalled that during that era, the Egyptians and the surrounding nations were primarily idolatrous. Joseph's brothers also had to be punished for dealing unfairly with him by threatening to kill him and eventually selling him to slave traders. In addition, God used this period to show His people that He can protect them, in that Joseph was deliberately sent to Egypt to preserve the lives of his relatives and other Israelites.

There are many examples in the Old Testament where believers were involved in business ventures such as cattle rearing, farming, carpentry, trading, weaving and selling of cloth. God grants a special favour that enables His people to progress in business activity, providing that they are glorifying Him in this and other areas of their lives. In Genesis Chapter 30, we read about Jacob, who used a 'scientific' method that produced an increase in the number of speckled and spotted sheep and goats and black lambs. These animals were to be given to Jacob as final settlement of his wages for working for Laban.

Old Testament believers were expected to fulfil several requirements before they received God's favour. They included:

(a) Produce from the first harvest of the crops and flock, and even human being (who had to be redeemed, that is repurchased by their parents) had to be given to the high priest as a love offering or 'gifts of first fruit' to the Lord. The Lord then blesses the producers of the product and/or services.

(b) When harvesting crops, farmers were instructed to leave a remnant for the poor, widows and orphans to glean for their own use. Boaz demonstrated this principle when Ruth, who was a widowed daughter-in-law of Naomi, gleaned in his field. This benevolent act caused Boaz to expand his wealth when he married Ruth since he inherited the land that belonged to her deceased husband. Boaz and Ruth were also blessed spiritually in that Jesus was their descendant.

(c) During the year of the Jubilee, debts were forgiven. During this year, there was also provision to free persons held as slaves because of unpaid debt.

Irrespective of how small or large a business undertaking is, the basic principle of effective budgeting requires that a realistic projection be made of the effect of the activities that are likely to occur during the year or even longer. We must be able to ascertain in the **short, medium and long term**, what we are aiming to achieve. Some businesses also have an **operational budget** which is computed over a month, week or even day, depending on the nature of the business. Factors which have to be considered before establishing a business include:

(a) **Selecting the best product to be manufactured, process conducted, crop planted and/or service provided,** where cheap raw materials and other resources which are needed for its success are available in abundance.

(b) **Employing the best possible technology** which is within the financial capability of the business is essential. Important factors to consider in this area include efficiency in the production process, operating with the lowest possible cost of production so as to consistently produce high quality output.

(c) **Recruiting and maintaining suitable qualified staff** is essential to ensure that the necessary skills to man the operations are readily available at a realistic rate to ensure the continual profitability of the business.

Many Christians omit the important principle of recording a **vision statement** for their business. In the same way as a vision is essential in our personal lives and that of the church, it is also important in business undertakings. The *modus operandi* of the business may change over time, but very often the vision remains the same or it may be expanded. For this reason, when starting a business, entrepreneurs must ensure that their Memorandum and Articles of Association are not restrictive, but will allow them latitude to conduct their business activities that are within their vision without the need to incur additional legal and other expenses to register a new business.

MANAGING THE FAMILY BUSINESS

Business activities such as commercial farming, the sale of groceries, hardware and other products and the manufacturing of items and the provision of services have been the primary source of income for many families. These businesses may be wholly managed by members of the family or they occupy key positions, or at least the major shareholders of such entities. As alluded to earlier, business entities operated by Christian families who are walking with the Lord, paying their tithes, giving of their offerings, and obeying the other commands of the Bible, will prosper. However, there is a tendency for such businesses to lose the autonomy which the family had as they expand.

In many traditional societies it is advantageous when there are many children in a family. The more persons there are in the family, the greater the number of pairs of hands which are available to provide a cheap labour force on the farm or other form of family business. The advantage of using family members in a business includes the fact that it enables them to retain the wealth in the family. In addition, trade secrets and the confidentiality of unique business practices are also protected.

There are extreme cases in countries such as India, Brazil, and in several African countries, where child labour is still exploited. Children are often used as major sources of providing income to their families by working as labourers on farms or factory, for example. There are also instances where children are forced to beg and even engage in stealing and prostitution to support their parents who may or may not be disabled, sick and/or very old. Children are also used as herders for cattle, to sell in shops and engage in other income-generating activities for their parents and in some instances for themselves, as occurs with street children.

In farming communities in lesser developed countries (LDCs), boys above a given age may have to accompany elders to the farm to learn basic techniques such as clearing the land and planting crops, while adults perform the more strenuous tasks such as ploughing the land. As the child matures, he will be given more strenuous tasks and may eventually be given his own plot to manage.

In some traditional societies the ownership of land, animals reared by the family and other major assets are handed down from the father to the eldest son when the father is unable to continue his role as breadwinner of the family due to sickness or death. The inheritance of such properties is usually saddled with the responsibility of caring for his immediate and extended family. Provision is usually made for the brother of the deceased to inherit such properties in circumstances such as when the deceased did not have a son. In some polygamous societies, such proprieties are given to the brother of the deceased who may have to marry the widow of the deceased and continue his lineage. This practice has resulted in disastrous consequences when the deceased died from AIDS, for example.

Chapter 4 of the Book of Ruth relates where the most eligible relative of Naomi's late husband, Elimelech, was willing to purchase the land which belonged to her deceased husband, but he was unwilling to marry her. (Marriage was a prerequisite of a Jewish tradition for the transfer of land and her husband's inheritance).

Therefore, Boaz, who was mentioned in the line of relationship of Elimelech, decided to redeem the land and married Ruth.

Family businesses are often inherited from ancestors. In many instances older relatives are reluctant to release the reigns of control of such entities to younger relatives. The rationale very often is that they are fearful that the younger generation would not appreciate the amount of sacrifice, planning, energy and resources which were expended in establishing the entity to its present status. The fear is often that the person inheriting the business which the founder and subsequent generations may have laboured extensively for, often does not appreciate its value. The result is that such assets are often depleted or abandoned in a very callous manner because of factors such as, the new owners:

(a) Could not appreciate the potential which is in the business. In such examples persons who are aware of its full value may deceive the new owner into disposing of it cheaply, as illustrated in the maxim 'easy come, easy go'.

(b) Might be unable to manage it and are reluctant or unable to secure competent personnel to do so,

(c) May be interested in financing another business venture or engage in other activities, hence, the interest to carry on the family tradition may not be very appealing or even financially viable,

Abandoning a family traditional business which may have dated back several decades is often a sad event. In some instances it is necessary to change several of the methods used by one's predecessors in order to increase production and productivity or the output of the service. This becomes necessary because of factors such as the introduction of new technology and increasing competition due to globalization. This can be a very painful experience for family members who have been in the business for a number of years. This process of modernization may include the construction of a new building or the renovation of the existing one, the establishment of a new plant and the procurement of additional equipment, changes in the management structure and the recruitment of more academically and/or professionally qualified staff.

Disagreements in a family business may cause a rift in the family, with elders clambering for family loyalty, while the younger generation may be supporting the necessity for modernization. The youths may advocate that the change is the only, or at least the most feasible way of surviving in an increasingly competitive business environment. Once the necessity for modernization is marketed properly, the elders in the family may eventually be convinced of the wisdom of adopting the new strategy. In fact, the primary concern of the elders of the family may be to ensure that the family retains the ownership of the business and that it continues to generate substantial returns for the family.

There are examples where a privately owned business is forced to go public because of the need to secure a high percentage of capital for necessary investment needed in order to make the company profitable and to remain competitive. In many instances the company goes public by selling ordinary shares. The family may retain a significant percentage of the capital and ownership of the company in the form of preferential shares and a large amount of ordinary shares. There may also be clauses in the Articles of Association of the company which entitles preferential shareholders to receive some form of financial remuneration regardless of whether or not the company realizes a profit in a given year.

Unpaid dividends for the years of loss may have to be paid with an agreed interest during the year of profitability. It is noted that companies which have a large percentage of preferential shares are usually not as attractive to private investors. This is because preferential shareholders usually receive a disproportionately higher percentage of dividends of the company relative to ordinary shareholders.

The management of a family business is prone to several more problems than those encountered by non-family owned businesses. They include:

(a) Suggestions of younger members of the family may be overruled by the elderly members of the family not necessarily on the basis of the soundness of the recommendation. The objection may be primarily on the basis of elders of the family believing that younger family members are not likely to be as knowledgeable as the elderly. This situation may occur when elders maintain an autocratic management style which demonstrates that being older is synonymous to being wiser since they have a large number of years of experience of working with the institution and they are the ones controlling the finances of the business.

In such instances younger members of the family may not be given senior appointments in the business even though they may be highly qualified. This sad occurrence is evident in several instances where the family may have invested much in educating a family member in specialized strategic areas of the business. This is usually done in order to maintain the control of the business in the family and to provide a lucrative career opportunity for the child.

After being qualified, the young person may take advantage of more lucrative job opportunities which are available in other agencies which offer more attractive benefits. This may be an attractive alternative particularly if the elders in the family business are not very receptive to accepting sound business proposals from younger relatives.

(b) Introducing changes or hiring more experienced persons which may result in the displacement of family members could result in major family disputes since there are emotional implications and family loyalty considerations which may take precedence over purely business decisions,

(c) Family members may be underpaid and promotion may be based on chronological order of seniority and years of service rather than on competence and qualification,

(d) There is also the disadvantage where serious disagreements on the worksite may transcend to their personal lives. The effect could be that of having to live in an environment where there is much tension from the home as well as place of employment. This mental agony could have a serious negative effect on a person's judgment, particularly for persons who are not Christians.

(e) Younger members of the family, after seeing the success of their elders, may decide to embark on their own line of business which may even be in competition with the family business,

The more established family businesses have been maintained primarily because there is a conscious effort on the part of the management of the business to promote excellence in the mode of operation of the entity, with less importance given to family loyalty. This process may be facilitated by maintaining the services of only the most competent family members in the work force and emphasizing that those family members should be highly trained in vital areas of operations of the business. In some instances, much effort is placed on maintaining the control of the family on the board of directors and in very senior and strategic positions in the business. The family may also employ the services of renowned lawyers and financial and other advisors in an attempt to ensure that the interest of the family is well protected.

The Christian family business has the potential to become a very profitable entity if they allow the Spirit of the Lord to lead it. There are examples of such families having morning devotion at home and/or at the work site to start the workday in the correct way. As expected, all transactions of the Christian business have to be conducted in a manner which reflects the practices of high Christian values. The management of some of these businesses also engages in the practice of tithing from the net income of the business. This practice will be more difficult once the business goes public and the laws of the country may not facilitate such practices, yet companies have sought to circumvent barriers of this nature by making contributions to charitable organizations. In addition, individual shareholders can also tithe from their dividend and other returns from the business, and employees can tithe from their salaries. These practices will attract the blessings of the Lord in the personal lives of the employees and owners of the business and also lead to the expansion and greater profitability and viability of the business.

> **'Jack of all trade'** individuals and investors with highly diversified portfolios are seldom successful financially. Persons and institutions which specialize in managing one or a few activities are more often successful.

STARTING YOUR OWN BUSINESS

Many Christians are desirous of starting their own business or expanding on a small-scale operation. Many entrepreneurs do not know the essential criteria which must be satisfied to ensure that the business succeeds and generates the high level of financial returns which they envisage. It is a fact that there is a high rate of business failures particularly in their first five years of operations. After the first few critical years, as the management becomes versed in managing the business, once they remain proactive in their business decisions, their chances of survival are usually increased. However, exogenous factors (which are beyond the normal control of management) such as the level of interest rates, inflation, exchange rate, the stability of the economy and other factors must be taken into account when planning such undertakings.

There are several factors which influence persons who decide to embark on a business activity and the type of business they undertake. They include:

(a) A vision or some other form of revelation from the Lord of a specific direction in this area. This may include the type of business activity which one should be involved in, the method of raising finance, the location of the business and the staff to be hired. Businesses are also formed when someone recognizes a demand for a particular product or service which is in short supply or which has the potential to offer lucrative profits.

(b) A thorough **feasibility study** should be conducted to ensure that the business venture is viable; being cognizant of the **cost/benefit analysis** of the business to ensure that it is not merely an 'impossible dream.' If it is, one may awake one day to realize that a large amount of money, times and other scarce resources were wasted and there is much frustration when persons have to be laid off because of a failed business venture.

(c) **Knowing who the major competitors will be.**

Unless it is a product for which one will have a monopoly, or be able to capture a niche market, account must be taken of what competitors are doing and what should be done to capture the required percentage of the market to ensure that the business is profitable.

(d) The entrepreneur/s will have to decide on **the best method to be employed to raise capital**. This may include using personal savings, borrowing from friends and other business associates and/or the church, borrowing from a financial institution such as a commercial bank or issuing shares to the public.

(e) Depending on the type of business, account has to be taken of the **cost of securing the level of technology** which is required to make the business competitive. Some types of businesses require that the company keep abreast with current levels of technology which might require that a large company establish a Research and Development Department to ensure that the company stays one step ahead of, or at least abreast with competitors.

(f) Identifying and securing the **best possible location for the business** is very important. Consideration must be taken of the cost of transporting the raw materials to the business and the finished product to the market or directly to customers must be realized.

(g) Depending on the magnitude of the size of the business, it may be necessary to at least **register the business as a sole proprietorship or as a company** and verify that the company is authorized by the state to conduct the business for which it has been licensed. Companies in some countries would have to formulate an Article and Memorandum of Association. There documents outline features such as who are the shareholders, the scope of the business, the amount of share capital injected by each partner and the method of distribution of profits.

(h) It is important that **competent contractors are hired to construct the building for the factory**, or the best possible building is secured to house the business operations. In addition, machinery purchased must be of the correct type and quality to ensure that the production process is at the required standard and quantity and other specification must be met.

(i) **The organization's vision, objective, mission statement and other management framework** must be formulated to ensure that the direction of management is maintained and developed as required.

(j) **The best possible staff must be recruited and any relevant training provided** to ensure that the required product and service targets are met with as little disruptions as possible.

(k) **The larger businesses would have to recruit specialists** in areas such as Marketing, Financial Analysts, Accountants, Personnel Officers and other specialists and junior staff to manage the daily operations of the business. For smaller businesses, it would be necessary that the persons managing the business at least be familiar with basic book keeping principles, marketing and other practices which will enhance their success.

(l) **It is important to maintain an excellent working relationship between management and employees** to foster minimal disruptions due to industrial actions and also that employees would maximize their production since they are confident that management has their best interest at heart and that every effort is being done to cater to their well being. Medical insurance, pension and other amenities should be made available.

(m) **Efficient marketing of products or services** is absolutely necessary since it would be futile to produce a product or service which is not in demand by customers. If the **entrepreneur/manager is not very educated** and is unwilling to take advice from, or employ experts who would be able to assist management to take the business to the level where it is needed, in order to service.

(n) **Essential features such as formulating and adhering to a strategic or business plan is lacking in many of these businesses**.

(o) **Management is unable to secure the additional capital** needed to purchase the working capital requirements and fixed assets needed to expand the business,

(p) **The inappropriate use of finance**, where management diverts the funds from the overdraft to finance long-term investment. The result may be that when the management of the bank recognizes this, they may cancel the overdraft limit and/or foreclose on any security held as surety for the overdraft.

(q) **The cost of capital was too expensive**; this factor is illustrated where the project return was over-ambitious and management is unable to adequately service the credit facility,

(r) **Difficulties** required level to make the operations profitable. The packaging of the product also has a very significant effect on attracting and maintaining customers.

(s) For larger businesses, primarily those which are involved in export, it would be necessary to secure ISO certification or at least the certification of a competent local authority. The product should meet national standard specification. This is absolutely important since it gives consumers from foreign countries the confidence that the product is not one of questionable character.

It is a fact that a large percentage of businesses, and in particular small businesses, fail in their first year of operation. A primary reason being that many of the lofty ideas which the entrepreneurs had when the business was conceptualized, were not as easy or may be to be realized or even unrealistic. The owner of a business which failed classified the business climate as a '**dog-eat-dog world**' since his experience was that the atmosphere was not conducive to the successful operations of new businesses. Of course this is not a general view since each year many new businesses strive and become major operations. Another reason why new businesses fail is due to industrial and other actions by employees which result in contracts being cancelled and embezzlement by dishonest employees.

Luke 14:28-30 stares: "28**For which of you, intending to build a tower, does not first sit down and establish the cost, to see whether he has enough it complete it? 29Otherwise, when he has laid a foundation and is not able to finish, all who see it will begin to ridicule him, 30saying, 'This fellow began to build and was not able to finish.'"**

Similarly, a person has to count the cost of establishing the business and keeping it in operation before embarking on such a course. If it is not working out as expected, it may be necessary to abandon the operation rather than consistently operating it at a loss. It is true that at the initial stage of the operation of a business it may be necessary to operate at breakeven point (where the cost of production is equal to the sale) in the short run. However, it is expected that the profitability of the business will increase, as its product becomes popular on the market and as the company is operated more efficiently and management attains other positive attributes.

There are at least three financial reporting statements which entrepreneurs should be familiar with when starting a business. They are the:
(a) **Balance sheet,**
(b) **Income statement and,**
(c) **Cash flow statement.** The cash flow statement presents a more concise picture of the source and uses of cash transactions in the business. The nature and details of these financial statements is dependent on the type and size of the business.

(a) For the **balance sheet** important areas are:
  (i) The **assets** of the business may include current assets such as the amount of cash which the company has on its premises and in the bank and working capital items such as stocks which would be used for future production and/or items to be sold. There may also be fixed assets such as building, furniture and fixtures, plant and machinery. There may also be other assets such as motor vehicles.
  (ii) The **liability** identifies the sources and uses of funds from external sources such as loans from a bank which were used to finance the operations of the business,
  (iii) The **shareholder's equity** on the other hand, identifies items such as the amount of cash injected by the shareholders, and the amount of the net profit which has been retained by the business for future investment.

  The balance sheet identifies the value of the assets, liabilities and the shareholder's equity (the input and/or ownership by the owners of the business).

(b) **The income statement** identifies the amount of revenue earned by the business and the amount of expenditure which was incurred in order to generate the level of net income of the business.

A typical income statement would have the following table. Even though the net income or net profit after tax of $2,430.49 represents the amount of profit for the year which the company will be able to retain or used as directed by its management. The company may not have all of this as cash since the company may have outstanding payments due from its customers and have outstanding payments to suppliers, for example.

The income statement relates the amount of sales and/or other sources of income which was generated by the business and how it was spent and allocated. Many large businesses do not sell and purchase only on a cash basis. Hence, accounting categories such as Accounts Receivable and Accounts Payable and other non-cash transactions are shown in the Balance Sheet and Income Statements. The concept of **Gross Income (sales, less cost of goods sold) and** depreciation expenses, for example, were also omitted to simplify the table.

(c) ***The cash flow statement*** is very critical since it presents the actual cash position of the business at a given point. Whereas the income statement may include items such as accounts receivable and accounts payable, the income statement records cash inflows and outflows of the business.

Phoenix Small Business Inc.
Income Statement
Year Ending December 2014

Sales Revenue		$5,550.65
Cost of goods sold:		
Salaries	$398.85	
Administrative and other general expenses	$425.76	
Purchases	$675.23	$1,499.84
Net income before Taxation		$4,050.81
Income Tax (at 40% of NI before tax)		$1,620.32
Net Income after tax		$2,430.49

Table 3.1 Summary Income Statement of the Phoenix Small Business Inc.

RAISING CAPITAL

There are several methods which investors use to raise capital. The primary methods are:

(a) **Debt instruments** - this is the financing of the operations of a business with capital which is not owned by the business. Common debt instruments are the various types of loan facilities such as term, pinnacle or personal and other types of loans. **Commercial Loans** are usually to finance capital investments and a repayment schedule is computed based on the ability of the payee or the commercial activity to generate the cash flow necessary to adequately service the debt. Commercial banks would usually charge interest rate of prime for their best customers and on facilities which are secured by cash or other highly liquid assets which can be realized if the customer is delinquent on servicing the credit facility. An **overdraft**, on the other hand, is usually allocated for working capital requirements. This is where the bank agrees to grant permission for a current account to be overdrawn to the extent of an authorized limit. The customers would only pay interest on the amount which they use. Other debt instruments include **guarantees** and ***letters of credit.***

A disadvantage of debt financing is that the cost of debt is usually more expensive than equity financing. In addition, if the borrower is unable to honour the repayment schedule as per the credit agreement, the credit institution may levy on the asset which is pledged as surety for the facility.

(b) **Equity** - equity represents the assets owned by the shareholders of the business. This would include cash injection, land, building, machinery, entrepreneurial skills, goodwill and other assets which belong to the owner/s of the business. There are several companies which specialize in injecting equity into a company which may be unable to raise capital otherwise or which prefer equity than debt financing. This is a very useful avenue where an investor or company is unable to raise the equity required to satisfy the requirement of a credit institution which is not prepared to lend beyond a stipulated amount, usually between seventy to ninety percent of the project cost. If they are able to secure equity financing they would have to satisfy the financial requirement of the credit institution and thus, secure the loan and commence the operation. They may be able to repay the equity injection over a number of years and thus maintain total control of the business.

Some of the advantages of equity financing are:

(i) Since the owners inject the capital, there is usually no compulsion to repay the capital over a short time span or at all, as is common with debt financing. The result is that management has more scope to turn over the capital over a longer time span without the added pressure to repay it.

(ii) The business has the opportunity to reinvest the retained earnings (and profit made which is not paid to shareholders) of the business to further generate profit,

(iii) The cost of capital is usually cheaper with equity financing since the interest rates of most commercial institutions are very high,

(iv) The shareholders of limited liability companies, for example, are only normally liable to the extent of their shareholding in the company,

There are however, several disadvantages of holding shares and other assets in a company. They include:

(i) In the event of the failure of the company, shareholders are usually the last to be repaid from the sale of any remaining assets,

(ii) The payment of a dividend, and the amount which is paid, even when the company realizes a huge profit is at the discretion of the management of that company,

(iii) The value of the shares is often determined by factors which are beyond the control of the company. This includes inflation, the exchange rate of the country and even the world market prices.

(c) **Leasing** - to some extent, is an extension of the hire purchase arrangement where the owner allows the leaser to use the asset for a fee. At the end of the period of the lease the leaser may negotiate to extend the contract, purchase the asset at a discount price or acquire another. This arrangement is attractive to many investors who may be able to negotiate the servicing of assets such as machinery, vehicles and the maintenance of building to be at the expense of the leaser.

It is important that one carefully read the lease contract before signing it. It may seem an attractive option to secure a lease for a motor car, for example, without having to make a large cash injection before securing the vehicle. All that one may be required to do is to sign the necessary documentation, pay the first monthly installment, and drive away with the vehicle. The attractiveness of this option often obscures the leaser from reading the 'fine prints' of the lease contract.

One document which is usually presented is an authorization from the employer of the leaser to continue paying the monthly installment until the entire sum is paid or when the institution presents written consent to discontinue the payment. The latter clause is particularly applicable if the leaser is desirous of breaking the contract. Even if one changes job, the mere fact that one is indebted, carries an obligation to repay.

Leasing companies usually have a battery of crack solicitors who would pursue clients who refuse to pay or who attempt to get out of the contract. Of course there are circumstances which most leasing companies would consider as being genuine enough to warrant a cancellation of a contract. This may include if the leaser becomes unemployed and is unable to secure another job after a number of months or the death of a spouse.

When the leaser is desirous of trading in the vehicle or discontinuing the agreement, one may encounter penalties. Penalties such as the leaser having to pay the company the equivalent of one year; nine, six or three month instalments for breaking the contract in year one, two, three or four, respectively. In some instances there may be some concession which is granted to the leaser, such as if the vehicle is defective, the customer decides to trade the vehicle in for another or the leaser becomes seriously incapacitated, for example.

MANAGING TAXATION

The use of taxes by governments and other statutory bodies has been enforced in one form or another from the early period of civilization to present day. There are several reasons why taxes are imposed by the government and other statutory bodies. Taxes are:-

(a) **A method of recovering some of the money from persons and agencies which utilize the resources of the jurisdiction for their own benefit and/or to make a profit.**

(b) **A way of recovering some of the wealth from persons or agencies which utilizes the resources of the state for their own benefit and/or to make a profit.**

(c) **Used by the executing agency to finance activities which other sectors of the country or community would not be willing to, or are unable to undertake.** These include the payment of the salaries of civil servants, the construction of public roads, the provision of health, educational and other public services.

(d) **A method of redistribution of the wealth of the society.** Personal income, corporate (taxation on businesses) and other activities are taxed and the proceeds allocated for the payment to old age pensioners, unemployment benefits and to other destitute groups.

(e) **Used to assist in the management of economic aggregates such as inflation and devaluation of the local currency.** Where there is an excess liquidity in the financial system which can induce inflation, the government through the Ministry of Finance or other monetary authority may increase taxes with the intention of reducing the amount of money circulating in the economy. This method is often used in conjunction with monetary policies such as the management of interest rates and the foreign exchange system of the country.

The payment of taxes is frequently resisted by persons and institutions. There are several references in the Bible of the animosity which existed between the tax collectors and the tax payers. Tax collectors often demanded more than the statutory amount and convert the difference to personal use. They also had the power to execute judgment such as imprisonment, confiscation of the property, and enslavement of members of the defaulting family. Not-withstanding these defects Jesus admonished His disciples to adhere to the laws of taxation and other just laws.

There are several types of taxes, such as:

(a) **Personal income taxes** where persons who earn above a statutory minimum income are required by law to pay a given amount of taxes on their salary to the government or state regulated tax authority. Employers usually make the appropriate deduction from the gross income of their employees and send it to the tax authority. Persons who are self-employed are also required to pay their personal income tax monthly, quarterly or as stipulated by law.

Persons and corporate entities usually have to submit annual income tax returns to the regulatory body for an assessment of whether or not they have paid the correct amount of taxes. A refund is usually made to persons who contributed more than they were required to contribute while persons who have paid less than they were required, would have to pay the additional amount.

The importance of filing correct income tax returns cannot be overemphasized. If a person defrauds the system and is caught, he may be prosecuted. They are convicted; they may be fined and/or their assets confiscated by the state. It is often not easy to receive a prompt refund when one overpays his income tax. In some countries, before a person is allowed to leave the country or transfer the title of major assets such as a motor vehicle or house which is being sold or even being offered as a gift to another person, an income tax clearance certificate must be obtained to certify that no outstanding tax payment is owed.

(a) **Property taxes** to the government, state or municipality are payable on land, houses, motor vehicles and other assets by the owner/s of the assets. These taxes are usually allocated to defray the cost of providing services which are directly related to the upkeep of these assets. These would include the provision and maintenance of drainage and irrigation facilities for farmland and the provision and maintenance of roads and other facilities.

(b) **Corporate taxes** such as capital gains taxes are paid by commercial agencies in most countries. The tax is usually levelled by government on the net profit of the business.

(c) **Valued Added Tax (VAT)** is a very effective method used by many governments to ensure that the adequate amount of revenue is generated to finance capital and other national, state or municipality expenditure. This method ensures that a wider cross section of the public is contributing to the financing of the expenditure of the economy since VAT is allocated to consumer, capital and other items. The VAT, usually an addition to the mark-up of the seller, is usually collected by the seller and paid to the VAT office monthly or as otherwise directed.

There are several methods which persons and organizations use to avoid, or reduce the amount of money which they pay in taxes. Persons and organizations employ the services of tax consultants, accountants, lawyers and other professionals who are versed in interpreting the income tax laws. They would recommend that their client employ strategies to reduce the taxable income.

An accountant can use accounting principles to prepare a financial statement where **a company declares a loss for income tax purposes.** That same Accountant may produce **a financial statement for the bank** which shows the company generating a meager profit or even a loss, which may not be as large as the loss which was declared for the purpose of income tax. This may be in an attempt to justify the need for or the continuation or increase in bank financing. **The 'true' financial statement which is presented to the management of the company** may declare a huge profit. This of course is an illegal act which can result in the imprisonment of the persons who supported this declaration. Christians should not participate in such illegal practices.

Some organizations are also able to negotiate tax-free traveling, housing, entertainment, clothing and other benefits for their staff. Where possible, employees often opt to receive a low percentage taxable income and a high non-taxable income.

A popular strategy of the tax policy of several countries is imposition of a disproportionately higher level of income tax on the larger section of the poorer persons of society who earn above the minimum wage (which may be tax exempt) and the middle income earners. Conversely tax and other incentives are granted to the rich and business sector. One of the primary reasons for this strategy is the belief that the poor spend more on consumption rather than on investment. This is similar to the hierarchical Pyramid which has been popularized by Abraham Maslow, where the majority of the population is poor and falls at the base of the pyramid. They are more focused on meeting their basic requirements such as obtaining food, clothing and housing for themselves and their family. However, as one progresses up the pyramid, increasing priority is usually focused on investment. He however, deviates from scriptural principles in concluding that the smaller percentage of the community at the apex of the pyramid would be more focused on self-actualization and on spiritual matters.

Several aspects of the principles of Maslow's pyramid are contradictory in many societies in that the poor are often the ones to turn to the Lord since they come to realize that the Lord is their only source. The rich on the other hand may place their confidence in their own entrepreneurial abilities and the security in their material possessions and influences in society. This statement is supported by Jesus' exposition in Matthew 19:24 that it was easier for a camel to pass through the eye of a needle than for a rich man to enter the Kingdom of Heaven.

A high consumption pattern is good for the growth of the economy, particularly if they are consuming more locally produced commodities. Priority is usually granted to the productive sector since they would generate foreign exchange earnings by exporting their products and/or they save valuable foreign exchange since they produce substitutes for imported commodities. In return for the high tax on the poor, economies such as the USA have established welfare systems which seek to assist the unemployed and other impoverished groups.

The months of April or May in many countries are anxious months for most employees and business entities as they prepare to file their income tax returns. The forms are usually not very complex to fill and the income tax offices of many countries would provide officers, conduct advertisements and other education programs to guide persons to be able to complete the income tax form correctly. Many persons would retain a copy of the forms which were filled for previous years for their personal record and to enable them to fill the forms for subsequent years consistent with previous applications.

Common features on most income tax forms include the name, address, date of birth, national registration and national insurance numbers. What makes the filling of the forms complex for many persons is that they may not be conversant with issues such as what constitutes income, since they may be deriving income from rental, the interest on savings account/s, dividends from shares and from an estate which they may have inherited. There are a number of transactions from which they may be able to derive a tax rebate. They may include a stated amount on:

(a) **The support of the spouse who is not working,**
(b) **A maximum of two children under the age of eighteen years, or if they are over eighteen years old but undertaking full time education and are being supported by the applicant,**
(c) **Contribution made to charitable, religious or other organizations.** Usually the applicant has to produce evidence that such a contribution

was received by the recipient. It may be demanded that a **Covenant** must be presented by the applicant and endorsed by the recipient that the contribution was indeed received. These may include a commitment made to contribute ten percent of his gross income to the church as his tithe. If he fails to fulfil this commitment but still claims the amount of tax exemption which is allowed for the contribution, he has committed a fraud and thus a gross sin. The penalty for fraudulent disclosure is punishable by a huge fine and even imprisonment in some countries.

(d) **Support made to dependant relative or other person directly under one's care**,
(e) **Interest paid on mortgage, life insurance policies**, and other acceptable claims,

At the end of the computation, the calculation would identify whether the applicant has to submit a payment to the income tax office or whether a tax rebate is due. If the form is submitted after the official deadline for the submission of the application, there is usually a penalty fee even if the Inland Revenue office is to provide a tax refund to the applicant. If on the other hand an amount was payable by the applicant, a penalty fee is usually added on the amount due by the applicant unless there were extenuating circumstances such as the hospitalization of the applicant which resulted in the delay.

Some Christians do not complete this section of the income tax form where they have to disclose how much tithes and offerings they contributed, since they are of the opinion that their 'giving should be done in secret' and not disclosed to a public organization. Failure to do this would mean that they would forgo the rebate which they were entitled to which could have been given back to the church or to a charitable organization. The question which should be addressed on this issue is whether it is more prudent for the government to spend this amount or should we use it for the work of the Lord? The disclosure of the amount contributed in tithes and offerings to the Inland Revenue Department should not necessarily be viewed as a public disclosure since it is not likely to be used for a public disclosure unless there are extreme circumstances such as the applicant is brought before the court due to an allegation of false disclosure, for example.

> **Taxation Avoidance Verses Tax Evasion**
> **Tax avoidance** is the use of legitimate accounting and other methods to avoid or at least reduce the amount of money which one pays in taxation.
> **Tax evasion** is deliberately dodging or illegally refusing to pay taxes.

MANAGING INFLATION

It should be noted that the blessings of the Lord are not inhibited by economic and other limitations which affect man. His word transcends the boundaries of conditions which we may deem as being beyond our control. If Jehovah could have taken millions of Hebrews forty years through the wilderness, surely He is well able to sustain His children through the most difficult economic, climatic and other catastrophes.

There are several prominent symptoms which are common in an economy which is experiencing inflation. First, the price of items, interest rates and the cost of production are high. Secondly, there is usually an economic downturn with high rates of unemployment. Some of the strategies which individuals and institutions have employed to manage inflation include:

(a) Indulging in more saving than investment, particularly in activities which will not generate very high returns. This is because the cost of

borrowing is high while the interest rate on savings is high. It is therefore more lucrative to save more than to invest in activities which generate low rates of return on investment.
(b) Purchasing foreign currencies and save them or engage in **trading on the foreign currency market as a hedge against the instability of the local currency**. This strategy is particularly advantageous for large investors.
(c) The sale of fixed assets such as property, since the prices are usually very high,
(d) Investing in an investment fund where the interest rate is floating. Once the economy is doing well they will usually benefit from high returns on their investment. The converse also holds.

Debt, and the fear of debt, has trapped millions of persons into being focused on financial security rather than pursuing financial freedom which can be achieved by being in the perfect will of the Lord for our lives.

MANAGING DEBT

The Bible highlights several important issues on debt management. They include:

(a) **If debt is secured among His people, they should be short term**. Deuteronomy 15:1-3 highlights that every seven years a remission should be granted where debtors forgive any outstanding debt of their creditors. However, the Jews were allowed to demand the entire amount from foreigners,

(b) **Lending to fellow believers should be interest free** - Exodus 22:25,
(c) **A blessing from the Lord is manifested in His people lending to many nations instead of borrowing** - Deuteronomy 15:6,
(d) **Borrowing is financial enslavement** - Proverbs 22:7,
(e) **His method of provision does not include a person getting into debt.** Even though debt per sé is not classified as a sinful act unless it is a manifestation of greed or other sinful acts, it is not His best method of provision when we walk in His ways and trust Him.
(f) **We should not stand as guarantor (surety) for strangers.** Sadly in today's world strangers may be our own children, for many parents unwisely give a credit card to a youth only to find that he went on a massive spending spree and incurred a huge debt. When the person who incurred the debt is unable to pay, payment will be demanded from the guarantor.
(g) **We should not incur so much debt that we are unable to pay our tithes and give our offering.** If we cannot give to the Lord but we have to pay our creditors, it could be an indication that we are idolaters in putting the satisfaction of material desire before being obedient to the command of the Lord.

It is sad to see that many churches encourage their members to incur debt to finance the building fund of the church or other projects, when they should be assisting members to be debt free. Nevertheless, for many Christians the admonishment of a borrower being a 'slave to a lender' is strong enough a deterrent for us to seek to avoid incurring debt, particularly when it can be comfortably avoided. Philippians 4:19 states: "[19]**And my God will fully satisfy every need of yours according to His riches in glory in Christ Jesus.**" If Jehovah is able to supply, according to His riches, isn't it a contradiction to

His word when we jump ahead of His provision and incur huge debt on our own?

Debt related issues are the primary financial problem which affects a majority of persons directly or indirectly. One of the indirect effects of debt on nations is that the government of both developed and developing countries impose huge taxes on their income earners, consumers and other groups in order to defray debt incurred by the government. The national debt of the USA, for example, is computed by the second and displayed on monitors around Time Square. In most countries a newborn child is saddled with a debt repayment schedule for debt which the child knows nothing about. The justification by some governments for this practice is that the infrastructure programs such as significantly improved medical facilities, roads, and education programs which has in some way contributed to the safe delivery of the child and during its growth, is testimony that the child has already began to benefit from the proceeds of government loans which were secured in the past.

> **Two methods which can be used to get us out of debt are:**
> - **Increase our inflow of income and/or,**
> - **Reduce our expenditure to the level which would enable us to have enough money to honour the repayment of the debt.**

Debt is usually the symptom of a deeper problem experienced by a person, family and even a corporate entity and nation. There are several reasons why persons get into debt. They include one or a combination of factors such as:

(a) Many persons are living beyond their means, in that their expenditure consistently exceeds their income because of greed etc.

(c) There is an acute shortage of job opportunities in the society and they cannot find a higher paying job to enable them to provide enough funds to support their family,

(d) Persons are not making a realistic budget and are not adhering to the discipline of a budget,

(e) Major catastrophes or large expenses such as the death or major illness of the only or a major breadwinner of the family and survivors are saddled with major debt/s which they are unable to adequately service,

Once a person falls into uncontrolled debt, unless he receives a large injection of money, possibly from an inheritance, it usually would take a much longer time to get out of the debt, even with the implementation of a strict adherence to a disciplined budget. The difficult question which often goes unanswered until it is too late is how does a person recognize that he is experiencing a debt problem? We often make promises that we will make this last purchase on the credit card or hire purchases, for example, and it goes on perpetually. Some of the first symptoms that a person caught in the debt trap may identify are:

(a) One is unable to meet monthly repayments and have enough money remaining to purchase food and other necessities for the month,

(b) The inability of the holder of credit cards to fully repay it at the end of the month without being able to meet other important expenditure,

(c) Many persons seek to emerge out of debt by obtaining a **home equity loan (or using the unencumbered value of their property as collateral for a loan)** or refinancing their mortgage to secure the money they need to repay their debt,

Once the persons involved are prepared to adopt a disciplined spending program, they may be able to emerge out of the debt. Sadly, many persons end up incurring more debt and may even lose their home since they are unable to maintain the repayment. This is an example where the debt was a symptom of a deep rooted problem which the couple may not have been willing to seek or adhere to Godly counsel and to adopt a disciplined budgetary program. For this reason, women in particular usually are very hesitant about mortgaging their home to repay a debt or even to use it as surety for an investment, unless there is concrete evidence that they may not end up losing their home.

Many persons and corporate bodies use the avenue of declaring **bankruptcy** in order to avoid repaying a debt which they incurred. There are genuine instances where this is the only way out because of circumstances which were beyond the control of the debtor. For Christians, this should be the last resort, since we are obligated to honor our pledge since this is a good testimony and a direct command from the Lord. A person who declares bankruptcy would have that record on his credit record for five to ten years, depending on the country. This becomes public knowledge and it hinders one's testimony of God's provision, one's prudence and financial discipline. For these reasons many Christians endeavour to repay outstanding debt, even if it entails having to sell some of their assets and live at a lower level or take another job, for example.

Many persons incur short term debt in order to invest over the long term. If one is a skilful investor and is able to secure a lucrative investment then this could be profitable. Commercial banks, for example, derive much profit by mismatching deposits and investments. The interest on short term credit is usually higher than on long term investments. For this reason when commercial banks experience liquidity difficulties they have to purchase certificate of deposits (CDs) and inter-bank loans which carry high rate of interest. This reduces their profitability.

A question which a Christian who is heavily in debt frequently asks is if they should make the repayment of the debt a priority over their tithes, offering, saving and investing? It is true that the debt burden is quite heavy; particularly when it is past due and creditors are calling you on the phone, visiting your home and may even be in contact with your employer. Three popular methods which a person may be able to use to managing his cash flow are:

(a) **Increase his income** - this includes methods such as taking a second job, securing a higher paying job and engaging in some business activity which generates additional income. A wife who was previously working from home may secure a part time or permanent job. These options must be attempted carefully since they will have a negative effect on other areas of our lives. Parents who, for example, spend lengthy hours working away from home would have far less time to spend with their children and each other. Unless they are able to secure a babysitter who it is cost effective to have, or a relative who possible volunteers to do so, the family will encounter financial, discipline and other problems.

(b) **Decrease the expenditure** - this process will not be achieved instantaneously since the person may have become accustomed to a certain standard of living and even reducing it gradually may demand several major adjustments,

(c) **Renegotiate the terms of repayment** - this could range from requesting an amortization of the principal payments over a favourable period to extending the repayment period, therefore, reducing the monthly repayment. The wisdom of this strategy must be weighed against the additional interest charge which will be incurred.

Particularly for business entities, two additional features are usually added. They are: **increasing the time** *for the settlement of accounts payable*, that is, **delay in making payments to suppliers**; and **reducing the time for accounts receivable, where they demand cash or payment within a week or so, when purchases are made by customers**. This practice is questionable from a scriptural perspective, since we should "do unto others as we would expect them to do unto us". However, if the suppliers are prepared to accept those conditions, they can be effective in reducing severe cash flow difficulties which a company is experiencing.

A businesses which is in a '**cash strapped**' position (where they may have healthy non-current assets in their balance sheet, but low in liquid assets, and cash in particular) but would still like to maintain their good relationship with a supplier would request that the **payment be made on a pre-dated check.** Even though the check is issued it will not be cashed until the date stated. Some suppliers may negotiate with a financial institution to have the check discounted and they will receive the funds even though the customer's account will not be debited until the date written on the check. A standard check also has an inherent credit element associated with it. A check issued on a Friday afternoon, for example, actually provides credit to the purchaser until it is cashed, say on Monday. Other important debt management techniques include:

(a) **It is always better to contact the agency before the repayment is due and negotiate a prudent rescheduling of the repayment.** This may include negotiating a lower monthly repayment and/or a period of moratorium where you service the interest only, for example. Efforts should be made to have the additional finance to meet future payments.

(b) **Some persons adopt the prudent strategy of consolidating their debt with one institution** which offers a lower monthly repayment than the individual creditors from several institutions.

(c) **As far as possible, persons on a tight budget should avoid purchasing items over a given amount, say one hundred dollars, on impulse.** It is better to pray about the wisdom of the purchase and discuss it with your spouse or other persons before purchasing it. Very often the moment of reflection allows us to exam other options of payment, or whether or not a cheaper substitute can be secured. This principle is highlighted in Proverbs 21:5 which states: "⁵**The plans of the diligent lead surely to abundance, but everyone who is hasty comes only to want (poverty)**."

(d) **Increase the time in paying debtors and increase the time frame to pay creditors.** There are two principles which are commonly used by business entities to manage their cash flow. The benefit may not be as significant for an individual where the transition is small. It can be advantageous if we are able to delay payment for a month or two with the concern of the debtor, particularly if it does not include incurring additional charges.

(e) **Where possible solicit assistance from a relative, friend or even a fellow Christian or the church council. It may also be possible to secure a short term loan from a relative or friend.** These may be methods to alleviate the predicament temporarily. The longer term solutions would usually be more discipline in managing the budget.

> **Debt to most persons is like the Venus flytrap to insects, easy to get in but very often impossible to get out.** (A Venus flytrap is a flower which traps and kills insects which enter its enfolding petals. The flower would shut tightly and suffocate the insect which was attracted by the sweet smell of the flower and its quest to collect nectar. The flower would then absorb the nutrients from the body of the decaying insect).

We have established that it is the perfect will of God that His children are free from financial debt since we are not to remain slaves but live in the liberty that Christ has set us free. This freedom is not only spiritual, but includes the liberation from financial bondage such as the hideous burden of debt. We have an obligation to give our tithes and offerings and to be faithful to the Lord in every other aspect of our lives. In return, He will provide protection, health, material, other blessings and benefits to us and our family and to the wider community. An important criterion which enables us to emerge out of debt is that of **sowing our way out of Debt.**

> *Once we stay committed and focused on fulfilling God's will for our lives and we are walking in accordance with His will, then we have nothing to worry about. We can cast all of our cares on Him since He empowers us to succeed.*

The ability of persons to live on their salaries is often not as feasible as they would like. As a result, a number of persons and financial institutions have existed on the basis that they have been providing credit to persons and institutions which have immediate financial needs which they cannot currently meet, but which they have the potential to honour at a future date. The credit culture is dominant in the US and several other countries where credit agencies offer attractive bargains to members of the public who would end up in many instances in a worse financial position than before they accepted the credit offer. The credit card industry and 'loan sharks' are two agencies which have contributed to the serious financial difficulties of many families in these societies.

Deuteronomy 32:30 states: "**³⁰How could one have routed a thousand, and two put a myriad (ten**

thousand) to flight unless their Rock had sold them, the Lord has given them up." This verse is often used when referring to the compounded strength which unity produces. A couple who is united in Christ will be able to achieve ten times more success if they operate together. This law is demonstrated naturally in several ways. It is stated that two horses that are able to synchronize their efforts, will be able to pull as much as seven times more weight than they would have been able to pull independently.

> *Very often we make unwise financial decisions primarily because we had the option to purchase the item on credit. When we have to make cash payments, the average person would automatically be forced to review other more lucrative ways of spending the money.*

Married couples can also apply the principle of the two being able to achieve far more than they would have individually and reap substantial benefits. For this reason, members of a family who budget together and pool their financial and other resources will be able to achieve substantially more than spouses who are doing so independently. When spouses save independently and are very cagy about disclosing their financial plans and resources, it leads to much distrust and disharmony. They may only be collective in emergencies and even then, they may still be apprehensive about disclosing the full extent of their resources and what they can do to assist. Therefore, they conduct independent financial and other transactions and they may actually be competing to out-save each other or to secure various assets.

The devil obviously delights in such situations, for there will be so many avenues for him to create distrust and animosity in such a family. When couples pool their financial and other resources, they will be able to purchase items cash, for example, instead of paying the huge hire purchase interest when one person purchases it on hire purchase. Collectively, they could have purchased the item cash and use the saving from the transaction to invest in a venture which realizes significant gains. The couple will also be able to save and invest far more and generate higher levels of return together than if they were doing so independently. Very often the return from the accumulated resources of the couple would be compounded instead of a linear return from one spouse.

Credit card companies are known to offer clients easy access to credit. As a result, the undisciplined and the desperate persons often utilize these facilities to the maximum in anticipation that they will be able to fully repay the debt in the short-run. The reality is that they have often become so addicted to using credit cards that they go on frequent shopping sprees with the honest intention of repaying in due course. Often such persons end up having to take out several credit cards and other forms of credit facilities in an attempt to repay outstanding debts. In other words, they 'dig a hole to fill a hole'. It is customary to find such persons accumulating credit on one card to repay outstanding debt on another.

It is often much easier to acquire a credit card without having to undergo extensive background checks in some countries, that young adults who are not even working and cannot adequately service such a facility are offered credit cards. Such persons often obtain a bad credit rating even before they had the opportunity to start earning a decent wage. The question is often asked who is to be blamed for such an unfortunate situation. The answer is usually both the credit card companies whose primary concern is usually to issue as much credit as possible and the gullible customer for accepting these offers at face value without seeking wise counsel and carefully weighing the consequences of their actions.

It is true that a credit card may come in very handy in situations such as purchasing items on the internet. Even though the risk of using it to purchase on some sites may be risky, since it may be illegally debited for other unsolicited purchases or the site may not be secure and other persons may have access to the number. It is very convenient and safe to use a credit card when one is travelling since it offers safety where if it is stolen, it is usually easy to stop any payment on the card by merely reporting it to the credit card company. However, a debit card offers the same facilities without the additional high interest charge on transactions undertaken since the cost of the transaction is merely debited from the account of the users.

Particularly for the undisciplined spender, the best ways of managing a credit card may be:
    (a)   Not to purchase any item on credit unless it can be promptly repaid for by the end of the current month,
    (b)   Simply cut it and throw it in the bin,

Proverbs 11:15 states: "[15]**To guarantee loans for a stranger bring trouble, but there is safety in refusing to do so**." It is true that not every stranger will be dishonest but there is a higher probability that a person with whom one is familiar, will usually endeavour to honour a commitment which is guaranteed by a relative or at least someone who knows them. Failure to do so may result in members of one family, friends and other persons pressurizing the defaulter to honour their commitment. This may not be possible with a stranger and one may end up losing his surety or good name may be tarnished.

Unless a person can exercise prudent financial discipline, it is wise that credit cards and other forms of credit, particularly for consumer items which may be desired in an attempt to 'live like the Jones', should be avoided. The important consideration should be a commitment to live within the confines of a well-structured budget and for each family member to endeavour to live within the confines of the budget. There should also be a commitment from the parents to endeavour to enhance their earnings.

There was a recent advertisement for a washing machine where consumers were offered the follow options:

(a) A cash payment of $1,999.00.
(b) Term payment as follows:
 (i) Down payment of $1.00, or an amount that one can afford to pay,
 (ii) 30 monthly payments of $100.00. (The monthly payment would be smaller with a higher deposit, since a smaller interest will be payable).

Many persons would be attracted to the second offer since it does not put immediate pressure on them to find the cash payment. In taking this option they have to consider issues such as:

(a) They would enjoy the privilege of using the washer even though they were not willing or able to expend all of the money immediately,
(b) They may be able to negotiate to have the warranty on the washer extended to at least the life of the repayment for it. They may enable the purchaser to be better able to

negotiate that any problem which may be encountered is repaired quickly by even threatening to withhold further payments until the problem is rectified.

(c) The total cost of the washing machine at the end of the two and a half years is $3,001.00. The cost of the washer would be $1,001.00 or 14.3% more that if it was to be bought cash.

(d) If the purchaser is unable to meet the full payment of the washing machine and the company is forced to repossess it, it would affect one's credit rating. This may jeopardize one's chances of securing further credit from other companies in the future. The purchaser would also lose the amount paid to date on the washer.

(e) Once one is able to invest the $2,000.00 and generate a net profit of more than 14.3% for two and a half years, it may be a worthy investment to secure the item on credit.

> **The word mortgage comes from the French word 'mortir' which can be translated as an agreement until death.** This is very much a reality for a large number of persons who are so stressed out from working hard to meet their monthly mortgage payment; they die young due to stress related illnesses.

If a person or family were to secure a **mortgage for a property**, some of the initial costs which would be incurred are as follows:

(a) Valuation of the property,
(b) Solicitor fees,
(c) The legal registration of the mortgage over the property in favour of the mortgage company,
(d) Facility fee charged by the mortgage company,
(e) Insurance of the building,

(f) Transportation of furniture and utensils from one's old home, and/or the purchase of new furniture, utensils, blinds and other necessities,

The major consideration once the applicant qualifies for the mortgage is the obligation to honour the monthly payments, failing which they could lose the property, unless they are able to negotiate for a moratorium on their repayment until they are in a better financial position to resume their repayment. Many persons also take a second mortgage on their home in order to conduct repairs, renovation or for other purposes.

Many persons debate which institution to secure a mortgage to purchase or build a house. The options which are available include a credit union, building society, insurance company and commercial bank. There are also some agencies which provide housing loans for staff of the institution with highly concessional terms. In many instances the credit union and the building societies would offer attractive interest rates even though the maximum amount which these institutions lend to a given customer may be lower than that of commercial banks. The interest rates on mortgages from a commercial bank may be higher than other financial institutions and they may require a higher percentage contribution than other financial institutions. Customers may also have to pay commitment and other fees, and their interest rates may be floating at a given percentage above the bank's prime interest rate. Unless a cap is agreed to, this would prove to be very expensive once the interest rates increase significantly.

The purchase of one or several homes is the biggest financial investment for a large number of couples. This may only be second to the investment in business ventures which some couples or a member of a family manages. For this reason it is imperative that the couple be very careful in choosing which house to purchase since factors such as the architectural design, number of rooms, size of the land, and neighbourhood where it is located are important.

Many persons debate whether to accept a **fixed rate or an adjustable rate mortgage**. For most persons it is more advantageous to secure an adjustable rate mortgage since they will benefit from having to pay less interest when the interest rate is low. They will also have to pay a higher rate when the interest rate is high. For this reason, even with an adjustable rate of interest mortgage, it is prudent to negotiate an interest rate cap, where charges will not exceed a given amount, say 3% above prime.

It is usually better to repay the mortgages or other credit facilities by consistently making the monthly payment along with additional payments to the principle. Once the principle is reduced, then the interest charge will also be reduced. There are, however, some credit facilities where there is a penalty for early repayment. This is usually done since the institution would lose by not being able to collect the projected income.

In an effort to avoid paying a high mortgage, while securing the asset of a home, many families purchase a mobile home or purchase a condominium or flat. One advantage of purchasing a condominium or flat is that the maintenance of these facilities may be done by the maintenance department which is managing the complex. This may be particularly attractive for persons who do not want the worry of contacting the services of individual maintenance persons. When they are more financially secured they may choose to rent the former facility or sell it and use the proceeds for a down payment on a mortgage for a house.

Many couples have more than two motor cars in their lifetime. The amount of money spent on the purchase, maintenance and repairs of motor vehicles, cause motor vehicles to be rated as the second largest expenditure for many families. The model of vehicle which a person purchases is usually determined by factors such as his preference for a particular make of vehicle and the availability of cheap spares. There are the wealthy persons who purchase vintage vehicles because of their love for a particular model of classical vehicle, their resale value and/or merely as collector items.

For many persons it is prudent to purchase a good second hand vehicle rather than to purchase a new one which is too expensive and would deplete their personal savings, and/or the monthly repayment is too high for their budget to accommodate. It is also important to know when it is better to trade in or sell a vehicle. For persons with a serious budgetary constraint, this decision should not be arrived at as fashion dictates but in accordance with the peace which a person receives when the decision is consistent with the will of the Lord. Very often a vehicle which is more than ten years old would carry a very high maintenance cost which makes it uneconomical to maintain. Factors such as the level of pollution which it emits and the consumption of petrol are also important considerations. Important tips to observe when purchasing a motor vehicle on hire purchase, similar to any other credit scheme is that, the higher the down payment, the lower the monthly payment and charges will be.

There are several prominent preachers and other Biblical scholars who have several publications and also preach extensively on the importance that **Christians should be debt free and stay out of debt**. They have expounded on several scripture verses which reiterates the fact that it is the will of Yahweh that His children should rely on His provision and not be 'enslaved' by the burden of debt. It is true that the inability of persons to manage debt has led to the disintegration of many families and individuals resorting to illegal activities in an attempt to repay their debt. However, when we are able to manage personal and corporate debt, it contributes significantly to the acquisition and expansion of our assets. This does not infer that we should not rely on the provision of the Lord to enable us to acquire and manage our assets.

If a person feels that it is essential to engage in a debt transaction, it is always better to have the direction of the Lord before indulging in it. In embarking on, or expanding a business entity for example, the option is usually either to utilize a debt instrument or expand the ownership of the business in the form of issuing shares. Since the present owners may not be desirous of extending the ownership of the entity to other persons, (as in the offer of additional shares, for example.) to whom they would have to share their profit and then the option is usually to engage in debt.

The perfect will of the Lord's is for us to be debt free and be able to have abundance to give for the furtherance of His work. Nevertheless, Christians still incur several types of debt in order to survive in this world where easy credit is the order of the day. As a matter of fact, very often if a person does not have a credit history it is difficult for them to secure a large credit facility when they need it the most. This is no doubt the prelude to the era where unless a person has the 'mark of the beast' - (666) inscribed on him, he would not be able to engage in economic activity.

There are several factors which we should take into consideration before borrowing money. They include:
- (a) Whether or not the item to be purchased or investment made is not fuelled from greed, lust, or other unscriptural practices,
- (b) Before the credit is negotiated, at least the primary parties who are involved in the transaction prayed about the matter, discussed it thoroughly with competent persons and they are assured that it was not inconsistent with the will of the Lord for their lives. Hence, the transaction was not undertaken on impulse without receiving a release in their spirit, the Holy Spirit approved of the transaction.
- (c) There is/was a clear and workable strategy to servicing the facility which would not place them and/or their family or other persons concerned, in major difficulties,
- (d) That all the parties concerned are aware of the possibility of losing any asset which may have been lodged in the event that the borrower defaults and that they are able to forgo the asset, or are willing to 'bail out' the debtor, where possible.
- (e) That a person or persons with technical knowledge on the item to be purchased were invited in to review the purchase and to submit an unbiased opinion of the wisdom of the purchase and we are willing to accept their recommendations.

Three important criteria which established financial creditors use to determine the credit worthiness of an applicant include:

(a) **Character** - in order to verify whether past credit has been honoured satisfactorily, credit institutions usually access the credit scores of the applicant which highlights factors such as the promptness of honouring payment, whether the person filed for bankruptcy, or record of honesty in repaying other creditors punctually, for example. Character references are also usually contacted.

(b) **Capacity** - for salaried employees, the applicant usually has to submit a copy of a recent pay slip or statement of employment, at least one Income Statement, and for some institutions a Statement of Indebtedness to other institutions.

(c) **Collateral** - most commercial creditors would maintain ownership of the asset being sold or take a lien over other collateral with a greater value that the amount being lent or an item purchased. A lien is usually taken over the collateral so that in the event that the debtor is unable, or refuses to honour his repayment obligation, then the creditor would be able to confiscate the security or repossess the item bought under the credit arrangement.

It is recognized that it is the perfect will of God for Christians to not only be debt free, but for us to have enough that we can be a blessing to those around us and to engage in the financing of the gospel nationally and internationally, where possible, for not all of us will have the financial resources to impact significantly. However, even so we have to play our part in prayer, and other activities to spread the Word.

Having recognized that we can and should be debt free, there are several principles which we can follow in order to be debt free and stay out of unnecessary debt permanently. They include:

(a) **Stage 1** - Recognize that you have a debt problem and be committed to get out of debt with the help of the Lord, prudent management of the debt and adhering to Godly counsel.

(b) **Stage 2** - List the extent of the debt. This can be done in a format as highlighted in Table 4.2.

This table presents a dismal picture of a family who is likely to be straddled with a huge debt burden for over ten years, unless the family is able to generate a large enough income to enable them to emerge from this debt trap. This is not a very healthy position for a lower or middle income family to be in. There are several negative criticisms which can be levelled at this schedule:

(a) The huge monthly credit card payment is evidence of financial impropriety by the family. Instead of using a credit card, other lower interest rate sources should be utilized.

(b) The largest monthly payment is that of the car payment. This could be an indication that the family is living above their means. Unless the car and/or other motor vehicles are absolutely necessary because of the distance, one or several members of the family commutes, cheaper means of transportation is often a better alternative, at least over the short run.

(c) Even though substantial amounts of loan repayments have been made, the outstanding amount is more than 44% of the principle borrowed.

A debt schedule does not have to be as complex as this one, it is important to know who your creditors are so that the eradication of the debt can be tackled in a systematic way. As the family recognizes the magnitude of the debt problem they can prayerfully attack the total eradication of all of them. Depending on the financial resources of the family, discipline and other factors of an individual family, this process may take a few months for some families and a number of years for others. As each debt is repaid and it is scratched off the list, it would be a source of joy for the attainment of a milestone and also a challenge to eliminate the others.

(d) **Stage 3** - work ardently to eliminate each debt. In the process, it would take much discipline and faith in the Lord to avoid getting into new debt.

The issue of being debt free is particularly difficult for poorer families to embrace, even though many richer families also adopt a lifestyle which is beyond their means because of greed and other lifestyle patterns. However, the solution to being debt free is reinforced by the fact that in every aspect of our lives, the Lord expects us to work conscientiously and also to trust Him to see us through every difficult situation. We cannot please Him without having faith in Him.

Each person experiences financial and other difficulties in one form or another at various occasions. This dilemma is not only applicable to persons who are living below the poverty line in third world countries but also for persons in affluent societies. Very often a person who is born in an impoverished family is better able to cope with financial difficulties since they have been accustomed to stretching the little which they have. Conversely, many persons in affluent societies are prone to experience mental depression and may even commit suicide when confronted with financial difficulties since they cannot imagine living well below the affluence which they have been accustomed to and the prestige which their status commands.

Debt Schedule of the Robertson Family

Debtors	Purpose	Amount Borrowed $	Total Loan Payment $	Outstanding Balance $	Payment to Date	Monthly Repayment $	Interest Rate %	Maturity Date
A&B Credit Card Co.	Miscellaneous	5,000		3,564		250.00	23%	N/A
Uncle Jake	Wedding expenses	4,500	5,227	1,742.43	3,485	$145.20	10%	30-Dec-13
A to Z Variety Store	Vanity set & bed	15,625	20,854	8,342	12,513	$347.57	12%	31-Dec-15
	Fridge & stove	5,500	6,214	3,107	3,107	$258.90	12%	28-Dec-14
Rest Motors Inc.	Motor car	65,000	171,769	85,885	85,885	$715.71	12%	28-Dec-22
Ace College	School fee	48,000	63,928	37,292	26,637	$443.95	5%	07-Dec-19
Family Mortgage Inc.	Mortgage	250,000	539,595	359,730	179,865	$1,498.88	6%	28-Dec-32
Total		393,625	807,588	499,662	311,491	3,660.21		

Notes: 1. The Monthly Payment for the Credit Card account is computed using 5% of the limit of the card but will vary depending on the amount used.

Table 4.2 Hypothetical Schedule of the Debt of the Robertson Family

A famous cliché states that the only good debt is one which someone else is paying for you. Examples of these are:
- Purchasing a house large enough that you are able to rent sections of it for more than the monthly mortgage payment.
- Securing a large enough mortgage to build other houses, and the monthly rent from the two are enough to pay for the one that you live in.
- Invest a part of the loan in an economic venture with a high rate of return that will service the entire debt.

MANAGING FINANCIAL CRISES

The devastating effect of financial difficulties is so profound on the lives of individuals, families and nations that it has continued to be one of the primary reasons for much of the difficulties which adversely affect our society. As alluded to earlier, money is important because of factors such as:

(a) It enables us to conduct the financial transactions which enable us to get the essential, hence, for our sustenance such as food and the adequate type of clothing,

(b) It determines to a great extent the educational status we will be able to attain, the level of health care we will receive, the neighbourhood in which we live, the type of house we live in and the furnishing and other amenities which we can afford,

Our social status in society is to a great extent influenced by our financial position. Very often political and other prominent positions in society are influenced by the financial standing of both the incumbent candidate and his/her supporters. This is often so because the person who is able to get things done would have to inject personal funds or at least be influential enough to secure the financial support of rich persons and institutions.

Several financial problems which affect families have been highlighted in various sections of this book. However, it will be useful to have a section which focuses exclusively on some of the more common ones and on methods which have been successfully used to resolve them. They include:

(a) Living in an impoverished society where there are very limited opportunities to earn a reasonable standard of living,

(b) The inability of the income of the breadwinner/s of the family to satisfy the basic requirements of the family such as the provision of adequate amount of food, clothing, housing, education, health and other essential items.

(c) Spouses who are grossly dissatisfied with the standard of living of the family and are working for long hours, neglect each other and the children or have resorted to extramarital affairs or other sinful methods of securing money,

(d) Is it wrong for a wife who is working to request or even demand that her husband provides her with a separate 'spouse allowance' even if he is meeting other financial needs of the family? If there is efficient budgeting in the family and everyone is reasonably satisfied, one would not normally expect such episodes. However, if the husband is a miser, stingy, not earning enough to meet the financial needs of the family, for example, such situations are common.

(e) Children who are dissatisfied with the standard of living of their family and have become rebellious and may even resort to a life of crime to satisfy their financial wants,

(f) One or both partners of a marriage who are lavish spenders and would not adhere to the discipline of a well-planned budget and living within their means.

(g) A spouse who is domineering and would seek to impose his/her dictates in financial and other matters on the other. Husbands who are the sole breadwinner of the family are particularly prone to this practice.

(h) A person, and more seriously, a family going through life without concrete financial and other material goals which would challenge them to structure their financial and other resources to achieve them.

(i) Members of a family having to prostitute their bodies, beg and indulge in menial acts in order to survive,

(j) Members of a family who have to live in perpetual debt in order to survive. This may be as a result of having to finance an addiction such as illegal drugs and greed, which propel them to make credit purchases which are far beyond their ability to service adequately.

(k) Some families suffer from financial difficulties due to severe sickness and other forms of incapacitation of one or several members of the family,

(l) Crises such as finding money for weddings, to purchase a home, engage in the establishment or expansion of a business, the burial of a member of the family, to finance the cost of a member or several members of the family travelling to a foreign country are merely a few of the other large financial demands which confronts many families.

Some Christian families go through life so poverty-stricken that there is hardly a time when they can truly enjoy spending money to enjoy the simple things in life, instead they are perpetually bowed-down scavenging to exist from moment-to-moment, day-to-day. Yet we are serving a God who has created the world and all that is in it. Whatever the need, we serve a God who is well able to meet all of our financial and other needs which are consistent with His will. We also have Christian financial counsellors and other professionals who are specially trained to guide us in this and other important areas of our lives. God has given us His Word; we have the direct access to Him via the channel of prayer, praise and worship. We also have intercessors, the body ministry of the church, the five-fold ministry, our spiritual weapons and other assets to see us through financial and other difficulties.

> God is our source. He may change the supplier, which may include our job, business, a widow or even a raven (Elijah). However, all good gifts come from Him.

PURCHASING FROM MAIL ORDER SALES AND VIA THE INTERNET

The method of purchasing items by mail order has been popular for decades. The modus operandi of these businesses is predominantly that they are usually able to purchase items in large quantities and thus receive dramatically low prices. Therefore, they are able to present attractive offers to perspective customers who are lured to subscribe as members. Usually, offers which would appear 'too good to be true' are presented as an introduction for membership on condition that the member is willing to purchase at least a given minimum number of the products over a year or some other time span. A feature selection of the month is usually presented to members and if they do not wish to order it, they have to return the form which describes the feature selection by a given date or contact the company by some other method. Members usually have the option of replying via mail, telephone, fax or email.

It is usually stipulated that if the member does not inform the company that they do not wish to be mailed the offer, it would be interpreted that the item is requested. If there is no communication on the decline of the offer, (we will assume that they are honest and would not post the item even if the decline was received before the deadline), the item is mailed to members. The 'catch' in this system is that if the member does not wish to use or keep the item, it is often more expensive to return it by post than to pay for it. In addition, since the member would have responded to a questionnaire, indicating one's choice of the particular item being sold, and the item presented may be irresistible.

Some of the items offered by mail order companies are CDs and DVDs which are shipped by air, sea or land.

These clubs can be sourced online and in several magazines and other publications. This is a well organized network and once a person is a member of one such club, his name and address is usually circulated to others and they will send their introductory offer to him also. This system can become very addictive as a person is lured to accept the attractive introductory offer. Very often getting out is not as easy, unless the member is prepared to purchase the mandatory offer to satisfy the prerequisite for membership. The system is further compounded when the member sends his credit card number. The payments for items shipped are often deducted automatically.

Persons who decide to make payments by sending money order or check (cash payments are usually not recommended) have a greater scope to avoid making a payment if they so desire. These clubs also would offer members free gifts and other special offers if they introduce a friend to join the club. There are also sales and other special offers which members can benefit from. Many of them also offer members sweepstakes, lotteries and other drawings from which members can enter if they so desire. The record of success of persons winning the jackpot is assumed to be the same as other games of chance since they have to register with the state before making such announcements. Many persons would receive at least 'consolation' prices of token gifts and discounts if members accept offers to purchase other items.

Many of these clubs present so many attractive offers that many persons have been subscribing with them for over a decade. When a member refuses to honour a payment, they would usually have to pay late fee penalty. The name and address of delinquent customers are usually handed over to debt collectors who would make demands for the settlement of the debt. At the extreme, and depending on the amount, legal actions may be taken for the settlement of the debt.

The names of some of these companies are:
(a) Bookspan Club,
(b) History Book Club,
(d) Music Heritage Society,
(e) Book-of-the-Month Club,
(f) Sound and Spirit,

Membership to these clubs is usually restricted to persons from the country from which the company operates. However, persons from other countries are able to secure them by opening a **sky box**. There are several courier and other services which offer membership to subscribers who are given the address of the company in the US and other countries. Members quote the overseas address, fax and telephone number and their mails are delivered to that address and transported by the courier service to the local address of its member. There may be some element of illegality in this practice since the person does not live at the stated address, even though this system is widely used. Any tax and other expenses other than that of the supplier for transporting the item are usually paid by the management of the courier service and this charge, along with delivery and other charges passed to the customer. This service is widely used in several countries and the price for the item is usually significantly cheaper this way than if it were to be purchased locally.

CHRISTIANS AND THE LAW, AS IT RELATES TO FINANCIAL ISSUES

Christians, like other persons, sometimes encounter circumstances which involve litigation. For most persons having to take a civil matter to court would only occur if all other methods of resolving the matter fail. One factor which deters persons from pursuing civil legal recourse is because the court system in many jurisdictions has a huge back log of cases, thus, new ones have a lengthy wait before they are heard and finally resolved. There is also the cost associated with hiring the services of one or several attorneys, depending on the severity of the case. There are instances such as some traffic violations, robberies, fraud, violation of a contract and other public crimes where it becomes mandatory that legal actions be taken against a Christian, or a Christian has to seek legal actions against someone else.

The Bible discourages Christians from taking a fellow Christian to court. There are however, instances where attempts to forge a resolution of the conflict fail and resorting to the court seem to be the only option. There is a sequence of events which should occur before a Christian is spiritually authorized to take another Christian to court.

In 1 Corinthians 6:1-8 Apostle Paul discourages Christians from taking fellow believes to court to be tried by an unrighteous judge. He admonishes that such matter, as far as possible, should be resolved amicably within the Christian community since the saints will judge angels. The sequences of activities used by many churches in an attempt to resolve a serious conflict between two believers:

(a) The two or more persons attempt to resolve the matter among themselves,
(b) Invite a mutual believer to mediate on the issue,
(c) Call at least two elders of the church to mediate on the issue,
(d) The church council would meet the two believers and any other of their representatives,

Hopefully the matter is amicably resolved before they have incurred the expense of engaging the services of a solicitor and the time wasting process of having to attend several court hearings. When two Christians cannot resolve a matter before it goes to court, it does not bring glory to the Lord. Verse 8 identifies that it is blessed to accept the loss as a result of a wrong committed by another believer rather than to go to court. The reward of the Lord for such a person would be fair, since that person protected the damage which would be done when two Christians go to court, and would far exceed that which the earthly judge would allow.

There are many instances when it may become necessary for a person to secure the assistance of another person to act on their behalf in matters which they may be unable or unwilling to attend themselves. They would have to secure the services of a **power of attorney** by signing a legal document prepared by or at least notarized by a Justice of Peace, solicitor or other persons designated by the law of the country, depending on the nature of the service requested. In instances where the request is for the representative to act only on a specific matter such as to represent the person on a court matter since he will be out of the country or is ill and would not be able to attend the hearing, for example, a **limited power of attorney** can be granted specifically for that purpose.

A **general power of attorney** may also be appointed to manage all of the affairs as specified in the document. This may include the collection of rent, dividends which are payable to the person whom he is representing, sign on his behalf, represent him in court and on other matters as stipulated in the agreement. Depending on the laws of the country, this document is subject to be renewed annually and may be revoked by any of the parties.

A spouse may have been a rational spender but suddenly decides to engage in lavish spending. Lavish spending from such a person is often an indication that he is suffering from depression, insecurity or other forms of disturbances or may even be having an extramarital affair. The couple has to discuss the issue, pray about it and even seek council if it persists over an extended time. It may be a relatively harmless phase if, for example, the husband is undergoing a mild mid-life crisis or the wife is experiencing menopause. If it is a prolonged phase, corrective actions have to be taken such as seeking counselling, or in the extreme, in instances such as senility, a restraining order may have to be secured from the court to prevent the person from conducting further depletion of the assets of the family.

CONCLUSION

This chapter reviewed several aspects of financial management from a macro and micro perspective as it relates to the family. It reiterates that the wider cross-section of us have emerged from misconceptions such as that poverty is synonymous with Christianity. Therefore, we have to manage our financial and other material resources so that there is enough remaining to enable us to contribute towards the spreading of the gospel to persons all over the world. For this principle to become effective, it is important that every Christian be aware that financial management is not merely a textbook or academic vocation. In fact the Bible is the best financial manual.

Although some readers may have found some

issues discussed in this chapter a bit 'over their heads' the intention was to challenge our awareness that Christianity is not only shouting 'glory hallelujah', although this is an important attribute. It also entails studying the scriptures, studying finance, taking the scriptures literally and allowing the Holy Spirit to guide us into managing our finances, investing prudently and reaping harvests in abundance, to the glory of the Only Wise God.

It is hoped that you did not have the impression that the fun stops after the wedding day, since the couple will be facing what some sceptics deem the reality of the marriage. What is presented is a candid perspective of some important issues which, when they are managed, will lengthen the joy of courtship where romance transcends and matures in marriage. It is recognized that the mis-management of financial resources is one of the primary sources of millions of divorces. Therefore, we have to rebuke the devourer from controlling our finances and indeed from every aspect of our lives.

A family can and should be budgeting, investing prudently and happily banking huge profits from their business ventures and/or enjoying promotions from their job. We should not be a people who are merely surviving from one pay check to another, or on a meagre wage. We should rather be helping the poor, going on vacation, and attending conventions in various countries, for example. **No Christian family should be living in poverty, when the Lord has promised us abundance even while we are on earth.** However, wealth is not only material since spiritual wealth very often is the answer to many of the world's problems as highlighted by Peter at the gate called Beautiful where instead of offering alms, he prayed and God restored sight to the blind man.

NOTES

****

Chapter 4 **FINANCIAL MANAGEMENTBY THE FAMILY**

INTRODUCTION

Traditionally, men have been the main breadwinners for the home in most societies. Women were primarily involved in activities such as child bearing and rearing, subsistent animal husbandry and farming, and other duties around the home. There are, however, several references to entrepreneurial women in the Bible and today women are also playing a vital role as single parents and also as the sole or main breadwinner and co-financiers of many families. Women also engage in financing the work of the Lord directly. There are also several examples of women in current Christian ministries who make vital contribution to the work of the Lord and to society.

There is no doubt that both sexes have an important role to play in the development of society. Women have also shattered the norms in several societies and have achieved prominence in several vital areas. They are, for example, chief executive officers (CEOs) of major international corporations, senior functionaries in the military of some countries, heads of governments and other prominent political offices and also serve as professionals in traditionally male dominated careers such as engineers, agriculturists, labourers and other careers. Even if a woman homemaker, her role should not be underestimated. Even though many of the contributions made by women may not be quantified in monetary terms, their significance should not be underrated.

Women are often more outstanding than their male colleagues at the office as business executives, at the technical workshop, as astronauts, in the market place, as shop stewards and just about every occupation. Some men who are not as matured to accept this God given truth that women are just as 'brainy' as men, often retaliate by being sexist and may indulge in sexual harassment and even subjugate them to rape and other demeaning acts. Thankfully, the law-enforcement agencies in most countries are waking to the reality that women have to be protected from such unscrupulous practices by chauvinistic men, who obviously are not born-again.

The Christian male will know that a fundamental aspect of the Gospel is that all human beings are equal in the sight of God. A person who fails to accept this reality infers that even though one may be called a Christian, one's mind has not been renewed to this truth. The spiritually matured Christian woman would not walk around with a label saying to men that 'anything you can do, I can do better'. Yet the reality is often that they command higher wages than their male counterparts and are better financial managers, despite the noise made by some men. Amen!

FINANCIAL PREPARATION FOR MARRIAGE

Apart from being spiritually and emotionally prepared to enter marriage, most pre-marital counsellors will emphasize the importance of the couple outlining their principles on the management of money and other

material possessions. This is so because, as was alluded to previously, serious disagreements on financial issues have the potential to undermine even the stronger foundation which a couple may have established in other vital areas of their marriage.

The faith of the Christian couple is expected to be strong enough to trust Jehovah for financial and other blessings which they need. However, Jehovah would not usually perform a miracle for things which He has already placed under our control. He has given us wisdom and the necessary blessings which are required to enable us to attain the best we can in this life. He may nudge us when we go astray, but He expects us to use what is already in our possession to progress in every aspect of our lives. These principles were highlighted in several parables which Jesus presented.

Before a Christian man contemplates entering the noble institution of marriage, he must be in a position, or unquestionably have the potential in the short-run to adequately cater for the financial and other demands of his future family. There are several examples where a wife may finance her husband during his studies at medical school, seminary and other institutions. Some persons marry while attending a training institution such as college, university, a technical institution, or while they are undergoing a period of apprenticeship to learn a trade. Once the area of study is marketable in the society where one is residing or intends to reside, there is hope for one's financial success. In such situations the intended wife may be prepared to support her husband financially where necessary to enable him to complete his training, after which he will be expected to take his rightful place in supporting his family.

If a man cannot adequately cater for his financial needs as a single person, it would be difficult for him to adequately cater for his future family unless he drastically changed his lifestyle to cater for the additional financial responsibility of marriage. There are several arguments pertaining to what are the basic material possessions which a man should have before he seriously contemplates getting married. This to a great extent is determined by factors such as the society in which the couple lives, the material philosophy of the couple and the influence of others over their lives. In an affluent society, it may be necessary that the husband has a well-furnished house or apartment, a car and other amenities which may be considered as a luxury by persons from poorer societies. In the latter example, all that might be required is that the husband has the basic furniture for the home, rented room or apartment. Many couples also begin their marriage by living with their in-laws until they are financially independent enough to go on their own.

It is possible for the couples from rich and poor societies to be just as happy, since their environment usually has a large influence on what is classified as a satisfactory standard of living. It is even possible for the marriage between the poorer couple to be happier than the richer couple since material possession is not a very tangible yardstick to determine the level of success, or the degree of happiness and stability of a marriage. Having stated this, **it must be reiterated that money and financial security is a major contributor to happiness in most marriages**. It is more comfortable to drive to church with one's family rather than having to change three buses to get there, as occurs in some affluent countries, or having to walk or paddle a canoe over a long distance.

Three advantages of the rich over the poor couples include:

(a) A higher standard of health, education and

other facilities for family are more accessible,
(b) They are usually able to bequeath their affluence to their children, relatives and even leave a subsequent inheritance for their dependants,
(c) On an average, the richer families tend to have a fewer number of children than poorer families. This is often because the richer families have more scope to enjoy leisure and other facilities which take the couple away from their homes. Hence, there is often a greater tendency for them to want to avoid the complication and additional expenses of travelling with a large family.

The above analogy does not infer that all is bleak for the poorer family. In many instances there is a very close bond between members of such families which propels the children to achieve prominence in society and other spheres of life. This is often because parents take quality time to instil high morals and spiritual values in their children. The parents of poorer children often admonish them that they should seek to emerge from a state of poverty. They are encouraged to be honest, hard working and dedicated, and that they should strive to their utmost with the guidance of the Lord, to substantially improve their standard of living and that of their relatives.

Very often, even with their limited financial resources, poorer children strive and attain prominence in society. Notable examples of this practice are the life of Abraham Lincoln and Nelson Mandela, who emerged from humble parentage to the office of President of the United States and South Africa, respectively.

One of the first barriers children from poorer parentage often encounter is a feeling of lack of self-confidence since the richer children are often boastful of their affluence. This is not always a glorious picture since there are many poor families where the parents do not care or they are so preoccupied on survival that they neglect their children and the children are left to the mercy of human predators who exploit them sexually and otherwise.

Some men contend that they should not marry until they have attained a given level of material affluence in an attempt to avoid unnecessary conflicts which can emanate because of shortage of finances in the home. Even though there are many positive aspects of such a philosophy, it also has several negative connotations. In the first place, the couple will be missing the unique joy in achievement which couples derive when they plan and work together to acquire material and spiritual targets from the inception of the marital relationship. This sense of achievement often brings the couple closer. In years to come, the couple will be able to reminisce with pride at what they have achieved over the years of working hard and building together. Such reminders are often a good spiritual lesson of the work of the Lord instilling patience and perseverance in their lives. Secondly, many wives have a higher sense of appreciation for what they have achieved as a couple when they plan and execute their plans and achieved their goals, rather than having everything 'ready-made.

The attitude which a person inculcates in the preparation for marriage is primarily dependent on factors such as one's social upbringing, financial strength and relationship with the Lord. Since the Lord gives His children the desires of their hearts, He would usually provide a suitable partner who complements one's financial orientation. If it is misguided, He will send someone along or situations will occur to assist us to get on the right path. This principle is also applicable to Christian women.

There are some women who would not marry a man unless he has acquired her prescribed standard of material possessions. This may include the fact that he must be a highly qualified professional, be an official in a senior position in a well established organization; own a well furnished home, a car and other material amenities along with stipulated spiritual and other qualifications. On the surface one may condemn such a woman as possibly being too materialistic and exacting. However, if the woman in question has matured, say over 35 years old, then she would possibly marry a man in his late 30's to early 40's. At that age an ambitious man, particularly in an affluent society, should have acquired at least the basic material possessions which might be consistent with the stipulated material and other qualifications of the sister whom he is courting. Therefore, he is in a position to satisfy the preconditions which she expects of him. Once the sister is faithful to the Lord, He will provide 'Mr. Right' with those material and other possessions, along with the spiritual and other qualifications.

It is important that a couple contemplating marriage master the principle of being frank and maintaining effective communication in dealing with money and other sensitive issues. The couple will become aware that the freedom with which they utilize their finances during courtship may become somewhat restricted after they are married and as they plan seriously for their children and to acquire material and other items. This will not necessarily cause conflict once they are fully aware of and are in agreement with the sacrifices which they have to make in order to achieve their goals. Problems in this area may arise if a false sense of financial affluence was created by either or both partners during courtship in their attempt to impress each other.

The excitement of courtship would cause most couples to do and say things which they might have genuine intentions of sustaining after marriage. Unfortunately, it is often very easy for one to be carried away with the excitement of the period. After all, this is often a once in a lifetime experience for many Christian couples and one may feel that one is walking on 'cloud nine.' Hence, even though courtship should be very enjoyable, the couple should endeavour not to create false impressions which cannot be realistically sustained after marriage.

Many societies still maintain the tradition of the payment of dowry to the parents of the male or female. The amount of the dowry varies in societies as well as with individual families. Even where such practices do not exist, the engagement, wedding and other ceremonies pertaining to the union of a man and woman in holy matrimony are usually elaborate. The expenses include:

(a) The purchase of special wedding garments and other costumes, ring/s and other items.,

(b) The purchase of food and beverages for the wedding reception and provision to hire caterers, if required,

(c) The hiring of the hall for the reception, car, limousines or other modes of transportation,

(d) The payment of the officiating registrar or pastor (in some instances) who is conducting the wedding ceremony,

(e) The payments associated with the honeymoon such as the hotel, meals, transportation and tours,

Thankfully, very often relatives and friends would often assist in the purchase of many items, or provide the actual item which the couple need. Even so, the couple must be careful not to rely too much on promises from persons who have been habitual promise breakers in the past, or who may stipulate strenuous conditions which must be met by them before they fulfil their promise. There are instances where a couple will have to agree to serve alcoholic beverages and provide secular music for dancing before the gift would be provided. The prospect of receiving an expensive gift from a particular person or family may also be used to entice the couple as to whom they should invite to the wedding. For these and other reasons, much prayer and planning is important to ensure a successful marriage ceremony and honeymoon for the couple.

THE CHRISTIAN WOMAN AND FINANCE

Unlike most other religious teachings, the Bible does not discriminate on the basis of a person's sex, even though distinctive duties are assigned to both sexes based on factors such as their uniqueness, strengths and weaknesses. There are several scripture references which attest to the fact that men and women are equal in the sight of God. We are all wonderfully made, irrespective of our sex. As distasteful as this may sound, particularly to male chauvinists, God did not make women inferior to men. What is important for us to note is that there are distinct differences between the sexes which characterize their unique nature. It is a fact that differences do not generally connote inferiority of one over the other.

Genesis Chapter 1 illustrates that God - the triune being of God the Father, God the Son and God the Holy Spirit created a unique human being (one can assume that there was a male and female nature of the first human) whom He instructed to have **dominion** over every living creature and all the resources of the earth.

However, after Eve was separated from Adam, and they both sinned, as a part of the curse God told them in verse 16 that Adam would **rule** over her. It is noted that the style of leadership which God refers to in the Bible is illustrated in the life of Jesus who was prepared to wash His disciples' feet, to meet them at their level, to eat and sleep with them.

There are several references in the New Testament where the husband is instructed of his role as the **spiritual head of the family**. Even though the Old Testament is dominated with kings and rulers who were primarily men, there are a few outstanding examples of women who occupied prominence. They include the Queen of Sheba and the Prophetess Deborah. There is, however, a remarkable woman who taught her son King Lemuel some very important attributes of what has been popularized as the Virtuous Wife. Her dynamism is expounded in Proverbs 31.

Marriage is a symbiotic relationship where each spouse is assisting the other in areas of weaknesses and strengths instead of a **parasitic relationship** where one or both partners attempt to sap the maximum from the other without giving of their maximum. Hopefully, there is compatibility in the relationship, where as far as possible the strength of one spouse would assist the other to overcome their weaknesses. If both spouses are weak in the majority of areas, then they will have to rely more on the Holy Spirit to teach them to overcome these weaknesses. In some instances they may also have to seek external assistance and counselling from spiritual leaders such as the Pastor.

In a healthy marriage, both spouses should become better persons spiritually, intellectually, financially and every other area of their lives should be blessed. This is so because of the love and support of each other and also because of the special blessings which are embodied in marriage.

The second aspect of the important role of the wife as helper is to **support her husband** so that he fulfils God's calling on his life, performs creditably as a husband and father, be outstanding on his job and make a tangible contribution to society. These attributes can be illustrated by reviewing the characteristics of the 'virtuous wife' as illustrated in Proverbs 31:10-31. Though it is a long passage, its importance certainly warrants quoting the whole section. **It should be noted, however, that it is difficult to imagine one woman being able to consistently display all of these traits. Nevertheless, they are ideals which every woman should ardently seek to emulate as many as is possible**:

10: **"A capable wife who can find? She is far more precious than jewels.**
11: **The heart of her husband trusts in her, and will have no lack of gain.**
12: **She does him good, and not harm, all the days of her life.**
13: **She seeks wool and flax, and works with willing hands.**
14: **She is like the ship of the merchant; she brings her food from far away.**
15: **She rises while it is still night and provide food for her household and sets tasks for her servant girls.**
16: **She considers a field and buys it; with the fruits of her hands she plants a vineyard.**
17: **She girds herself with strength, and makes her arms strong.**
18: **She perceives that her merchandise is profitable; her lamp does not go out at night.**

19: **She puts her hands to the distaff and her hands hold the spindle.**
20: **She opens her hands to the poor, and reaches out her hands to the needy.**
21: **She is not afraid for her household when it snows, for her household is clothed with crimson.**
22: **She makes herself coverings: her clothing is fine linen and purple.**
23: **Her husband is known in the city gates, taking his seat among the elders of the land.**
24: **She makes linen garments and sells them; she supplies the merchants with sashes.**
25: **Strength and dignity are her clothing, and she laughs in time to come.**
26: **She opens her mouth with wisdom, and the teaching of kindness is on her tongue.**
27: **She looks well to the ways of her household, and does not eat the bread of idleness.**
28: **Her children rise up and call her happy; her husband too, and he praises her.**
29: **"Many women have done excellently, but you surpass them all."**
30: **Charm is deceitful and beauty is vain, but a woman who fears the Lord is to be praised.**
31: **Give her a share in the fruit of her hands and let her works praise her in the city."**

This is the making of a sermon; however, only a summary of some of the more important issues in the above passage will be presented. The word virtuous connotes a person who is chaste in her morals and one who exudes an aura which commands respect and demands that one be held in high esteem. Such a person displays a sense of direction and is strong in character. This quality should not be misinterpreted as being proud and haughty. Ruth, for example, (as illustrated in the Book of Ruth) comes readily to mind when referring to women who possessed several notable attributes of the virtuous wife in the Bible. These traits are not visible if one exhibits the deceptive trait of being an 'angel in the day and devil at night', that is, a very superficial or deceptive person.

Verse 10 implies **that not every woman or wife automatically fits this description**, even though most women can attain at least the major attributes if they are so motivated and the circumstances under which they live promote such attributes. Some critics present the argument that such a woman has to be 'bionic' and that it is not a realistic image which women should try to emulate. Even though today it may be difficult or not as important to replicate several of the attributes of the 'virtuous wife', it is very important that cognizance is taken of the principle behind her attitudes and actions. This verse implies that it is difficult to find a wife who categorically fits the above description. However, every Christian woman who is fully yielded to the leadership of the Holy Spirit has the capacity to attain such a noble state.

Verses 10-12 states that such a woman is presented as being **far more precious than jewels since her qualities are indeed rare**. Therefore, when they are demonstrated, they should be nurtured and guarded with utmost care and attention. Such a woman induces the trust of her husband in her as a person and also in her ability to be productive; not indulging in idle chatting or gossiping, but someone who spends her time gainfully employed to promote the spiritual, financial, intellectual and other positive attributes of her family. It is not difficult for us to find examples of husbands who have confidence in the judgment of their wives since their wives are 'level headed' and would not usually make irrational decisions. An industrious woman will cause her husband and children to be continuously benefiting from her prudent disposition in managing finances, in promoting their spiritual growth and in other areas.

The husband of a virtuous woman should not have the cause to harbour the thought that she is lavishly spending the money earned or allocated for other financial needs in the family budget in pursuit of selfish personal desires. The latter issue often means that the couple has to be committed to an effective system of planning, budgeting and control with both of them in agreement with the system and its implications. Trust also extends to the sensitive area of confidentiality in knowing that important issues which are discussed in confidence are not divulged to others.

The virtuous wife is **a model to her home and to society** in that she does good, promotes justice, is hospitable and genuinely displays all, or at least an overwhelming majority of the other positive traits of a god-fearing wife. The basic principle which is being propagated is that her actions, words and thoughts, are to bring blessings, and to strengthen and to support her husband, children and others, every day of her life.

The issue of '**doing her husband good**' can be extended to the area of encouraging him to exercise, eat a balanced diet, spend more time with the family and with God and other positive things, even if he does not like doing many of them. If she demonstrates this good quality by leading by example, it is usually far more effective than merely talking since he would be challenged by the positive effects of what she is advocating in her life. When the husband sees the benefits, particularly when he recognizes that such seemingly harsh principles are coming from a heart of love, it is often easier for him to appreciate the situation and to comply accordingly. The concept of doing good, does not always imply presenting him with 'breakfast in bed'. It often entails sacrificing short-term benefits for more enduring, long term gains.

The issue of the wife 'doing the husband good' is particularly important when things are not going well in the family, for whatever reason. It is usually very easy to reciprocate love and affection when the going is smooth. However, this attribute becomes even more important when the going is rough. This is when the real gem sparkles as the true character of her virtues is displayed. Practical areas where this sensitive value is demonstrated include:

(a) Encouraging him to eat a sensible diet and possibly be his partner in jogging and keeping his weight down,

(b) Assisting him to study and prepare himself to be successful at his secular job and also to be effective in ministry,

(c) Being a loving wife with a calm and gentle spirit but one who Is firm enough to tell her husband about his shortcomings without necessarily hurting his ego, and being able to offer wise counsel on how he may be able to overcome them,

(d) Being there for him, for example, when he needs a friend to talk with, a shoulder to cry on and a tower of strength when he is weak,

(e) Supporting him in areas such as disciplining the children when it is warranted, and not leave all of the difficult decisions for him to make, unless of course, his input is absolutely essential,

(f) Even if she has to criticize or rebuke him, it should be done, as far as possible, in private and in love,

(The question which may be asked is, "What do issues such as the above have to do with finance?" This issue can be addressed by reviewing the lives of the millions of couples who have lived well below the standards for happiness which Jehovah decrees for a marriage, couples who have divorced and the lives of children from such unions. Some of the financial implications include disorganized spending, leading to little or no saving; one or several members of the family have to secure medical and psychological and other forms of treatment due to depression, physical and mental abuse and other traumas; and the financial implications of a divorce. Several of these issues are reviewed in Chapter 5).

Verses13-19 describes the **industrious** nature which a wife is expected to display in her daily activities. Implicit in this section is the fact that she should be prudent in business transactions and thrifty in areas such as spending. This process becomes more effective as her husband gives her scope to develop in this area. Very often the wife is better able to budget for the family and she may be a more prudent controller of the financial resources of the family. Therefore, wives should be encouraged to develop the art of making wise choices in the family budget and also in investment decisions.

The virtuous wife is portrayed as an **entrepreneur** who is competent to make wise investment decisions. At the same time she does not neglect the affairs of her household. It is becoming increasingly common for wives who hold secular jobs or are self-employed, to earn a higher salary than their husbands. Even if the wife is unemployed, she may be performing the pivotal role of managing the affairs of the family in such a way that the monthly expenditure does not exceed the budget, thus, there is enough money for saving and investment. There is no room for a Christian wife to be treated as a 'second class citizen' in a marriage even if she is not holding a secular job. Very often her function of managing the affairs of the family from home could save the family more than if she held a secular job. This fact also extends to vital areas such as inculcating correct spiritual, moral and other favourable values in the children. Maids are usually unable to perform this important function in a manner which is satisfactory to parents. For these and other important reasons we should not look down upon a woman who stays at home to care for the family. Her functions are priceless.

Men who have working wives know of the difficulties of trying to maintain the stability of the family when both parents are concentrating on their careers. There is usually the hassle of who cooks (if they do not have a maid who does this) when both spouses come home from work and are tired. It is likely that there will be more tension in such a marriage since the process of unwinding from a strenuous day at work could be traumatic. However, this has to be balanced with the additional tension which might be present if the husband alone is unable to adequately cater for the financial needs of the family. On the other hand, there is the career-oriented woman who would be frustrated if she was compelled to stay at home as a housewife.

When parents are unable to adequately supervise their children, it often results in delinquency, particularly in affluent societies where the extended family concept may be very remote. Some mothers choose to leave their secular career and spend as much as the first five years of the life of their children at home in an attempt to ensure that at least the correct foundation is laid in their lives. For reasons such as these, the role of a wife who stays at home with the children should not be underestimated. Even if she holds a secular job, her role in caring for her family should not be seen (as is common in most societies) as her 'natural' function, so that the husband should not share equal responsibility in caring for the children.

Verse 20 presents some examples when the important quality of **hospitality** can be shown. This trait is often specially attributed to the wife, since she usually has the knack and time for organizing charity events and is often instrumental in identifying needs in neighbours, for example. Very often men are either too greedy or too busy to notice the needs of others. Hence, like Abigail, the wife of Nabal who was nearly killed by King David's army because of his greed (1 Samuel Chapter 25), God often gives the special tender heart to women so that His mercy is still extended to the family. This does not imply superiority of the feminine gender in this area, for the carnal woman can also display negative traits, such as being very greedy and mean.

Verse 23 relates the very important attribute which will be demonstrated by the virtuous wife in that she releases her husband to achieve recognition as a respected person in society. In this way, she releases her husband to be respected since the affairs of the home are well taken care of by her. She is respected among women. As a result, it is easy for her husband to be credited with having a well-managed family.

It is easier for society to respect a man whose wife is viewed as a faithful partner and whose children are well mannered and disciplined, than where there is much dispute in his family, delinquency among children and other undesirable behaviour. As a matter of fact, a man will be debarred from holding senior positions in the Church if his family is not well managed. The other side of this scenario is that a woman who is highly respected in society because of her professional achievements, her prominence in the church and/or her hospitable example, does much credit to her husband, children and her community. Her achievements should encourage her husband to fulfil his calling also. Nevertheless a, slothful husband may view such women as a threat to his 'masculinity.' Some men would even be vindictive and attempt to suppress her activities. If such a husband spends his time idly, he will be ridiculed by ambitious and progressive members of society.

Verses 25 to 27 reinforce the authority of the virtuous wife. She is not a person to indulge in idle gossip, but is someone who speaks with authority, knowing that her achievements are a testimony of the noble principles she upholds. However, her greatest virtue in this area is that she is not boastful or arrogant, but rather teaches with kindness and encouragement.

Verses 28-31 begin by highlighting the fact that the discipline which she has overflows onto every member of her family. They recognize her untiring work and praise her for it. The beauty of her disposition radiates among the family and there is a quest among each member for excellence. A well-balanced personality in such a vital area can only be genuinely displayed in a woman who knows the Lord and truly follows His direction.

One of the most important admonitions which a Christian wife has to respect is that of the **spiritual headship of a Christian husband**. While the husband is instructed to love his wife, she is instructed to submit to him since, as we discussed earlier, he is the head of the home. The issue of submitting and headship took a serious bashing with the advent of the era of Women's Liberation where women are advocated as being equal to men. It is noted that on the spiritual level, God does not differentiate between a man and a woman. Galatians 3:28 states: "²⁸**There is no longer Jews or Greek, there is no longer slave or free, there is no longer male and female; for all of you are one in Christ Jesus**."

Jehovah is the God of order, as we can see in the offices of the church. The apostle, for example, only has spiritual authority over the pastor of the church which he has founded, who is submitted under his ministry. Similarly, a pastor only has spiritual authority over the congregation which he shepherds. In the same way a wife should only be submitted to her own husband as Ephesians 5:22. Verses 23-24 states: "²³**For the husband is the head of the wife just as Christ is the head of the church, the body of which he is the Savoir. ²⁴Just as the church is subject to Christ, so also wives ought to be, <u>in everything</u>, to their husbands**." (underline, mine)

A popular (and I would add, frivolous) argument is usually centred on which of the sexes is better at managing finances at home, in the corporate world and also for the church. Supporters of the superiority of men in managing finances and other assets often state that men have the following advantages over women in this area. Men are often afforded a better opportunity to pursue studies in academic and professional disciplines such as accounting, auditing and financial analysis. Therefore, they are often able to bring these experiences to bear even in the management of their personal finances. Even though this is true in many societies, this trend is rapidly changing since it has been discovered that there are no distinct advantages of men over women in this and other disciplines. As a matter of fact, the management of many organizations contends that there is a distinct preference for female financial managers since it is often discovered that they tend to be more meticulous in highlighting details, as is expected from financial managers.

There is often the sexist approach which contends that women in general tend to be more temperamental and often make serious mistakes when dealing with stressful circumstances at home and menstruation and menopause. It is true that due to hormonal and other changes in the body chemistry of women during the various stages of their menstrual cycle, the period of childbearing and other phases would have a profound effect on their mood and how they interact with others. The Bible takes cognizance of the peculiarities of each sex. For this reason, several principles which are established on the way a husband should treat his wife can also be extended to the working environment and the wider society. 1 Peter 3:7 states: "**7Husbands, in the same way, show consideration for your wives in your life together, paying honour to the women as the weaker sex, since they too are also gracious gifts of life - so that nothing may hinder your prayer.**"

The issue of woman being the weaker sex (or vessel, as stated in other translations) has sparked much controversy. Several views have been expressed in an attempt to explain this phrase. They include:

(a) Due to the peculiar effect of the hormones in the body of the female, women are likely to be more temperamental than men,

(b) It is factual that on an average, women experience sporadic changes in their body chemistry and behavioural patterns than is common in men. In addition, the average woman is physically weaker than a man who is exposed to the same type of manual labour or sporting event. However, one wonder how many men would have been comfortable or able to carry a baby for nine months the way a woman does. In addition, some men behave far worse than their wives do when they are affected by sickness such as a common cold.

(d) Women are generally more 'soft natured' than men, that is, they are more gentle and kind and it may be easier for a man to dominate a woman than vice versa. This of course, is subject to extensive debates, for many women in all walks of life command the respect of men. This is seen in the life of female executives, female pastors and other professional women.

(e) Women are more likely to be lured into 'sex-sins' than men,

(f) Women are physically and emotionally weaker than men. The issue of men's perceived superior emotional stability is highly questionable since in many countries there is statistical evidence to support the fact that men have a higher rate of suicide and greater incidents of mental illness than women.

It should be noted that women are not presented as the weaker sex, rather, it is stated that they should be treated that way. This implies that a husband has to be extremely patient with his wife since she is often subject to physiological, emotional and other pressures to which he is not subject, or at least usually not to the same degree or severity. It is therefore important that men are consistently considerate, understanding, forgiving, patient, and demonstrate other forms of affections to their wives.

On the issue of sexual sins, men are usually (and this is rapidly changing in many societies) more aggressive in luring women to sexual and other forms of sin. However, the subtleties of the woman who is bent on attracting a man could be just as effective. This could be in the way she dresses, her body language, openly disclosing her intention and the other things which she may do, say and utilize to communicate her desires. Prostitutes and women who are desperate for a partner or committed to seducing a man display these features.

Regardless of the situation, men are instructed not to deal harshly with their wives but to be gentle with them. Disobedience to this decree is sin, thus, the Lord will not answer the husband's prayers unless the issue is resolved amicably particularly if her discord is based on sound scriptural principles. Unfair as it may seem on some occasions, even when a wife rages in a sudden fit of anger or quarrels over what may seem a trivial matter, one has to remember this scripture. However, even though Spirit-filled, the woman has to learn to overcome what may be considered as minor weaknesses which she should easily overcome. Assistance can also be found through methods such as studying and practicing the teaching of the Scriptures, prayer, fasting and counselling. Even if she does not overcome these weaknesses, her husband has to love her anyway.

WOMEN BREAKING THE GLASS CEILING IN THE CORPORATE WORLD

Increasingly, women are moving up the corporate ladder and occupying very senior positions in large corporate organizations. This phenomenon has caused many organizations to reorganize their policies of the hiring, training, promotion and working conditions of women. Many agencies still classify women as if they were a minority segment of society especially as marginalized ethnic groups and the disabled. Conversely, many organizations are faced with the challenge of having to reduce their entry requirements and basis of promotion for men to enable them to have a more equitable distribution of men on their work force. There are laws in many countries which attempt to prevent discrimination against women. However, many women find it too expensive to even attempt to bring a law suit against a major corporation and other agencies which have discriminated against them. As a result, hundreds of blatant sexual harassment and discrimination practices against women in the workforce and at other forums go undisclosed even in societies which prize themselves as being very liberal.

It is common to see women going to and from work dressed in suit and scarf, and other attire which is representative of their place of employment and culture. Thankfully, many church organizations have progressed beyond the dogma of prohibiting or looking down on a woman who is attired in pants and other garments which are befitting their working, sporting or other activities in which they are engaging. Objection in this area is usually if she reveals parts of her anatomy which should be concluded.

Many mothers are confronted with the difficult decision of whether to stay at home or work outside of the home when their children are very young. The major consideration is usually that of the poor financial status of the family. This is usually an unfortunate situation, for a large percentage of women would prefer to spend at least the first five years of the life of the child at home where more care and attention can be provided. Of course, there are women who are career oriented and even though they have a great sense of attachment to the child, would prefer to be back at work shortly after the delivery.

Some of the difficulties associated with being a working mother include:

(a) Apart from having to work on a full-time basis, many women have the additional responsibility of performing the major role of caring for their family at home. This often includes cooking, washing, purchasing and transporting the groceries home, and cleaning the home, ironing and caring for the children. The result of this is that she is in effect managing two full-time jobs along with responsibilities at church and other organizations. This could result in mental, physical and psychological collapse.

(b) Many women who have small children have to undergo the emotional pressure of feeling that they are neglecting their children by leaving them at a baby sitter, kindergarten, play school or other institutions instead of being at home with them. This pressure often comes from:

(i) The church sometimes contributes to this also by scheduling meetings during a period of the day when the working mom is at work,

    (ii)   Other women who may be better off financially and are able to be at home with their children until they are able to cope by themselves,

    (iii) There is the pressure from male colleagues who, particularly if they see her as a threat, would express the opinion that a woman should be at home with her children,

(c) The simple truth is that many women would indeed prefer to stay at home with their children. However, the financial situation of the home often forces them to work in an environment which they do not enjoy. Even if they do enjoy their career, there is also the feeling of guilt for being 'selfish' in enjoying their career, when the little ones at home or with a caregiver need them just as much.

Many women would confess to feeling hurt which they experience on a daily basis when they have to leave a crying or sick child in the care of someone else who could never be as loving and caring as themselves. There is also the pain of the child crying and begging not to be left at home. Many women have to undergo a period of counselling to assist them through this most traumatic period. In addition, the assistance of other members of the family in taking and collecting the child/children to and from the kindergarten or school, drastically reduces the pressure on the working mom.

(d) Women often have to work almost doubly as hard as their male counterparts to gain a promotion and recognition as being as competent as their male counterparts. Even though this practice is changing in many societies, it is slow to occur in others.

It should be noted that in some parts of the world women are discriminated against in order to allow men to enter educational institutions and to secure certain types of jobs. The reason which is given for this unfortunate practice is usually that the poor performance of boys and men academically and otherwise has resulted in them not being able to secure high paying jobs and in many instances employment. The result may be that his wife may be earning more than he is, or he may have to stay at home while she is the sole breadwinner. These occurrences often lead to an abusive relationship, since such a man may feel that his authority as a man and husband is not being reinforced by his financial contribution to the family.

There are also high instances of professional women who find it very difficult to find a suitable partner or they may marry a man who is not as academically or professionally qualified as they are. Men who find it difficult to relate to such women at home or on the job often resort to abusing such women. There is thus a need for law enforcement agents and other civic and religious groups to ensure that such practices are, as far as possible, prevented. Where they are perpetuated, stern punishment should be meted out and adequate rehabilitated facilities be made available. It is so sad when persons cannot recognize the true value of another human being because of their gender, race and religion. This distinction is made since even though God loves the homosexuals, lesbians, adulterer and other persons who indulge in other non-scriptural practices, He hates all sinful practices.

There are several important factors which are important when one aspires to achieve excellence in one's career. As Christians it is important that we seek excellence in all of our undertaking. Daniel 6:3 depicts this attitude: "³***Soon Daniel distinguished himself above all the other presidents and satraps because an excellent spirit was in him.***"

What was evident in the life of Daniel was that apart from his ardent pursuit in studying and applying wisdom in his endeavours, he also spent much time in praying thrice daily. Therefore, the Spirit of the Lord dwelt in him and he excelled in executing his duties as a ruler. This same Spirit dwells in the life of each Christian, thus, we have the ability to excel in all of our undertakings. The measure to which the Spirit will be manifested in our lives depends on how much of our lives we are willing to allow Him to direct. The Holy Spirit is so gentle that He will not force Himself on us but will only be manifested to the extent that we allow Him to. One of the major hindrances to His movement is if we are operating in an environment or area which is inconsistent to His will.

Some of ways in which a person can ensure progress in his chosen career path are:

(a) It is important that a person pursues a career path that is consistent to his calling as a Christian, particularly if this is a choice for a long-term career. Some of the indications of this path include the area of study/practice for which he has a 'natural' aptitude. Additional confirmation can be secured as he seeks the Lord for guidance in this direction. Church Council, the prayer group, the pastor and godly council can be sought to provide further direction in this area.

(b) One of the key secrets for success in pursuit of a career as well as in every area of life is a genuine love for what he is doing. If a person is genuinely enjoying his vocation then he will seek innovative ways of doing it better and this attribute will be reflected in the way he interacts with colleagues and other persons. If he is in a job where the primary outlook is to receive the pay check at the end of the month, there will be much discontent exhibited in the way he conducts the activities and also his relationship with others.

> A famous maxim states: "If you find a job which you enjoy doing, then you would not have to work a day of your life, and you will be paid for doing it."

(c) Being thankful for the opportunity which has been afforded to enable you to earn an acceptable remuneration and at the same time receiving fulfilment in the job is also important. If you are appreciative of what you are doing and it is reflected in what you say, do and your general attitude to the job, it will be reflected in your output and relationship with others. If the employee is unable to do so, then there might be a need to seek another form of employment.

(d) There is a famous maxim which states that **one's attitude determines one's altitude**. There is much validity in this statement since in many organizations a person who is less academically qualified may be promoted more rapidly than a co-worker who is more academically qualified, primarily because of the former employee's level of output, efficiency, mannerism and other positive attributes. Other important issues in this respect include:

(i) Being punctual,
(ii) Speaking clearly and being articulate.
(iii) Working beyond the 'normal call of duties,'

(iv) Being a dedicated and excellent performance,
(v) Seeking to progress in his area of work by learning others tasks in his area of work,
(vi) Assisting others in their work when possible or necessary,
(vii) Being adequately prepared academically, technically and/or having whatever aptitude it takes to enable him to attain the highest level of competence in his career path,
(viii) Time management, as alluded to in Chapter 1, is a very important factor. Some persons spend much time and effort trying to develop a system to distribute their time in the various aspects of their tasks in an efficient way. Very often employees can become distracted from completing assignments because they are consistently distracted by other activities in the office.
(ix) Carrying himself as professionals, including dressing appropriately for the job, desisting from encouraging sexist comments and actions,
(x) As far as possible, he should seek to consistently perform his duties at a higher standard than his colleagues, within the limits of not 'burning oneself out' and jeopardizing his health, family life and spirituality.
(xi) He should actively seek avenues of promotion. This does not infer that he would deliberately seek to belittle and undermine colleagues merely to attract the attention of senior management. However, there is no harm in expounding on his qualities in staff review and other forums to identify how much contribution he has made to the organization.

(xii) Being a very prayerful Christian and who is consistently a good witness in showing love and kindness to others and also in breaking the powers of darkness which attempt to block his career advancement,

(xiii) The prayers and support of his spouse, children, and fellow believers are also important,

(xiv) There should be an equitable balance between the number of employees conducting a particular task and their level of efficiency, hence, reducing the amount of time an employee has to spend conducting job-related activities particularly after the official working hours. There will be occasions when he has to work 'beyond the normal call of duties,' take work home and engage in other job-related activities. It is important that his family can appreciate the impact of such pressures, and seek to assist where possible.

(xv) Efforts must be made to secure on- and off-the-job training programs to advance his career path. Even if the place of employment does not afford such opportunities, he should take the initiative to upgrade his skills and aptitude in areas which are career related.

(e) He should seek areas of promotion, even if it may mean moving out of his current department or even location, where possible, once it is as the Lord directs. There are occasions where a person may have to decide to change jobs or even career path in order to earn a higher wage and also to progress in one's career. The implications of such a change often mean that the family may have to be relocated to another part of the country and even to a new country, in some instances. The support of the family is very important in such circumstances.

The consistent observation of these positive suggestions will contribute to his level of advancement up the corporate ladder.

Apart from a few highly specialized areas, there are usually very few professions and career paths which a woman cannot pursue and be at the helm. Women are just as competent as men are to manage senior positions in most organizations. Hence, the onus is on women to vigorously pursue legitimate careers and succeed in their pursuit of their chosen career paths.

THE CHRISTIAN MAN AND FINANCE

In most societies the husband is the only or, at least, the main breadwinner for the family. However, this trend is rapidly changing as wives are increasingly becoming co-partners in meeting the financial needs of the family. Notwithstanding this, as far as possible, men are still expected to be the primary provider for the material needs of the family and for managing resources.

It was alluded to earlier that the instruction that man will sweat to earn 'bread' to maintain his family is not restricted to manual labour. The executive in his air conditioned office is in fact 'sweating' when one has deadlines to meet, and one may have to take work home from the office and work until the wee hours of the morning to complete such schedules.

There are several basic qualifications which a prospective husband must satisfy before many pastors consent to preside over the wedding. They include:

(a) He is spiritually mature in that he is competent to be head of his home and execute the other functions of a husband as decreed in the Word of God,

(b) He is physically mature in that he can manage well beyond the basis responsibilities of marriage. These include the provision of the basic material amenities such as comfortable accommodation and an adequate standard of living for his family.

In some instances, men who are blatantly lazy will refuse to work even though there are lucrative employment opportunities available to them. This feature is evident in several Third World countries which depend on tourism or where there is high level of migration to developed countries. In such societies young men would congregate in areas which are frequented by foreign women with the intention of aligning themselves with a partner who may be willing to assist them to migrate. This is usually done in exchange for sexual and other favours. Christians are not expected to be 'bumsters' even though there are many instances where missionaries and other foreigners have assisted Christians from other countries to migrate or settle in their country.

There are instances where Christians legitimately cannot readily find suitable employment. While they are awaiting a reply from applications, many such persons would offer their services to voluntary organizations, their local church or other ministries where they can be gainfully occupied even though they may not even be receiving an allowance. In such instances, over a period of time, the Lord usually provides the job openings which will enable them to achieve their career objectives. If, as the saying goes, 'the devil finds work for idle hands,' is true, how much more will the Lord reward persons who use their talent, treasury and time gainfully for Him?

It is not automatic that every Christian man will immediately attain his ideal career objective of which he is convinced that the Lord has called him. Very often, the process of getting to God's best entails that one has to undergo a period of intensive preparation. Many persons, before they attain a position at the top, have to spend a painstaking number of years climbing the ladder of success. Isaiah 43:2 is particularly relevant to persons who are prone to pursue the 'quick-fix' method of getting things done. It states: "²**When you pass through the waters, I will be with you, and through the rivers, they will not overwhelm you. When you pass through the fire, you will not be burnt or scorched, nor will the flames kindle upon you**."

There is much depth in this verse which can be extensively elaborated on. However, in essence it refers to the period of preparation which **all** of God's people must undergo in order to attain the standard where God can use us as He desires. Some of us may be fortunate in that our period of preparation may not be as extensive and arduous as others because the correct attitude was adopted from the onset or during the early period of the process. Reference can be made to outstanding Biblical characters such as King David, Moses, Daniel, and the Apostle Paul, all of whom underwent intensive periods of preparation for the greatness which God had in store for them. In the same way as their success is of tremendous blessing to us, even so the success of our lives will also be a blessing to others as we make our lives available to Him. This usually entails a process of searching, revealing, breaking, melting, moulding, and filling as the writer of popular song 'Spirit of the Living God' prayerfully requested.

We should not expect that success will come on a platter; instead, we must be prepared to **work smart** in order to achieve success. The word "smart" was used since a person may be working hard and does not achieve the level of success as another who sought to master the most effective and efficient way of achieving a given target. The gap between the two spheres of working hard rather than working smart can be illustrated in an example of **a man working hard cutting a tree with a dull axe, versus another working smart by using a sharpened axe, or, even better, an electrical chain saw**.

Many persons have progressed from the position of office assistants to top executive positions in several organizations. Very often when a person has passed through the ranks, as it were, he is better equipped to manage a senior level since he is *au fait* with what happens at each level of the organization. On the contrary a person who has recently graduated from college, university or another technical or vocational training institution, and who has been given an executive position, very often is at a disadvantage in some areas to the person who has passed through the ranks. For this reason, recent graduates are usually employed as management trainees and often have to rely on less academically qualified persons to teach them the intricacies of the job which they will have to perform. This is not usually intended to demoralize the graduate since they have qualities which the unqualified employees would not be able to emulate.

The technical knowledge often affords the young graduate the discipline and analytical ability which the non-graduate may not have. In addition, the presentation of reports and other technical details and the repertoire of research material to which they may have been exposed and areas to which they may have been able to make reference and other attributes often places the graduate at an advantage in the technical aspects of the job. Since both categories of employees have their place of importance, management has to ensure that their job description, lines of authority, salary, chain of command and other structures are well organized so as not to cause frustration and other forms of dissatisfaction for both categories of employees.

A person who has been granted the privilege of entering an organization at the executive level often has to interact with colleagues who were in the organization for a number of years and who feel that the position should rightfully be theirs. The Christian employee in such as position would have to execute his duties with humility and allow the wisdom of the Holy Spirit to direct his path. It is important that in such circumstances that one adopts principles such as:

(a) Being committed to consistently be ahead of colleagues and effectively applying the mechanism or systems involved in executing the duties to which one has been assigned with excellence,

(b) Duties are completed well in advance of deadlines in the most efficient and effective manner,

(c) One's duties are conducted with a sense of genuine humility,

(d) As far as possible, one should endeavour to maintain a good rapport with every level of the work force, projecting the genuine image of being warm, friendly and social, yet being shrewd in the execution of one's duties,

(e) Being a witness of the Gospel verbally and more importantly by the manner in which one executes professional and other duties,

It is important for each Christian to have a well-defined career objective early in their lives. This necessity is often more demanding for the Christian male since unlike his female counterpart, he is obligated to be able to support his family. The female may be fortunate to be married to a rich husband and the couple may agree that she should not pursue a secular career. Many women do not like this option and feel that even if their husband is wealthy, then as an expression of her 'self-worth' she should still pursue her career.

Even if a man marries a woman who is materially wealthier than he is, it is usually rare to find such a man refraining from working for an extended period of time. Unless he genuinely cannot find a suitable job, this would be contravening one of the basic principles of Christianity and that of most societies. Even if he chooses not to maintain a secular job, at least he would endeavour to be involved in some business activity which would generate income for the family. He may, for example, choose to invest in the stock exchange or in some other activity which he can manage from home. There are instances in the more affluent countries, where the husband manages the assets of the wife /who owns an established company, an estate or some other huge income-generating activity. This may entail that he sits on the board of directors of the company and conduct other business activities for her. A husband may be the manager of his wife who is an actor, singer or sports personality. These activities should not preclude him from also actively pursuing the areas of the ministry to which he is called.

The ego of the average man seems to be more fragile than that of women. As a matter of fact, the word ego is more often associated with the emotional instability of men. If the ego is described as the innate nature in a man which causes him to feel inadequate if he does not achieve the tasks in his own strength, then it is not an acceptable emotion for Christians to inculcate. The positive aspect of the ego is that, it is often the nature of a man to ensure that he is gainfully employed in order to adequately cater for the financial and other material needs of his family which are within his domain as husband and father.

There are several consequences which may result if a man is unable to adequately cater for his family due to negligence on his part, sickness or other situations. The effect will primarily be dependent on the particular situation in which he finds himself and the society where he lives. They include:

(a) His wife may become very frustrated and may not be receptive even to counselling. On the extreme, she may divorce him. In many countries the consequence of such an action would be that the court may grant any major assets such as a car, house, furniture and bank account which they acquired during their marriage, to her, particularly if they have small children.

(b) Unless he is seriously incapacitated or genuinely unable to secure suitable work, he will be nagged from several angles, including his pastor and the Holy Spirit to seek gainful employment,

(c) If his wife is not a consecrated Christian, she may resort to securing financial and other forms of assistance from other men who may not be related to her. The devil often creates situations which may expose her to a man (or woman, since there are increasing incidents of lesbian activities) who is more than willing to satisfy this inadequacy of her husband. The 'uncovered' wife may eventually fall into the ploy of such an unscrupulous man who may initially create the impression that he is merely rendering assistance on the basis that he is a humanitarian and is merely expressing brotherly love (Phileo).

The subtleties of the devil's advocate may eventually be revealed when the demands become more emotional and sexual, which often results in an adulterous relationship. This is a recipe for disaster, for if this incident is revealed to her husband, the common reaction, particularly for unsaved men, is to divorce her or at the extreme he may kill her and possibly commit suicide. Even though the wife is to be blamed for allowing herself to be enticed by the attraction of the monetary gains, the husband is possibly more at fault for deliberately exposing his family to prolonged serious financial lack.

(d) She may defy the decree of her husband who may have insisted that she should not pursue a secular job. The converse principle has been demonstrated in the marriage of some Christians where the husband feels that the Lord has called him into full-time ministry. In some instances, the wife may be supportive at first, however, as the financial demands increase, unless he has enough faith to undergo serious financial pressures, he may decide to seek at least part-time employment until he is able to adequately finance his family from the ministry.

Even in desperate circumstances of recession, war, drought, flooding and other disasters, the Christian family must endeavour to adequately provide for themselves. A member of the family or the entire family may be able to establish a cottage industry and make items which can be sold in the neighbourhood, or they can expand a farming project or engage in petty trading, for example. Additional income may be secured from the sale of vegetables and fruits grown by the family or purchased from wholesalers. Income may be derived from the sale of animal products such as milk, for example. When items are sold, the seller must have accurate information such as the cost of the item and its shelf life and be able to arrive at a selling price which enables a lucrative profit to be made.

BUDGETING AND THE CHRISTIAN FAMILY

It is important to set goals which are realistic, attainable and measurable which are consistent with the will of the Lord for our lives. We must be willing to pursue them fervently, prayerfully and with commitment, even as the Lord enables us to achieve them.

Most of the above issues in this chapter focused on financial management from a macro perspective as they affect the Christian family. The first part of this section discusses various aspects of financial management that the family has to consider when preparing their budget. A vital part of a couple becoming one-flesh is that they must **plan and execute their plans in unison**. Even if a Christian husband is the sole breadwinner of the family, he is not expected to practice the outmoded dogma that he has the right to plan the family budget.

It is important that in instances where both parents are working, that the **correct disclosure** is made of each spouse's income, so that the budget is based on honesty. When a couple has not mastered the spiritual principle of cleaving (where the couple are united in body, soul and spirit; where they plan together and execute their plans in unison), the budget is one area where there will be much deception. In some instances one partner may believe that the other is a lavish spender, or may not be as prudent as is expected when it comes to saving. **Wives are particularly noted for hiding money in secret places** which they may use in the event of an emergency. The effect of this principle may be positive or negative, depending on several mitigating circumstances. Some advantages of one spouse saving in secret include:

(a) It often comes in handy in an emergency, when all other avenues of meeting the financial demands of a situation may have failed,

(b) It may force the other partner to rethink their attitude towards saving and encourage thriftiness,

There are also many disadvantages which are associated with saving in secret, including:

(a) It may harbour suspicion from one's partner that the secret saver is possibly having an extramarital relationship from which financial support is being received,

(b) The partner who is not saving may feel inadequate that they are not as prudent as the saver. This attitude could challenge the non-saver to improve in this area, or it could fuel further disillusion in a spouse who finds it difficult to be disciplined in this area,

(c) Both partners may become very cagey about their finances in an attempt to 'out-save' the other,

(d) The saver may become frustrated by the undisciplined nature of the other in this area and resort to lavish spending,

The system of undisclosed savings between spouses does not promote cleaving in their marriage since one or both partners may not be committed to working as a team. However, there are instances where one partner is really not as conscientious as the other in managing finance, despite genuine efforts made by the other to promote this discipline. Christians are not expected to be inconsiderate. However, unless a spouse is matured in spirit, soul and body, they are likely to show weakness in these and other vital areas of the marriage. With encouragement, prayer and loving guidance from each other, the church council and even professional help where necessary, each partner will achieve the correct discipline in financial management.

Another area that tests how much cleaving exists in a marriage is how the couple manages their savings. Several methods are available to save with a financial institution, including:

(a) All savings are made in the name of one spouse. It is usually the husband who does this in several traditional societies. This may be because the wife is illiterate and/or may not have identification documents, or she may feel that her husband can better manage situations such as banking, or he may be domineering, for example. In this situation it is advisable that the wife is kept abreast of all major financial transactions. She should also be encouraged to correct any deficiency which may prevent her from being involved in banking, for she should be an equal partner in this and every aspect of the marriage.

(b) The couple may have one or more joint accounts. In some instances a couple maintains separate accounts to finance individual projects such as to purchase a house and to educate the children.

(c) The couple has individual saving, current and/or other accounts,

It should be noted that any one of the above methods is not necessarily superior to others, for the strategy employed in saving is usually primarily influenced by the individual circumstances of the couple. In some instances it would be imperative that a couple have separate checking accounts, unless it is stipulated that either of them can be the sole signature to the account. At the same time, if the couple has a high level of understanding and commitment, they may find it useful to save in the name of one spouse who is responsible for accounting for all major transactions on the account.

The system of saving which has promoted much unity in many marriages involves the couple having a joint account into which they channel their savings. Once there is accurate disclosure of the income and expenditure of the family, funds budgeted for savings can be deposited there. The discussion of the bank statements will enable the couple to keep abreast of all transactions on the account. Among the disadvantages of having a joint account, particularly if the couple agree that both of them should have to authorize withdrawals, is that in any emergency one spouse may not be available to sign the check or may be indisposed to make the withdrawal.

The common system of saving, particularly, in affluent societies, is that even if the couple has a joint account, each spouse may also have individual accounts for personal transactions. On occasions, such as when a spouse is travelling on an extended journey, the need for one to make individual financial decisions will be necessary. The joint account may be used for the main savings of the family, while the individual account may be used to finance the individual expenditure of each spouse during the month.

> The family budget should be prayerfully formulated since our plans should be consistent with the will of the Lord for the lives of each member of the family.

An elderly friend related to me that from the time he was married he always give his wife his entire salary for her to formulate the budget. This he contends saves him from the tedious process of looking into minute details of the daily expenditure of the family. Since she does not have a secular job, she is more familiar with the detail financial requirements of the family. It also saves him, he contends, from the possibility of her blaming him when there is a shortfall of finance before the end of the month. In addition, since she is familiar with his average daily financial requirements, unless a major financial demand occurs, she places in his pants pocket each morning the amount she feels he would need to spend on that day.

Some persons would find this system commendable and congratulate him on his confidence in his wife's judgment and her prudence. In addition, this system must have been successful for them, since they have their own home, which is well furnished and they have a good car and several other major assets. This system obviously works for many other couples for there is a strong cultural and spiritual unity that fosters this level of commitment. On the contrary, some persons would deem this practice of the husband as irresponsible, since he is not taking full responsibility in assisting in the planning and implementation of the family budget. The converse scenario may occur where a wife willingly or is forced to give her husband her entire salary and the two of them, or he alone plans the budget of the family.

In some wealthier families, a husband may decide

that his wife should use her entire salary for her personal expenditure. This may be because he is well able to support his family. The wife may be working since she is bored staying at home or she prefers to pursue her career.

> ***God did not create all of us to generate fivefold financial returns, yet in His measuring scale we are all equal.*** It is important to find out where we fall on His measuring scale and perform at that level. A person who is at level 3, for example, should not envy a person who is to perform at level 5, or look down on another person who is to serve at level 1. Once we fulfil our calling, we will be rewarded in this life and in eternity. There are also specific rewards for persons who accomplish various tasks - Revelation 22:12.

Anything done forcefully against the willing consent of a Christian will one day become explosive. Hence, there is wisdom if the couple is committed to implement the system which is best suited to the unique situation of their family. It is important that the couple is at peace with the budget and that they are committed to ensure that it is successfully implemented as far as possible. Despite how systematic the budget is, provision has to be made for changes to the forecast. Therefore, contingency funds should be in place where necessary and/or possible, to cater for financial demands which were not budgeted for.

The couple must recognize that the salary which they earn is in fact the Lord's money, since we are His, and everything which we have belongs to Him. Therefore, what we are budgeting on is in fact God's money. We should be committed to being good stewards of God's property. We should seek His guidance in enabling us to formulate the best possible budget and to implement it with diligence and in love.

Several times, each day of our matured lives we are confronted with several basic financial decisions. They include:

(a) Should one engage in a consumption or investment with money at one's disposal?

(b) What would be the implications of delaying the decision to consume and instead engage in a prudent investment program?

(c) When the decision is to engage in consumption, we have to further consider whether or not the decision was based on a necessity or merely as a result of the quest to fulfil a want rather than a need.

> A dollar spent on prudent investment has the capacity to generate additional dollars in the future. A dollar spent on consumption, particularly on nonessential items, would actually cost the spender far more than a dollar when account is taken of the **opportunity cost** which is lost had the dollar been invested prudently.

Before embarking on the preparation of the budget, the couple must have preconceived objectives of what they intend to achieve in the short, medium and long run as a family. They must be able to prioritize their expenditure, giving more weight to items which are important to them. At the early stage of their marriage their priority may be to acquire furnishing for the home, commence saving for the children's education, purchasing a house and a car. They must be able to allocate enough funds in these areas, while not neglecting important considerations such as the need for leisure, making provision for adequate health care and for personal development such as the payment of night classes.

We all budget in one form or another even though we may not have a structured approach to allocate the money at our disposal. An incorrect way of budgeting is to **spend all of the money we earn as soon as we are paid, and have to endure a minimal amount for the remainder of the month or rely on credit cards and other forms of credit to supplement the shortfall until the next payday.** I can recall the philosophy of former colleague who would have a lavish meal at a restaurant the day after she received her salary. Her rationale was that after budgeting she would most likely not be able to spend so much on a meal for the remainder of the month. Of course with prudent budgeting, she may be able to enjoy at least another restaurant meal before the end of the month.

Many financial counsellors advocate that we should **pay ourselves** before allocating funds to any other source. For some persons this means spending ten percent or more on entertainment since they feel that they have worked hard enough to have some time and for relaxation, be involved in sporting and other activities of one's choice. For others it infers engaging in saving and investing a given amount per month in preparation for retirement or to achieve other goals. Even though the latter strategy seems plausible, there are several possible flaws which must be considered, particularly for Christians:

(a) Our first consideration should be the tithes and offering which go towards the financing of the work of the Lord. Without Him, we have no guarantee of even waking the next morning. This is an act of obedience and love for Him.

(b) As a rule, as far as possible, every dollar of the budget, particularly for a couple, should be spent on the collective needs of the family, and only a small amount should be unaccounted for. Even in allocating a percentage of the salary for personal expenditure, an account should be given to the other on how each person spent their allowance.

(c) The richer segment of the population earns so much that they do not have to worry about overspending in any given month. However, even if they do not manage their resources, they will face financial difficulties over the long run. Hence, the more prudent will attempt to structure their spending to enable them to achieve the financial objectives which they are aiming for.

A common error which many persons make when they begin to work with a budget is that they expect to see an instantaneous change in the amount of money they can save and in the reduction of the debt. The process of achieving the ultimate objective usually takes some time every year since there may also be bits of indiscipline by one or both spouses and also factors which are beyond their control as the couple attempt to implement a disciplined spending habit.

Some persons, particularly those who are paid in cash, use the **envelope method** to assist them to achieve disciple in their spending. They would have several labelled envelopes in which they put in the amount of money budgeted for each of the various categories of the budget. As a part of the expenditure is paid, they would record on the envelope the amount spend and reduce the total amount of money recorded on the envelope by that amount. Categories such as **House Rent/Mortgage Payment, Car Expenses, Food, Transportation, Entertainment, Medical Expenses and other Emergencies would be recorded on the respective envelopes.**

Some persons would have an envelope for saving which they would retain during the month in the event that there is an emergency. Once they are able to maintain balance in any envelope at the end of the month, they would save that amount. The disadvantage of this method is that unless they are very disciplined, the additional amount of money could be a source of temptation to overspend, as against if it was in the bank, then they would not have ready access to it. Money kept at home may also be stolen.

> **The experiences of consistence financial difficulties by a couple, is usually a manifestation of difficulties in other areas of their lives such as communication, commitment and cooperation, which are adversely affecting their lives.**

Even though fear is not the best method that should be used in an attempt to motivate persons to adhere to the discipline of as far as possible, to work in accordance with the budge; we can be reminded of some of the consequences of not adhering to a well-structured budget. They include huge debt, the failure to attain realistic financial goals, disunity in the family and divorce. Many persons are encouraged when they realize how much they are able to save, the amount of debt they are able to pay off and other positive results achieved as they undertake the discipline of implementing the guidance of the budget.

A parallel can be drawn with a budget and a well structured fitness program which include the adherence to a discipline spiritual life, a sensible diet program, exercise, eating healthy and other disciplines to reduce weight and maintain a healthy soul, spirit and body. (Many programs rely on the balancing of **Ying** and **Yang**, Yoga and other methods which even though they contain some healthy practices, are founded on numerous unscriptural practices to 'discipline' their minds to assist in this process). Highly visible results may not be seen during the first month of the program. However, as the program is consistently maintained over a number of months, tangible evidence of the program becomes noticeable in ways such as a fit body, an alert mind and nicely fitted clothing. This discipline has to be continued over the greater part of a person's life time for it to achieve the best results.

The question is often asked what we should do after we have been successful in getting out of debt and achieve other objectives of the budget our short, medium and long term objectives? Some of the prudent strategies are:

(a) Increase your giving to the Lord since this will be a seed for financial and other blessings. We should not be ungrateful and neglect to honour God in acknowledging Him as the source of all blessings and to give back to Him and instead merely aspire and embark on a program to 'build bigger barns.'

(b) Increase savings and investment in mutual funds, certificate of deposit, shares and in one or several business ventures,

(c) Avoid getting into other unnecessary debt,

There are several **difficulties associated with the budget** of some persons. They include:

(a) **Budgeting on an irregular income** such as causal workers, seasonal workers and persons who are frequently ill or not being able to secure or maintain fulltime employment,

(b) **Budgeting on a reduced income** such as instances when a person is demoted or loses his job or due to retirement. This is usually a traumatic process as the family is forced to restructure their life style to cope with the reduced income.

(c) **One spouse, who opposed the formulation of a budget, would not assist in formulating and the implementation of the budget.** These are usually difficult situations to manage and can be overcome by prayer, counselling and the partner who is pro-budget can lovingly explain and demonstrate the benefits which are derived from working with a budget.

The process of preparing the budget is viewed by some opponents as being merely a futile period of worrying before we do our own thing and spend the money as we please, since most of us do not earn enough to be able to afford a comfortable standard of living at any rate. A large number of individuals, families, corporate entities and governments and other entities can attest to the significant achievements which are attained as a result of budgeting and executing the mandate of the budget.

It is surprising how many persons overspend simply because they cannot **balance a check book**. At the back of most check books there is usually a section where a number of items can be recorded. They include the check number, date of issue of the check, who the check is paid to, the amount of the check, deposits make on the account, and a running balance can be recorded on the current balance of the account.

In this way the holder of a check book can keep an accurate account of what is happening on the account. Deductions must be made of amounts withdrawn with an automatic teller machine (ATM) card or other methods and any service or other charges deducted from the account. The process of balancing the check book is also assisted by the use of a system whereby the account holders can have access to information on the account via mediums such as the telephone, fax machine and internet. The bank statement which is usually posted to customers at the end of each month also assists in this process.

Several financial planners have computed formulas which seek to guide individuals, families and corporate entities to structure their budgets in such a way that they are able to achieve their long term financial and other objectives. Much of this is highlighted in a table format with various percentages used in an attempt to present a realistic distribution of income and expenditure in such a way that they are able to enjoy a fairly comfortable life even though it entails the practice of a disciplined life style. Some of the major items which are usually considered in formulating a family budget are:

(a) **Disposable Income:** This includes deductions which the salary earner may not have control over. Income Tax, National Insurance payment, contribution to the personal pension scheme (the organization usually contributes a given percentage after an employee meets the stipulated criteria such as unbroken service with the company over a given number of years). Other deductions may include contribution towards a group medical scheme, monthly loan deduction on a staff loan and/or other deductions which are sent to another institution such as payment of a car loan, mortgage or even alimony and/or child support by a man who is forced to do so by the court, for example. For many salaried earners these deductions consist of more than

25% of their gross income. Income tax alone is usually more than 15% of the gross income of many salaried earners.

(b) **Tithes:** For Christians this is the mandatory 10% of our income. Some persons compute their tithes based on their gross income (which is the Scriptural definition) rather than their net income. The **offering** is usually dependent on factors such as one's love and commitment to the Lord.

(c) **Housing expense** is the largest expenditure for most families. It is absolutely important that we live in at least comfortable homes. However, the level of comfort which we enjoy is primarily premised on our lifestyle. Many persons do not seek to rent or purchase a home which they can comfortably afford, but this is premised on factors such as their future income increasing substantially to enable them to eventually live at their perceived level of affluence. There are millions of persons the world over who cannot find a home or live in one which they are forced to occupy since they do not have a choice. However, the percentage of our income spent on housing often supports an inflated lifestyle. For this reason it is prudent that we live within our means, even as we seek to increase our disposable income.

(d) **Food expenses** is another large expenditure which we have to balance and arrive at a realistic balance between eating sensible and avoid wastage and improper purchases due to the influence of advertisement, lifestyle practices and unnecessary expenses on food,

(e) **Transportation expenses** are high for most persons who have to commute a far distance between home and work, church, market and other locations. Our mode of transportation can also be influenced by our lifestyle. Many persons purchase a car which they feel is consistent with the image which they would like to exuberate rather than for the comfort and necessity of that specific type of vehicle/s.

(f) **Utilities** such as the payment of electricity, water, cooking gas and other utilities, where they are available and for persons who can afford one, several or all of these facilities, is a huge expense for many persons.

(g) **Servicing debt** is a huge expense in a large percentage of families all over the world. The inability to manage debt will significantly decrease our ability to enjoy a comfortable life.

(h) **Other expenses** such as the payment of school fees, medical expenses, insurance coverage, the purchase of clothing, entertainment expenses is also significant in most families,

(i) **Savings** - irrespective of how bleak our financial situation, it is important to budget in such a way that, where possible, we are able to save at least five percent of our income each month. The percentage saved could be small initially but efforts should be made to increase savings over time.

(j) **Investment** would not be prudent to allocate all of the 'excess cash' which we are able to generate only for saving. Savings should not be kept at a level which satisfies precautionary needs such as emergencies, and to fulfil specific targets such as the education of children, to make a down payment on a house. However, where possible, funds should be set aside to engage in prudent investment which would generate additional income for the family and for the work of the Lord.

It does not matter how small or large is our income,

it is important to budget wisely. Persons who start with small targets are usually challenged to increase their targets in areas such as increasing their income, reducing their expenditure, increasing saving and investing. Reducing expenditure may entail adjusting lifestyle practices such as not driving an expensive car, purchasing a house and have to pay a mortgage which is beyond our means. Most importantly, we have to rely on the Lord for direction in this and every area of our life.

It is advisable that the tithe of the family is the first expenditure that should be deducted and paid. As far as possible we should not indulge in borrowing from our tithes to fulfil other expenditure. The principle of tithing, even when there is a budgetary shortfall is putting God to the test; since we can be assured that He is no man's debtor. We also have to first lend to Him in our offering, after which we will reap His financial and other forms of abundance.

Care has to be taken that there is no blatant discrimination in the allocation of the budget to the disadvantage of any member of the family. Hence, care must be taken to ensure that every member of the family has enough clothing and other essential items. When there is an acute shortfall in the budget, nonessential items and those which can be delayed may be omitted.

There are several methods which couples use to allocate the budget.

    (a)   In a marriage where the wife is not working, an allowance may be allocated each month for her to take care of her personal effects and whatever else she chooses to use it for. This may be in keeping with the principle that the husband should be a better provider than his wife's father in that he has the solemn responsibility of providing for her material needs. This is a commendable gesture. Many husbands are unable to meet this criterion, at least in the initial stage of the marriage, even though most Christian men would be happy if this were possible.

(b) A man may still provide an allowance for his wife even though she is working, since he feels obligated to ensure that all of her financial needs are met. Once there is agreement between the couple and they are committed to using this system to their advantage it is a commendable system. It is particularly beneficial if the wife could become involved in some form of lucrative investment and the profit from such a venture can be ploughed back for the benefit of the family.

Proverbs 16:3 states: "³**Commit your works to the Lord, and your plans will be established.**"

Whatever the method of budgeting and the system used for distributing the finances of the family, it is important that as far as possible, there is agreement between the members of the family on this issue. It is commendable where each spouse have enough personal cash at their disposal where they can bless each other in purchasing even if it is merely little gifts for each other as a demonstration of love and appreciation for each other. The sad thing is that far too many Christian couples cannot meet the basic necessities of life and the area of giving is often stifled. Even then, the couple should squeeze some money in the budget on leisure and on ensuring that the personal effects of each member of the family are met.

Some of the ways by which we can be guided on the correct budgetary and other decisions is by answering questions such as the following:

(a) Is it consistent with the principles of the Bible?
(b) Is one's conscience at peace with the decision? Care must be taken that one's

conscience is in tune with spiritual matters and that one was not given up to a reprobate because of one's consistent disobedience.
(c) As far as possible, there should be agreement between the spouses, where applicable, and other members of the family. Care must also be taken to ensure that when there are disagreements, that the decision which is adopted is consistent with the leadership of the Lord for the specific issue.
(d) As far as possible, priority should be given to the fulfilment of long-term goals, particularly when it is possible to forgo some short-term, less important pleasures.

It is very important that we engage in saving and investing not only for the immediate future but **our planning should also be medium and long term also**. For many persons the stages are 1 to 5, 5 to 10, and above 10 years, respectively. The emphasis which is placed on the various stages is usually dependent on factors such as the period of our lives, our financial strength and investment and other opportunities which are available to us. To many persons short, medium and long-term goals include:

(a) **Short-term goals** include meeting immediate consumption such as food, clothing, medical, utilities, transportation and other expenses,
(b) **Medium-term goals** for the newlywed may include saving to accumulate enough money for the down payment and closing expenses on a mortgage, securing one or two cars, commence saving for the secondary and tertiary education of the children,
(c) **Long-term goals** may include accumulating, say, $500,000 for retirement; have enough capital to establish a business which generates adequate net income to support the family.

It is not enough to have lofty ideas if we are not disciplined enough or willing to seek the council of the Lord and other believers and implement the best strategies at our disposal in order to achieve them. Planning without implementing then is tantamount to building sand castles on the beach. They will either be washed away by the sea or destroyed by others if we do not destroy them ourselves.

Another important area in financial planning is in **whose name items such as the house, car, furniture and other major assets will be bought.** This is another area which shows the level of cleaving in marriage, particularly in societies where the title of properties does not go automatically to the husband. Usually, it is better if major assets are purchased jointly in the name of both spouses to avoid complications that occur after the death of a spouse in whose name items were bought and a will was not prepared. If the motive for joint ownership, on the other hand is an insurance against loss of possession in the event of a divorce, the couple is standing of shaky grounds.

Wives should be familiar with items such as budgeting for the family, knowing where the title deeds for the property, the bank book, birth, academic and other certificates and other documents concerning the affairs of the family are stored for safe keeping. This is not only as a precaution for eventualities such as death of the husband, if indeed she outlives him, but rather she has the right to such important information since there is no such roles as major and minor shareholders in marriage, but rather they are equal partners.

Even if the husband is viewed as the Chief Executive Officer (CEO), it is noted that in most corporate organizations it is the Deputy CEO who manages the daily operations, while the CEO attends external meetings, much like the Virtuous Wife, who was alluded to earlier. This is not a dogmatic approach since a husband may choose to, since he may have been made redundant, or because of sickness, for example, he stays at home while his wife pursues a secular career.

Proverbs 11:29 states: "²⁹**Those who trouble their households will inherit wind, and fools will be servant to the wise.**" There is clear evidence that persons who deliberately promote disharmony in the home will be severely punished by the Lord, for the Lord places a high premium on the fostering of harmony in the home.

We have to be good stewards of the financial and other resources which God has placed at our disposal. When we master this principle, it will be transmitted to our children and to their children. When parents fail to do their part in this and other important areas, it may hinder the fulfilment of the plan of God for future generations. Many parents believe the Biblical interpretation of training up a child in the way of the Lord relates only to spiritual matters. The fact is that God is concerned that each child has a well-rounded personality.

We have a solemn responsibility to set good examples to our children in managing our financial and other resources and be good mentors to our children in every area of our lives. Instead of spending our income in attempting to maintain a lavish life style, care must be taken that we are prudent so that our children can learn from our success.

> *The family budget is the format which highlights the financial resources which are available to execute particular aims and objectives of the family. The budget may include the allocation of time, financial, personnel and other resources for the fulfilment of particular goals.*

Prudent financial management principles which

should be reviewed by Christian families include:
- (a) Seek to invest more than ten percent (10%) of our income on prudent future income generating activities. Since **the Lord blesses the work of our hands**, persons who are employed by an organization should ensure that some of these blessings come directly to us rather than if it accruing primarily to the owners of the organization. The blessing of promotion given by one's employer is not all that God has in store for us.
- (b) **Avoid getting into debt as far as possible**, primarily for consumer items which we can forgo and purchase when we have accumulated the cash price. Very often what is advertised as a bargain, pay later plan and other attractions, has some hidden costs such as high interest rates and high penalties for defaulting on payments.
- (c) **It is unwise to seek to follow the 'Jones' and purchase items merely to keep up with the lavish life style of other persons.** This does not infer that a family should not thrive to 'move up the social ladder' and improve their standard of living. Rather, the family must be committed to, for example:
    - (i) Budgeting wisely,
    - (ii) Living as far as possible within their means,
    - (iii) Ensure that they engage in rigorous saving and investment programs,
- (d) **Encourage our children to start saving at an early age. They also have to be groomed to make prudent, independent financial and other decisions. Children should be encouraged to tithe from their allowance as well as to forgo the purchase of nonessential items for a good book and other items which will have a more profound influence on their lives in the future.** Parents should also provide

financial and other forms of support when the child shows an inclination to engage in an investment that may generate substantial returns in the future. Preparation for life is not only emphasizing academic excellence but also the development of a well-rounded personality.

(e) Ensure that **saving for future expenditure** such as for the higher education of the children commences early in the marriage. Where possible parents should secure adequate medical and life insurance coverage for each member of the family.

(f) **Investments in shares and other securities** in the name of the children are also practices of the more affluent families,

The way we shop have a profound influence on the management of the family budget. Important considerations which are observed by several families which have been able to manage their budget include:

(a) It is important that a grocery list is made of all of the important, and particularly the expensive items which have to be purchased. It may be necessary to include the price of the larger items so that an approximate cost can be allocated to the items to be purchased from particular stores or the market. It is not uncommon to find persons going to the cashier only to find that the cost of the items is more than the amount of money which they took with them.

The embarrassment is usually in deciding which items to return while there is a line of other customers who are impatient. For this reason some persons would take a pocket calculator with them to avoid such embarrassing situations. Adhering to the items on the list can be a mammoth task, particularly if there are small children who are demanding items which they may have been lured to by television advertisements. There will be items which may have been omitted from the grocery list which may have to be purchased. However, this should be limited based on the budgetary constraint.

Some families choose to leave their small children at home when they are going shopping at the supermarket in order to avoid the temptation of patronizing them to the disadvantage of adhering to the budget, particularly if the child/children are liable to misbehave in the store. They may be taken to the store on occasions when there is excess money budgeted for them. Some wives extend this principle of leaving their husbands at home or in the car, particularly if he is prone to purchase items which may not be absolutely necessary at that time. Men often overextend themselves in an effort to purchase items which they would deem that their family deserves, even though it may not be in their budget. There are also wives who are compulsive spenders and who would not adhere to the discipline of a budget.

(b) It is important when purchasing vegetables and fruits and other items that careful consideration is given to purchasing those which are in season and are thus fresh and cheap. Very often local produced items are also cheaper than imported items even though the imported items may be better packaged.

(c) Principles such as purchasing items at a sale and storing it for when it is needed also proves to be cost effective. This is particularly useful in purchasing summer items when there is a sale by stores which are stocking up on winter items. Persons are often able to secure lucrative bargains by purchasing items at a jumble, garage and/or auction sales. Many persons purchase items such as a car and house at an auction by making prior arrangement with a bank or mortgage company, for example. These items may be sold due to the inability of the previous owner to meet their mortgage payments.

(d) Purchasing items in bulk at whole sale depots has proven to be a huge cost advantage for persons with adequate storage facilities. Some persons indulge in group purchases to enjoy the cost advantage and subdivide the items according to their individual needs.

> When we can keep our focus on the achievement of long-term goals, the more likely we are to forsake less important short-term objectives.

This is a complex way of expressing the insatiable desire of persons to consume more and more as their affluence increases. **Very often we are deceived into believing that if we are able to acquire a few basic necessities we will be satisfied and begin to enjoy life.** However, we will find that as our salary increases and we are able to 'live in comfort' with the material possessions which we envisioned would have been 'enough,' we find that our vision becomes expanded and we aspire to achieve more material possessions. Very often this is so similar to the parable of the farmer who desired to build larger barns and enjoy his materially secured life.

Very often, as a person's income increases, his taste and life style increases at a level which is beyond the scope of the immediate income. As such, when an employee is promoted from a supervisor to a manager, for example, the employees would now be interacting with persons of a higher income and social bracket. The status of the position may entail entertaining senior managers at one's home, or at least be associated with persons who live in the 'posh' neighbourhoods, drive the latest models of vehicles, and dress in a fashionable way. This additional pressure often forces many persons to seek to live at a higher, or at least comparable life style as one's peers. The result is often that one ends up overextending one's financial capabilities. The weak natured person may even engage in illegal practices to support one's 'uplifted' lifestyle.

> **A popular economic principal state: "The propensity to consume is a function of one's income."** The simplified explanation to this phenomenon is that for most persons, as their income increases, their consumption pattern also increases to match, and in most instances surpass their new income. Hence, the perpetuation of the 'debt trap' – continue to borrow to satisfy one's life style.

There is an ongoing debate in many politicians, academics and other analysts on whether or not the wealthy and businesses should be taxed higher, and if so to what extent. This policy is opposed by some analysts primarily on the economic philosophy that the lower the taxes which are allocated to the wealthy and to businesses, the more they are induced to invest in the economy, which would increase the GDP of the country, create thousands of additional jobs and other benefits to the economy. In addition, with high taxes, the wealthy would seek to move more of their savings and other liquid assets to tax havens overseas and engage in more tax avoidance, and for the dishonest – tax evasion practices. Conversely, the higher the disposable income of the poor and middle class, the more they will seek to spend on consumptions and meeting lifestyle practices, rather than investing. Therefore, the economy would be more disadvantaged when the rich and businesses are taxed heavily.

Most governments rely heavily on taxes to support the budgetary expenditure of the economy. There is therefore a delicate balance of governments seeking to raise as much taxes as they can from the income of workers and from corporate entities. However, if income earners are taxed heavily, it decreases their disposable income, hence, their consumption decreases and there will be a fall in the demand for goods and services produced locally, but may be advantageous to the economy if consumers rely heavily on imported products. (This discussion can be reviewed in-depth in the relevant Economics text and on the internet).

History has so many examples of persons who engaged in an extravagant lifestyle as their status in life increased. Notable examples are found among pop stars, actors and other celebrities, royalties, government officials and other persons. Imelda Marcus, the former First Lady of the Philippines, for example, is remembered for her extravagance in the collection of shoes. For other persons it is the collection of vintage sports cars, purchasing a mansion and other 'extravagance.'

Many families aspire to have basic necessities, depending on the society where they live. They include:
- (b) A well furnished and comfortable home with enough room to adequately accommodate the family and visitors,
- (c) One or several motor vehicles,
- (c) Enough money for their children's education and to save for a 'rainy-day,'

(d) Be able to have enough money to spend on food, clothing, leisure, sporting and other activities,

(e) Engage in investment programs which would significantly increase their income and provide them with the future financial security which they desire,

(f) Enough money accumulating for their pension and to take care of the family after the retirement of one or both partners, enough to maintain their home and live comfortable after retirement,

(g) Enough money for the medical, funeral and other expenses of loved ones and to sustain the family after the death of the breadwinner/s,

(h) To be able to leave some tangible items such as a house, jewellery and other assets for their survivors,

> God has never promised us a 'bed of roses' in the present life. As a matter of fact, Jesus told His disciples that His followers must be prepared to suffer afflictions and adversities as a result of following Him. Nevertheless, He has promised 'peace' even when the 'waters' of life are troubled.

FORMULATING AND ACHIEVING GOALS

It is very important that we formulate goals in every aspect of our lives. The sad thing is that many persons establish goals for the type of person they would like to marry, what career they would like to pursue, but when it comes to financial goals they are often deficient in several vital areas. Very often the vision of the young when it come to financial matters, stops at completing one's education, securing a well paying job, purchasing a home, car, living a 'good' life, travelling etc. Thankfully, as many persons mature and start a family they become more focused and begin to plan their life beyond living a flashy lifestyle and plan for their future family. Planning for retirement usually become a reality for most persons after their thirtieth birthday or even later, possibly when they see their parents and other persons undergoing hardship when they retired without making adequate financial and other forms of provision for the remainder of their lives and that of their loved ones.

It is important that we set realistic financial and other goals as individuals, a family and the wider community. If the question of what are some of our financial goals is asked to a young person, it is common to hear responses such as:

(a) The desire to be a millionaire before age twenty,
(b) To have enough money to be able to purchase a home and furnish it before getting married,
(c) Ownership of the latest model of motor vehicle/s,

For the married couple it is customary to hear goals such as:

(a) Being debt free within a year,
(b) Having enough money to pay for the education of the children,
(c) To be able to save enough so that they can enjoy a comfortable retirement, meet any medical and other expenses which may arise and to be able to travel and enjoy the many things which they were unable to afford, or

had the time to do because of their schedule during the years of employment.

Even though it is absolutely necessary that we plan, we must first seek the direction of the Lord in this and every other area of our lives.

Thankfully, several ministries have been established to assist believers to manage their financial and other resources. A prominent ministry in this area is Crow Financial Ministries which is an international ministry which has established groups in several countries and in several communities. They also distribute literature to assist believers to manage their financial resources. They also have a website (crownfinance.org) which can be contacted for further information.

It is important that a couple analyze their personal and collective goals in areas such as their ministries, material acquisition, financial management principles, family planning methods, the rearing of children and other vital areas of their lives before marriage.

There are several important aspects of the establishment of financial goals which are vital to our lives. Irrespective of how good we feel our plan is, we have to rely on the miracle working power of the Lord in order to achieve the goals which He has specifically burdened our hearts to fulfil. The maxim which states that **if a person aims for the sky, that even if he falls short, he would have at least landed on the cloud**, comes to mind. However, if one is consistently pushed beyond one's capacity, it could result in severe mental and other problems.

Proverbs 4:7 states: "**⁷Wisdom is the principal thing: therefore get wisdom and with all your getting, get understanding.**"

Important considerations for formulating goals include the fact that they:

(a) **Challenging,** in that they should take a reasonable amount of effort, discipline and other positive attributes to attain them. If important goals are not challenging, one tends to under-perform. On the other hand, if they are too demanding, they could cause much mental anguish, frustration and other negative effects on the family.
(b) **Time specific**, where a realistic timeframe must be given in which to achieve the goals,
(c) **Quantifiable**, in that one must be able to compute the amount of necessary resources to achieve the goals,
(d) **Measurable,** in that it should be possible to ascertain the extent to which they are on, or off course towards attaining the goals over the time span allocated for their completion,
(e) **Realistic**, in that they should be attainable given the available time, finance and other resources at their disposal,
(f) **Specific,** where the persons conducting the activity would be precisely aware of what they are aiming to achieve, rather than merely working with no specific goal to direct them,

Most goals (apart for spiritual goals such as to live a holy life, winning the lost and walking in the calling of the Lord) are not 'set in stone.' Therefore, there will be occasions when it may be necessary to adjust the parameters of the goals in order to arrive at a realistic outcome. Some of the long-term financial goals which are established by some Christian families are:
(a) The acquisition of their own home, furniture, car and other assets,
(b) The financing of the education of their children,
(c) Investment and saving schemes which should realistically afford the family a comfortable standard of living,

(d) Saving and investment programs for their retirement,

(e) Leaving an inheritance for their children and children's children,

There are several obstacles which can prevent us from attaining our objectives. These may include the economic condition of the country, health and other personal issues in the lives of the couple and even the change in the direction which they have received from the Lord. A typical example of the latter issue was illustrated in the life of Abraham and Sarah, when God instructed Abraham to move his family and possessions. Abraham's obedience resulted in God commending him and Abraham was called the father of the nation of Israel.

There are several attributes of a vision which have been popularized. They include the ability to:

(a) **Think creatively**; this ability is not only limited to artists and entrepreneurs, but is found in every individual who is prepared to extend his mind beyond merely existing. Persons use their immediate environment and the wider community and engage in practices which improve their standard of living, make chores lighter, become more efficient at what they do, and participate in other activities which contribute to the solution of national and international problems. **One of the fundamental principles of many persons who have been successful in business, politics, medicine and other disciplines, is to identify an important need which has to be met provide a product and/or service and/or system to satisfy that need.** This does not only apply to the invention of commercial ideas but is also the basis for many individuals and ministries achieving recognition in their community and beyond.

(b) **To explore possibilities**; there is a famous cliché which states, '**nothing ventured, nothing gained**.' We may also be familiar with the maxim which states that **it is better to try and fail than to fail to try**, for in so doing, even if we fail to complete the task, even if we fail to complete the task, someone else may be able to improve on the effort and complete the product/program.

(c) **Tap into potential**; God has created in each of us the ability to fulfil a purpose which only we can achieve. The process of actualizing that potential requires that we undergo a period of preparation in forms such as academic training, physical and/or mental exercise. It may also require that we align ourselves at least initially with others, access funding and other resources to be able to put into effect that which the Lord has burdened our hearts to fulfil.

Vision is absolutely essential in order to foster progress. This is also the ingredient which causes persons to remain young even though they may be physically old. It is the vision of having an active body, winning a marathon or other competition which propel athletes and even persons who exercise as a leisure activity, to keep pounding their bodies to run or walk for a number of kilometres each week.

> After we have, what we thought was to asked, knocked, and sought, we may still be financially poor, as demonstrated in the lives of so many Christians (even though blessings are not only financial in nature). We must have the discernment, capacity, wisdom and revelation to:
> - Use wisely what the Lord has already given to us.
> - Pursue what we can achieve by, for example, furthering our education,
> - Aligning with mentors and strategic business partners,
> - Receive blessings from the Lord and others,

There are several examples in the Bible and in our history where the fulfilment of a vision which may have been birthed a number of years, only becomes a reality after one or several major catastrophes. Examples in the Bible include the life of Samuel whose vision which the Lord revealed to him when he was a small boy only became a reality after God killed Eli's sons who were exploiting the people when they offered their sacrifices. Joseph's vision of royalty only came into fruition after he was sold into slavery, imprisoned and suffered other misfortunes. Even so, we should not be over anxious to fulfil our vision but instead walk in the perfect timing and in the season which the Lord has established for its actualization.

COMMON ATTRIBUTES OF GODLY VISIONARIES

The Lord often reveals His purpose for the life of a person in the form of an inner vision which He makes known to them. Many persons have the experience of 'tapping into this vision' very early in their lives, and are able to live a fulfilled life, knowing that they have completed the task for which they were created. Sadly, a larger percentage of persons go through their lives without knowing, and hence fulfilling God's purpose for their lives.

For some persons a vision is imprinted on their mind as they humbly wait on the Lord for Him to reveal His perfect will for their lives. For others persons it is revealed at a time when they were not even seeking the Lord for this revelation, but they receive an inspiration for which they had an inner conviction that that was what the Lord requires them to fulfil. A person who has received a

Godly vision often finds that it is a lonely and painful journey which demands much sacrifice to carry the vision from conception to fulfilment. However, it is the most rewarding experience that a person can experience in this life. Some of the common attributes of Godly visionaries are:

(a) They are never satisfied with anything under the optimum fulfilment of the vision, least they become petrified and abort the completion of the full task,

(b) They are risk takers, even if it means initial or several failures along the way. This does not entail taking foolish risks or gambling but diligently, and with the wisdom of the Lord operating in their lives, persevere until success is achieved.

(c) They must be willing to venture into areas even if they are unchartered,

(d) They have a passion to fulfil their calling; they never say that it is over until God says so,

(e) They prefer to experience extensive physical and even mental exertion rather than to be satisfied with mediocrity,

(f) They align themselves with the right person/s who are able channel their potential or provide the necessary assistance needed to fulfil the task ahead,

(g) They position themselves at a 'high place' where they can see the extent of the 'land to be conquered' (Habakkuk 2:1),

(h) They recognize that success comes after work (the converse occurs only in the dictionary),

(i) They realize that it is often a lonely road to carry a vision to the stage where it becomes a reality, particularly since others may not have the same vision or empathize with your vision or feel that you are the right person or qualified enough to fulfil such a vision.

(j) They have to adapt the mindset of living the life of the end product as the fulfilment of the vision progresses so that by the time it is fulfilled, they are not overwhelmed by the magnitude of the success. (Not being prepared has caused many persons to mismanage funds, for example, when the blessing start coming, since they did not spend time to recognize that their success in a particular area is not an end in itself, but merely a means to graduate to a higher calling).

(k) They accept that it takes faith, patience and other godly characteristics to fulfil many a vision,

(l) They are careful not to disclose their vision to persons who are jealous or not able or willing to support the vision, for they may even attempt to stifle the fulfilment of the vision or steal the idea from you,

(m) A true visionary would not be reluctant to accept God's rebuke, reproof and discipline as He fashions him to the place where we can receive the tools needed to fulfil that vision.

GETTING OUT AND STAYING OUT OF POVERTY

Many of us have had the experience of reading a Biblical passage and nothing seem to register in our spirit. This may be as a result of how awake our spirit was to hear the word of God, and our physical state since tiredness and other distractions could cause us to miss what the Lord is saying in a particular passage. Then there are times when a passage, verse and even a word from the Bible has such a profound impact on us, that it wakes us up even if we were sleeping. The latter experience occurred as I read Matthew 11:4, 5: "*4Jesus* answered and said to them, "Go and tell John the things which you hear and see: ⁵The blind see and the lame walk; the leapers are cleansed and the deaf hear; the dead are risen up and the poor have the gospel preached to them."

What is evident in the first categories of physical challenges was that Jesus provided the solution to the challenge which these persons were suffering. Then Jesus tells us that He preached to the poor. A casual observer may ask of what significance is the issue of Jesus preaching to the poor? Was Jesus' preaching in some way designed to enable them to emerge from their state of impoverishment? It had to be that the acceptance of the teaching of Jesus caused them to emerge from poverty materially.

Even though there is also a spiritual aspect of the emergence from poverty; the theme of verse 5 is that there were physical manifestations of the solution to the undesirable physical condition which that person suffered. We can thus return to the earlier statement that indeed **the righteousness of God empowers us to emerge from poverty**. This occurs since we are now able to tap into the '**Source of true wealth**.' It is incorrect to contend that the preaching of the gospel by Jesus pertained only to the salvation of our souls and to provide us a place in eternity. The gospel is holistic, in that it focuses on our spirit, soul and body. It also ministers to our wellbeing on earth and after death.

There are several things which are at the disposal of persons who desire to get out and stay out of poverty. They include:

(a) **Our spirit, soul and body must be renewed in Christ**, which enable us to become righteous and thus derive all the prerequisite benefits,

(b) **Consistently make positive confession of our renewed state and act on our confession.**

Simple confessions such as "I am no longer poor, but I have the riches which are in my Heavenly Father" should be made. We have to confess prosperity, eat, sleep, dress and in other ways live prosperity. This does not mean that we 'put-on' a foreign accent or copy the life style of the rich and famous, rather it means that we should, as it were, discard the trapping of the 'grave clothes.' It may entail investing some of the little which we have into upgrading our appearance, home and other aspects of our lives.

(c) **Renounce generation curses** since they may hinder us from coming into the full extent of our blessings,

(d) **Surround ourselves with persons who would assist us to realize the liberty which we have already received.** This does not infer that you will not associate with persons who are poor, for very often as we assist others, we receive the manifestation of the liberation which we desire.

(e) **It may require that even an adult undergo academic and/or specialized training in order to acquire the competence to enable us to tap into the resources which God has already made available to us**,

---

It is often better to be charitable after making a huge profit rather than making poor financial decision and have very little or nothing to give. The rich often provide charity and/or make a contribution to an educational institution or other charitable causes and claim it as a tax write-off. Our giving should be in accordance with the leading of the Lord, since He is not confined to the financial reasoning of man. He may chose to bless us only after in obedience we give in the amount and to whom He directs.

FINANCIAL IMPLICATIONS OF A DIVORCE

It is a fact that a couple who pool their resources will be able to amass far more material possessions than if they were to do so individually. Many persons would contend that being married to a spouse who may not be as industrious, who is a lavish spender, and who exhibits other negative financial management traits would be counterproductive. The primary consideration of couples contemplating marriage should not be material security to the extent that they are prepared to sacrifice their spiritual obligation, love and other important factors. However, a couple should not neglect the importance of financial security as an important ingredient in forging harmony in their marriage. The husband's concern should not only be focused on providing for his family, but an important consideration should be that there is harmony in their planning and execution of financial and other decisions. When these objectives are not achieved, the couple is likely to be confronted with serious financial and other problems.

Some of the common reasons why couples divorce are:

(a) Sexual infidelity,
(b) Physical and other forms of abuse,
(c) Incompatibility in their religious persuasions, outlook on life and financial impropriety,

It is sad that incidents of divorce are high even among Christians. As in the Church of Corinth in the Bible, there are still incidents of infidelity among Christians who also succumb to many of the same problems as non-Christians. Many Christian couples also quarrel, fight, engage in lavish spending and other activities which precipitate a divorce. Recognizing this fact, many churches have opened the doors and have allowed some persons who have been divorced to be remarried in their church and they are accepted as members of the congregation. This is not a universally accepted practice since many churches are still adamant and will not remarry a divorcee, regardless of the circumstances which caused the divorce.

The more liberal church would allow the spouse who is cited as the 'innocent' party to remarry. For example, if a man committed adultery and his wife files for a divorce and it is granted, and both former spouses decide to remarry, some churches will bless the marriage of the former divorced man and not that of the woman, since she filed for the divorce.

Some of the implications of a divorce are:

(a) Anger,
(b) Regret,
(c) Embarrassment,
(d) The breaking up of a happy home and family,
(e) A drastic reduction in the financial position of the wife and children in particular, since the amount of alimony which the father may have to pay his wife and the financial support for the children is usually not adequate enough to support them,
(f) The education of the children may have to be disrupted since there may not be adequate financial provision for them to continue their education, particularly if they attended a private educational institution after the father discontinue financing of the children's education,
(g) It is heartbreaking when a parent turns his back on his children because of a divorce. There may also be additional financial responsibilities such as one or both former partners may decide to remarry and there are additional financial and other demands which force one or both former partners to neglect their children and former spouse,
(h) The cost of retaining an attorney and the time that is wasted in securing or defending a divorce proceeding could be saved if the couple would have only nipped this situation in the bud and

allowed the Lord to minister to their particular situation,

(i) Even if the couple had a pre-nuptial agreement, where assets which they acquired individually before they were married is protected in the event of a divorce, a judge may award a settlement based on the total value of the assets of the individuals,

(j) Children who experience a divorce of their parents often grow up with poor self-esteem which may result in their parent (who can afford to and where this service is available) having to take the child/ren to a psychiatrist. The child may also suffer from psychological challenges for which medical attention has to be sought.

The family home and other major assets may have to be sold and the proceeds divided among the couple in accordance to the decree of the court. In some instances, these assets are auctioned well below the fair market value of the assets. Thus, assets which the couple may have worked very hard to achieve become the property of strangers at a price which is far lower than if the couple had sold it without the pressure of the court.

Where would the wife and children live? It is common that the amount of money after the divorce settlement or what the husband is prepared to give to his estranged family to exist on, is far less than they require to live on. This may demand that the wife seeks a source of employment outside of the home and in some instances she may have to secure a second job in order to maintain her and children. This could be quite a wakeup call for her, particularly if she was not pursuing a secular career since she was married. However, she may be able to move into the home of a relative at least temporarily, until she can be independent.

The court may have compelled the former husband to provide alimony for his ex-wife, possibly until she remarries, if she is so inclined. The father may also be forced to support his children until they attain the age of legal adulthood, usually at age eighteen. In such instances the presiding judge may decree that these deductions be made at the husband's place of employment and sent directly to his family. Whatever the system that is used, a failure to make them could result in the man being brought before the court and even incarcerated, as is popular among 'dead-beat' dads in the USA. There are also rare instances where a woman is brought before the court by her former husband and the judge rules that she should provide some form of financial assistance to her former husband and children in instances where she loses custody of the children.

The experience will also have serious repercussion for the former husband who may have to start to fend for himself, if another wife or at least another woman is not caring for him. Some men may reside with a relative or friend.

The only persons who benefit from a divorce are usually total strangers to the family. They may include:
1. Attorneys and other legal luminaries,
2. The purchasers of the assets which are often sold for a price which is lower than the true market price to meet legal and other expenses,
3. Medical practitioners and psychiatrists who may have to treat the physical and mental traumas which often ensue as a result of a divorce. On the contrary, the losers are the couple themselves who would have to, as it were, start their lives all over again with the additional baggage of hurt, distrust and fear of entering another relationship.

Children for the marriage will also suffer serious emotional scars unless they allow the love of the Lord to heals such negative scars. It is inevitable that the family will encounter problems in a marital union. However, as they allow the Holy Spirit to surge through their lives and take His rightful place as the center of their lives and marriage, He will resolve every conflict and see them through any difficult situation which they encounter. Even in instances of a divorce, it is expected that a Christian man would honor his spiritual, financial and other responsibilities and ensure that his children are adequately catered for.

In most divorces among couples with children, the negative effects of the disintegration of the marriage extend to the children, in that one parent may be alienated from them by his/her choice or even as a decree of the court in circumstances such as when violence, infidelity and other extremely unpleasant circumstances precipitated the divorce. The father may be obligated to support his children even if his former wife remarries. In some circumstances the new husband will adopt the child and legally request that the biological father ceases supporting his child. This may be because the former husband was using the medium of the support to come into contact with his former wife. In such circumstances it is usually advisable that direct support be stopped.

The church in a **polygamous society** has to deal with questions such as how to relate to the wife who is in a polygamous marriage and who is converted, who does not have an independent source of income to support herself and children, apart from that of her husband who may not be a believer. She may be desirous of leaving her husband when it has been revealed to her that she is living in an adulterous relationship, which obviously is not pleasing in the sight of the Lord. This complexity is compounded if the church does not have the financial resources to support her and her children once she decides to leave her husband. In such circumstances the advice given may be that the Christian wife should pray for the conversion of her husband, even though that does not solve the fundamental problem. The rationale for this is that when he is converted, his stand may be that he should only retain his first wife, which may result in his having to divorce his Christian wife if she is not his first wife. In such circumstances, even if he decides to continue to support his children, he might have to be separated from all of his other wives.

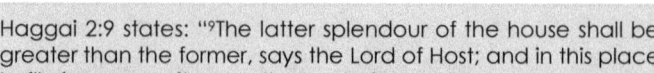

> Haggai 2:9 states: "⁹The latter splendour of the house shall be greater than the former, says the Lord of Host; and in this place I will give prosperity, says the Lord of Host."
> So, why should we allow past failures, discouragement, difficulties and other negative attributes to hinder us from achieving the best which God has in store for us? "For a Saint is just a sinner who fell down and was picked up by Christ."

CONCLUSION

This chapter reviewed several of the important financial issues which are critical for the harmonious relationship of the Christian family. We have seen that **money is a bad master but a good servant**, in other words, once the family is able to manage their financial affairs, it will assist them to manage other areas of their lives. Efficient financial management enables the couple to plan and execute their plan in an atmosphere of love and commitment to unite in other areas of their lives. On the other hand, problems in financial management will have devastating effects in possibly every other aspect of the life of the family. The primary principle which a couple must recognize is that **the money which is earned by one or both spouses does not belong to them; rather it is the Lord's**. He has given us the strength to earn it and also the wisdom to know how to manage it. When the couple recognizes this fact, then tithing and observing other financial disciplines will also be easy for them to submit to.

It does not matter how much income a family receives, if they are not submitted to Biblical principles they will always experience financial difficulties. **The Bible categorically stipulates that prudent financial management would not resolve many of the basic problems which confront man. Therefore, the first**

principle of lasting financial success is a submission of the will and ways of Lord. As we seek His face and follow His path He will direct us into financial and other aspects of prosperity.

We have the onus to do our part, which includes working, paying our tithes and giving of our offering, planning and executing our plans. It does not end there, since, irrespective of how efficient a financial planner we may be, we must leave room for His provision and intervention. He expects us to follow healthy practices such as eating right, exercise, not worrying and other positive attributes, yet He decides the extent of our years on the earth. ***He is also a miracle working God who sometimes spoils us with abundance which we could not have dreamt of having.*** Yet, He expects us to exercise discipline in the management of our financial and other resources with which He has blessed us.

It is common for a married couple to have different personalities, methods of analyzing and solving problems and other aspects of their lives. With love for each other, allowing the Spirit of God to work in their lives, Godly council and other positive influences, will foster the harmonization and synchronization of the similarities and differences and unite the couple into the unique 'single being' which God designated to occur in the marital relationship. The process of uniting is traumatic for many couples, in essential areas such as the management of money and other material resources. Very often one spouse is a worrier, while the other tends to be more pragmatic in approaching difficult situations. This relationship can create a health balance since one may look primarily for loopholes in the process while the other looks for the solution. The earlier a couple realizes that they have to accentuate the strengths of each other and assist each other to overcome weaknesses and other shortcomings, the better it would be for them.

The importance of one partner disclosing to the other that one is experiencing financial difficulties is absolutely important. This is so since very often a debt incurred by one partner may render the other liable, even if the other did not sign the contract. Even if this is not upheld in court, the estate of the debtor could be reduced by the outstanding debt in the event of the death of the debtor. Many persons attempt to hide the fact that they have incurred a debt, until it becomes unmanageable and a debt collection agency starts calling and even visit their home or place of employment, for example.

NOTES

Chapter 5 *FINANCIAL MANAGEMENT & THE GOLDEN OLD AGE*

INTRODUCTION

Many persons look forward to retirement as the period where they will be afforded the opportunity of doing with their lives the things which they are truly desirous of doing, which they feel would give them most enjoyment. For many persons, retirement is a period which is viewed with fear and apprehension as they approach the formative years of their working life. A senior officer, during a major part of his working life may have lived a flamboyant life style, enjoying the benefits of a chauffeur-driven office car, a large salary with housing, travelling, telephone and other allowances; a well furnished home and other amenities which are financed by his employers. Suddenly one faces the daunting reality of having to relinquish all of these benefits simply because one is no longer needed by the organization.

Many persons look forward to the golden years of our life with the same enthusiasm as we enjoyed the other stages of our lives. A couple who began saving for their retirement from the early stages of their marriage, may be able to enjoy the blessing of retiring as a second career and/or a period of relaxing to the pleasure of enjoying each day. There is, for example, no longer the pressure of having to force oneself to go to a place of employment which one may have grown to dislike. In addition, the financial and other demands of the children may have been reduced significantly since they may have all left home and started their own families.

For many persons, old age is characterized by much pains, suffering and sadness. They recognize that even though they may have aged, there is much pain as they resign themselves to the fact that they no longer can enjoy the standard of living which they may have been accustomed. This is due to a significant reduction of the income of one or both spouses. There are also the adverse effects of inflation, the high cost of living, neglect by relatives and friends, their vulnerability to confidence tricksters and robbers. This is just a short list of some of the negatives which often confront many elderly. This is also a period when many couples find that they can no longer live with each other since the escape route which work provided for most of their marriage life, has ceased to exist.

ENJOYING RETIREMENT

Many persons wake up one day to realize that they no longer have to go to the workplace which they have gone to over a number of years. This place may have been a 'home away from home,' in that they may have spent more than one-third of their waking time, Monday to Friday, and for other persons Saturdays and even a number of Sundays there. This is the place where they may have forged lasting friendships and good working relationships with persons from similar and/or different backgrounds and way of life. For others, their place of employment was one of constant battle, where over the last decade or so the fight to hold their job may have been an uphill battle. This may have stemmed from the quest of management to hire persons who were more academically qualified, younger and more energetic and who were more abreast with the use of modern technology such as the computer and other gadgetry. Yet one may have been retained because of the representation of unions and also the fact that management may have recognized that the thorough knowledge which one has of the procedures of the operations necessitated that there be a balance of the young and energetic and the old and experienced. But alas, all of this is about to end.

It is important that a person who is employed outside of the home ensures that their employer pays the National Insurance Scheme, Pension Scheme, Medical Insurance and other contributions which are particularly important as the employee becomes elderly and is nearing retirement. There are frequent incidents of dishonest employers who fail to make these payments on behalf of their employees over an extended period. This irregularity may only come to light when the employee is sick or in need of some form of assistance where it is revealed that the institution cannot honour the claim because the employer did not pay the contribution as prescribed in the contract of employment. Even though the court may fine and/or imprison the dishonest employer, the employee may have to sue the institution unless the labour authority or court decrees that the employer makes the relevant compensation.

The elderly are particularly vulnerable to be exploited by confidence tricksters who prey on the fact that the elderly often live by themselves and they may not have other relatives around to consult before making major financial decisions. For these reasons, dishonest sales representatives from some credit card companies, lotto and bingo and various types of investment schemes would deliberately target the elderly to sell their products and investment schemes. The elderly person may be encouraged to purchase a particular item, which will entitle them to enter a raffle or lottery which offers very attractive prizes to the winners. The elderly person may be told that they have won an attractive prize but in order to collect it they have to purchase other items. The result is often that the gullible elderly person ends up with a large number of items which they do not have any use for, but they continue to buy into the scheme in anticipation of one day collecting the jackpot. Such dishonest sales personnel may encourage the elderly to invest in schemes when they are aware that the elderly persons will be losing all or a greater part of their investment.

> *After the retirement of the breadwinner/s, a family may very well be forced to live on less that one-fifth of their income from state pension and gratuity, when the cost of living may have increased significantly. It is thus important to commence saving and investing specifically for retirement early in life.*

CONSUMER PROTECTION

Many countries have laws which protect consumers from unfair practices by sales agencies. Consumer protection bodies and other civic organizations may also render support to consumers such as the elderly who have fallen prey to dishonest sales personnel and organizations. In addition, persons who are elderly and are unable to manage their own affairs, should grant a Letter of Administration or Power of Attorney to a relative or someone else who they can trust to conduct and manage their financial affairs. This may include activities such as withdrawing money from the bank, the sale or purchase of property and the management of credit cards. It would really be devastating if the trustee is also fleecing the elderly of their hard earned cash.

Social Security laws in most countries require that the employer contributes a given amount of money to that of the employee's which is saved in a special account each month for the employee. Therefore, at the end of one's working life one receives one's personal contribution, that of the organization/s as well as the interest which has accrued on the pension. Some organizations allow employees to invest a part of their pension in approved investment schemes. This practice has proven to be very disastrous to thousands of employees who invested in the Savings and Loans Scheme in the US which was eventually declared bankrupt. The result was that these employees were faced with the unfortunate realization that their nest egg which they were accumulating for their retirement was gone, and there was nothing anyone could do to recover it.

Other organizations give their employees the option of utilizing a percentage of their pension for personal use or to invest in some authorized scheme such as for a down payment on a home. This is usually granted at a lower interest rate than a commercial loan. The employee is expected to repay the loan over a short period, usually below five years. Failure to do so will usually result in a penalty of the commercial rate being demanded on the outstanding balance.

It is not safe for an elderly person or even couple to live alone since they may suffer debilitating illnesses such as a stroke or heart attack when there is no one around to assist them. There are also instances where they suffer from heat stroke during the summer, and freeze to death during the winter in temperate countries, since their homes do not have adequate air conditioning and heating systems, respectively, or they may not be conversant on how to regulate these gadgets. The elderly are also often the target of robbers who may pose as utility personnel or other officials and enter into the home of the elderly or simply breach the security measures at the homes of the elderly. The elderly may receive assistance from their children, members of their church and other persons to assist in protecting them from unwanted intruders. In addition, the judicial system should deal harshly with persons who violate the privacy of the elderly, most of whom have made valuable contributions to the society in which they live.

> Many persons resolve to 'straighten' their financial and other affairs, but sadly, this is not done even when they have been 'straightened out' by the cold arms of death. Please start today!

The **registration of a will** is an issue which most persons are apprehensive about doing since it somehow connotes a sense of finality to our lives. However, since death can occur at any stage of our lives, it is prudent for anyone with valuable assets which they are desirous of passing on to someone specific to make a will at an early stage of their lives. The failure to write a will could have serious consequences including:

(a) The valuable asset which one was desirous of giving to someone who is dear to one's heart is coveted by someone else to whom one would not have considered giving the item/s to,

(b) The dependants of the deceased may have to secure the services of an attorney to make representation to the court for the assets of the deceased to be given to them,

(c) The state may value the assets of the deceased at their current market value, and the relatives of the deceased have to pay the allocated taxes before they can take possession of them,

(d) The state may appoint an executor who supervises the disposal of the assets of the deceased. The relatives of the deceased may have to obtain approval before they can take possession of, or disposal of the assets.

Some common problems which are associated with wills include:

(a) The will was not authenticated by a Notary Public, attorney or some other officer who is authorized by the judiciary of the country. This feature is important since there would have to be at least one other person whose testimony the court would accept as impartial and true and who would be in a position to authenticate that the decrees of the will were truly those of the deceased.

(b) The court normally accepts the final testimony before the person dies as over-ruling any other which may have been made before. However, account is normally taken of the condition under which the will was prepared. In instances where persons are contesting the final will, evidence may be presented to prove that the person may have been forced or tricked to affix their signature to a blank document and the contents filled in thereafter. Another accusation may be that the deceased may have been senile shortly before their death.

(c) There are incidents where an impostor along with a legal luminary forges a will, in some instances to prevent the estate of the deceased from being declared intestate. (That is, where a person dies without making a will for their estate and the state takes possession of the estate until the matter is amicably resolved). Of course if such fraudulent transactions are discovered both perpetuators will be sternly dealt with by the court.

(d) The decree of a will could be contested by persons who are of the opinion that they are entitled to a given section of the estate of the deceased. A common occurrence in this regard occurs when a man has separated from his wife and cohabited with another woman for a number of years. If he leaves all or most of his assets for his 'common-law wife,' his legally married wife may contest the will and claim her share of his assets which were accumulated during the period when they were living together. Additional amount of money, for example, may also be claimed as amounts to support any minor children and also in lieu of unpaid support for her children and herself.

Despite the apparent difficulties, it is prudent for owners of valuable assets to have a written will which can be updated as one feels it necessary to do so. There are instances when a person is killed by the person to whom they leave a substantial amount of their assets. In the same way, there are examples where a person is killed by another because he/she was omitted from the will or a substantial amount of the assets was not left to the killer. Once it is ascertained by the state that a person was killed and the accused is found guilty of the murder, even if the name of the killer was on the will, the state may confiscate the assets or distribute it to other members of the family.

It is usually a difficult task for parents to decide how to **allocate their assets among their children and/or other persons and organization in their will** or when they decide to give them as a present on occasions such as when a loved one is being married. Some of the factors which are taken into consideration are what criteria will be used to allocate assets to various persons and/or institutions. When bequeathing a part of their assets to children, the considerations which some parents use are:

(a) **The ability of the recipient to use the item in a manner which the giver would be proud of,**

(b) **The degree of love and affection which the child showed**, therefore, the gift is an extension of the love which the parents have for the child,

(c) **As a surety in the event that they need care and attention before they die;** would leave major assets such as their home to the child who they feel is more caring and attentive to them in the event they need special care before death,

> Failure to leave a will for the allocation of major assets to our loved ones is tantamount to giving the state the authority to allocate it to whoever they chose, very often at a great tax disadvantage to the estate of the deceased. The state may also appoint an administrator over the distribution of the assets, very often in a manner which is to the disadvantage of the family of the deceased.

No well meaning parent would be proud that they give their offspring assets before they die and they live to see that asset destroyed, squandered or sold for less than its market value, even though the spirit of giving is to release the item for the recipient to do with it what he/she wants. In attempt to safeguard this eventuality; some persons prescribe how the item is to be used. However, this is very often done in the wrong spirit since the giver has not fully released the item but still want to control how it is used. The more generous parent may even leave the family home to a child or children, purchase a smaller one or decide to live in a nursing home. Whatever the method used, it is important that there is goodwill between parents and children before the parents depart the world.

Some parents would leave the home for a son and possible a plot of land for a daughter. The rationale may be that they feel that the girl will/should marry an industrious husband who should be in a position to build or purchase his own home. These issues are often dependent on the social fabric of the society.

PENSION PLANS

There are several pension plans which a person can adopt to make a positive impact on their retirement. It is always advantageous if many of these programs commence early in the working life of a person so that the greatest benefits can be derived. There is, for example, several retirement programs in many countries where the government offers special guarantees that their contributions will be payable to them irrespective of the financial situation of the country. This commitment is usually honored upon the retirement of the person. Many of these programs offer participants special tax incentives if they are disciplined enough to leave their savings until retirement. The government would be able to invest the money which is deposited in this fund in long term investment since it is anticipated that a large percentage of the population would attain the retirement age and the average payment per month can be computed and made payable to the retirees.

The USA has several bonds and other investment programs which self-employed persons and even employees can choose to participate in. A popular one is the **Serial I Bond** (the, **I**, is an abbreviation for inflation). Government Bond currently pays interest of 5.92% per annum, which is tax deferred, in that the income which is contributed to this bond is not taxed from the inception, however, the payment on maturity is subject to taxation.

The US Treasury declares a fixed interest rate and adds an adjustment every six months to protect the savings against inflation. The current interest rate is 3% and 2.92% is added because that is the level of inflation currently. This adjustment guarantees that the real rate of return on the investment, as far as is possible, is not adversely affected by inflation. This is very attractive to many small and large investors. These bonds can be purchased from commercial banks and on the web from as little as fifty US dollars.

A popular retirement saving program in Barbados is the **Registered Retirement Savings Plan** (RRSP). Persons who earn a consistently good salary and who are disciplined enough can benefit tremendously from such a plan. It offers tax savings as well as a challenge to inculcate a saving program which will generate high dividends after retirement. Because of the high income tax regime in the country, 15% of a person's assessable income or Bds. $4,000.00, whichever is smaller.

A person who is desirous of saving Bds. $333.00 from one's income would in fact be losing money from saving, even in a high interest bearing account, as against saving on the RRSP. If that person were to participate in the RRSP one could contribute Bds. $333.00 per month from one's gross income (before tax) directly to this scheme. In 33 years of consistent saving under this program, assuming a fixed rate of interest of 10%, the contributor would have accumulated Bds. $1 million (approximately US $500,000). This is a highly hypothetical scenario, since it assumes that interest rates will remain constant at 10% over the thirty two years of the chart. In fact the savings interest rate for Barbados in 2005 is currently under 3% per annum.

There are several **Retirement Plan Options** which some companies offer their retiring employees. Two of these options are:

    (a)   **A lump sum** - where the company pays the retired employee the entire pension at one time and he is allowed to spend it as he pleases. Persons who take this option would have the responsibility and challenge of spending, saving and investing that amount in such a way that it would last them for the remainder of their lives and for them to achieve the financial benefits which they desire. This is a tremendous challenge particularly for persons who are accustomed to living a lifestyle which is commensurate with their salary. For many persons this amount only last a few years and they may have to resort to some form of employment such as a security guard to cater for the financial needs of the family.

(b) **Annuity** - this is where the retiree is paid a fixed amount per year over a given number of years. The **one-life annuity** will only pay the former employee a fixed amount until he dies, while the **two-life annuity** will pay the same amount to the spouse of the former employee in the event that he/she dies before his wife/husband. Many persons choose the latter option since it provides financial security for both spouses. However, the amount provided per year is usually less than if the retiree were to take the lump sum and place it on a fixed deposit.

CARING FOR THE ELDERLY

As we become elderly the cost of administrating medical attention usually increases. This occurs since the ability of the body to repair damaged tissues and recover from injury decreases. In addition, years of abuse of our bodies will take their toll as the immune system loses its effectiveness to successfully combat diseases. Unfortunately, a large majority of elderly persons are unable to pay for private medical attention which they need, thus, they have to rely on the free medical services provided by the government and in some countries by charitable organizations.

There are several non-governmental organizations (NGOs) that attempt to provide a high standard of medical and other services to communities when the government does not have the money and other facilities to do so or they may decide not to invest in that area. However, the services of these organizations are handicapped because of their limited financial and other resources. Many of them are also unable to attract a large number of high calibre medical and other staff to provide required services on low wages.

The medical care and other services offered by the government of most countries are far lower than that of private agencies. Services provided by the Medicare Service of the US, for example, is fraught with criticism that a large percentage of the medical staff deliberately reduce the quality of the services they provide since they are restricted on the quality, and more importantly, the cost of service which they are authorized to provide.

The elderly need special care and attention. This was highlighted centuries ago by the great author William Shakespeare when he coined the famous slogan **'once a man and twice a child.'** As a person becomes feeble and incapacitated, it is necessary that special care be provided. Consequently, many relatives of the elderly find it difficult to cope with them at home even though it is their desire to offer much love and support to their elderly relatives. The solution to this dilemma is often that loved ones may be forced to place their elderly relatives in a home for the elderly where they have specialist care and attention on a continuous basis. This is often a very painful decision for a son or daughter to make. The option of securing a live-in maid to specially care for their elderly parents may have proven to be inadequate.

Apart from the specialist care and attention which the elderly need, they usually find it difficult to relate comfortably on a continual basis even with their children and grandchildren. Very often they crave the company of persons of their own age group where they can relive some of the experiences and memories which have been dear to them. Depending on the age, physical and mental health of the elderly, relatives usually pursue options such as the following:

(a) A relative or family friend would care for the elderly at the home of the elderly or an offspring of the elderly or other relatives may take the elderly into their home,

(b) In affluent societies, the state may provide special caregivers to care for the elderly. This may include administrating medication, bathing, cooking for or providing free meals and other services for the elderly. In some instances special stairs may be constructed to accommodate the wheelchair of the elderly.

(c) Some persons choose the option of the elderly attending a day-nursing facility or community centre where the elderly spend the day interacting with their peers and also learning new skills and keeping active. They may also be providing specialist care such as the physiotherapist, and other medical personnel and enjoy sporting and other events.

(d) In some instances it is necessary that an elderly person is confined to a permanent nursing home, or in extreme cases, they may be hospitalized for an extended period, possibly until they die.

Many elderly are destitute at the end of their lives because of situations which were beyond their control. Many of them were prudent financial planners and were careful to set aside a sizable amount of money for themselves during their elderly years. However, there are several reasons for the failure of financial plan. They include:

(a) Relatives and even strangers may rob them of a sizable part of their savings,
(b) The high cost of medical facilities may have demanded that they spend a significant amount of their savings on personal medical expenses or that of a dependent,
(c) The effect of inflation and other economic factors significantly reduced the value of their savings,
(d) Natural and other disasters such as a fire and theft would rob them of hard earned assets in a matter of hours,

Some of the special costs which are associated with the elderly are:

(a) The cost of medication and other medical facilities,
(b) The cost of providing specialist care and attention such as the payment for a room in a private nursing home or attending to the elderly relative in a nursing home,
(c) The cost of burial and other associated expenses,

We should never despise the elderly, for among other factors, one day we too may be elderly and may be treated accordingly. There is so much we can learn from them if we would but take the time to listen to their life stories, their successes and failures and other interesting aspects of their lives. God has a special place in His heart for the elderly and we will be blessed if we inculcate this nurture and care for the elderly in our community and beyond also. Of course, there are many financial commitments which they have to bear themselves, and/or by relatives and in many countries, the state. However, our attitude in managing such situations is often a good testimony to others since it is a demonstration of us giving back to these dear ones who invested so much of their lives for us to be in the position in life where we are.

The Bible made mention of the ages of several person. Methuselah, for example, lived for nine hundred and sixty five years. **During the early period of the Bible, men generally outlived women, of course with the exception of men dying from unnatural causes such as death during a war, and of course the occasional persons being struck down by God. This trend has been reversed in modern day, where in most societies, women generally live longer than men**. Among the implications of this reality is the fact that many women are left to manage the affairs of the family.

Even though we may not have a choice as to when we die, in many instances we can prolong the quality of our lives by having a close walk with the Lord, a loving relationship with members of our family and other persons we come into close contact, good health practices and by practicing prudent financial management principles. There are several reasons which would have contributed to this reverse trend.

(a) Men are often so busy attempting to earn more money that they neglect important health rules such as drinking in excess of eight glasses of water each day, getting at least six hours of sleep each day, managing stressful situations so that one does not become a chronic worrier. They are often reluctant to observe simple health rules such as eating a healthy diet, taking an adequate amount of rest, using vitamin and mineral supplement, undergoing a regular exercise program.

(b) Men are often reluctant to undergo regular medical checkups, seek medical advice on what they may consider to be trivial ailments and even purchase and use the medication which may be prescribed to them.

(c) Men are often addicted to unhealthy lifestyles such as using excessive amounts of alcohol, fried foods, foods high in carbohydrates and other unhealthy practices,

(d) For a large percentage of men, work is their life and they measure their success in life based on their success at work. Hence, after retirement, life seems to lose its meaning and they simply wither away mentally, physically and spiritually and die.

(e) Medical problems such as colon, prostate and other forms of cancers kill a large percentage of men,

(f) The promiscuous lifestyle of a large percentage of men renders them susceptible to AIDS and other sexually transmitted diseases (STDs) which result in the death of millions of men each year,

(g) Men are more likely to go to war and/or engage in hazardous jobs such as coal mining, prospecting for minerals and deep sea fishing and be killed or seriously injured than women,

Christians of both genders must learn what it is to rest in the Lord, while they observe other healthy practices. Resting in the Lord entails among other attributes, being in the right place at the right time and doing God's will for one's life. It also encompasses trusting in the Lord, knowing that we have done our utmost and allow Him to take care of the rest. Among healthy lifestyle practices are eating a balance diet, having adequate amount of rest each day, engaging in organized exercise programs and/or being involved in active sports and consistently maintaining a healthy peace of mind.

Many ministries have a special arm which looks after the welfare of the destitute in their congregation and further afield. Funds are allocated to the needy from tithes and offering collected, from fund raising activities, soliciting the contribution of members in the form of cash and/or kind and in some instances from donation made by national and international agencies. The mandate of this ministry may be extended to include offering scholarship and providing other forms of financial support to children from destitute families. Individual members of the congregations may also be encouraged to adopt a family or individual and be committed to make regular or periodic contribution to their upkeep.

Many persons who are experiencing financial difficulties do not accept financial and other assistance which are offered by other persons. They may be ashamed that they will be mocked, and even exploited by uncaring and unregenerate persons who are in the congregation. Women who have been divorced, for example, may fear accepting what may be genuine kindness from males since they are afraid that this may be an overture for sexual and other forms of compensation. For this reason the organizers of such programs have to be very discreet in relating to such persons.

> The Christians community would be failing one of their most solemn responsibilities when the poorer members of the congregation have to depend solely on welfare and other forms of governmental support. The Body of Christ has the responsibility to care for the poor widows and widowers, orphans, abused and other destitute members of the congregation and the wider community.

RIGHT ENDING ATTITUDES

Many Christians emulate the attitude of the 'Rich Fool' (Luke 12) who among other things sought to build bigger barns to accommodate his bountiful harvest without giving thanks to the Lord for enabling him to achieve success or to give some of his increase to the poor. There are many factors which cause a large percentage of elderly persons to spend the latter part of their lives in a state of perpetual poverty and much unhappiness. These include:

(a) **Many persons were not diligent enough to save and invest wisely,** hence; they do not have enough personal resource to supplement whatever pension and other support they may be receiving from the government or their gratuity,

(b) **Severe sickness and other disasters which affect them,**

(c) **Neglect by children and relatives,** who they might have spent much of their money to educate and care for but who did not feel it was their responsibility to care for their elderly relative,

(d) **Poor economic conditions of the economy,**

After living a life of righteousness, many Christians leave this world without fulfilling their final responsibilities of being good stewards. Factors such as the following are prudent financial management strategies which will assist us to make a good end to our stewardship of God's resources which He entrusted to us to manage:

(a) **It is important that we make a will,** detailing how we want our assets to be distributed at least after we die. It is always better when we have enough so that we can distribute it to our loved ones, the needy and to other areas of the work of the Lord. When we distribute our resources before we die, we will be afforded the opportunity of seeing the joy expressed in the lives of persons who benefit from the blessing. Hopefully, givers would not discriminate to the extent where there will be much strife in the family. Some persons make their final will on their death bed and it is honoured by the court.

(b) There are many examples, however, where persons contest the fact that the deceased may have been senile, or may have been coerced into leaving assets for a particular person. It is noted that it is enshrined in the statutes of the laws of many countries that the court will not allocate any part of a will to the person who signs as a witness to the preparation of the will. A **holographic will** can be written on an ordinary piece of paper, dated and signed by the person making the will. In order to execute this, it is often necessary to probate the will, which may involve the sanctioning of a judge to verify the authenticity of the document.

(c) **Leave a part of his heritance for the spreading of the work of the Lord.** This is a prudent way for a Christian to end his days on earth knowing that he has treasures untold stored up in Eternity.

(d) **A person should not go on a spending spree and live a lavish lifestyle merely to spend it all.** Some elderly persons are of the opinion that since they earned it, they should use all of it for their benefit since if it is left for others they will not cherish the importance of achieving goals independent of the support of others. Even though this often occurs, some assets can be left in a trust managed by competent persons and in a worthy charity of one's choice.

(e) **Have enough put aside to cater for funeral, the settling of your estate and other expenses to ease the financial burden on relatives after you die**,

(f) **Similarly, parents should not use their finances and other resources to fuel division among their children.** This may be done in the form of leaving a part of their inheritance to a married child and debarring the spouse from partaking in it, particularly if there are no scriptural reasons for this practice. There are other circumstances where, for example, a person is not prudent at managing their finance, or is too young; it may be wise to **leave it in trust** where the spending is supervised by a competent person or authority.

CONCLUSION

The Bible proclaims the virtues of old age and praises the wisdom, understanding and other positive attributes which are usually associated with the elderly. The fact that they may have gone through the exact or similar experiences often places them in the position where they are better able to give advice than the younger person who has not been very experienced. This is not always the case, since there are many elderly persons who have not made good use of their youthful days and may only be putting on an 'air of wisdom' which they assume will automatically occur as they become older. (Conversely, there are some younger persons who are experienced well beyond their age). One area which this trait is displayed, is in the state of the financial affairs of millions of elderly persons. The sad thing is that financial security for the elderly is not often a tangible reflection of how prudent one was in managing one's material and other resources. For even if one was as miserly as the legendary Mr. Scrooge, factors such as expensive medical bills, wars, inflation, political, social and other external factors can destabilize the financial security which a person may have worked consciously to achieve.

We must make the Lord the center of our lives and allow Him to direct our paths. The path which He chooses to take us through to the 'greener pastures' may not always be smooth and trouble free. In order to bring out the gem in us, we usually have to go through the fire, water and other purification processes which will help to fashion us into the gems which are fit for use by the Master's hands.

There is no guarantee that every Christian will be materially rich at the end of their lives. There is evidence of this in the life of the Old Testament Prophet who died and his children were almost sold into slavery to repay his debt. There are also New Testament examples where the Apostle Paul, chose to forsake material wealth in favor of a ministry which transformed the lives of millions of persons. Yes, the Lord is well able to supply our every need, but what happens if we have to suffer for Him as a martyr or if He recognizes that supplying us with material wealth will lead to our eternal damnation?

Our preference should always be avoid placing priority on the temporal material wealth of this world in favor of the eternal wealth experienced from serving Jehovah in this world and for eternity. For those of us who achieve material prominence, we must be in the state like the early church after Pentecost, who were overjoyed to share the assets with the poor, help other believers and to assist in financing the spreading the gospel. Yes, we are obligated to provide the best we can materially and otherwise for our family, but we also have a responsibility to play an integral role in spreading the gospel in our homes, neighborhood and to the world.

NOTES

****

Chapter 6 ENJOYING MORETHAN ENOUGH

INTRODUCTION

Malachi 3:10 states: *"¹⁰Bring the full tithe into the storehouse, so that there may be food in my storehouse, and thus put me to the test, says the Lord of Host, see if I will not open the window of heaven for you and pour for you an overflowing blessing."* The overflowing blessings referred to here are not restricted to material things and many of them cannot be measured accurately in financial terms. They include protection from sicknesses and accidents, peace of mind, harmony in our home, our children growing up in the fear of the Lord and fulfilling their career and other Godly objectives.

Since we are focusing primarily on financial issues, the following section concentrates on highlighting some of the factors which have to be taken into account to enable us to achieve financial success. It is important to note that we do not tithe and give offering in order to satisfy some need of Jehovah to cause us to suffer deprivation. Once we adopt the correct attitude in giving, it places us in the position where we will be able to derive the benefits of giving. Our tithes and offerings are to be used for the furtherance of the work of the Lord which includes the upkeep and expansion of the local church, assisting the needy and to spread the gospel. It is also used by some churches to assist in the financing of entrepreneurial projects by members and the wider community.

We have reviewed in previous chapters that it is the will of Jehovah for His children to live happy and fulfilling lives. This does not mean that every Christian will experience, or should pursue a life of luxury. The Apostle Paul, for example, turned his back on a life of affluence to suffer for his faith. Yet, at the end of his life he was satisfied with his achievements in that his heavenly treasures far outweighed the earthly riches which he could have earned while he was on earth.

Our best example of a person who maintained a healthy balance between the material and spiritual is in the life of Jesus who gave up His glory in heaven to suffer and die for our sins. The story surely does not end there, for even though Jesus lived a materially humble life, His ministry was supported by wealthy believers. Jesus also taught us the importance of maximizing the talents which God has vested in us. Even though all of us have not received 'five talents' we are still expected to maximize what we have.

> **Financial success for a Christian entails being in the correct place where God wants him to be, and having enough money and other resources to achieve the things which Jehovah has ordained for him to complete. It also entails having enough for himself and/or family and relatives and to be able to give to bless the lives of others.**

There is no one formula which can unilaterally be applied by every person, family and/or corporate entity which would provide them the level of financial success which they desire. We all have different personalities, temperaments, spiritual and other callings on our lives. There are, however, several Biblical principles which we can apply which would guarantee the desired effect, providing we adhere to the conditions which must be met and maintained. For this reason what may constitute success for one person may be deemed as failure in another. Similarly, while one path may result in financial success in one person it may result in failure by another. The financial goals and the path to achieve these objectives differ among persons and institutions.

What may be constituted as financial success is usually dependent on factors such as the goals which the principals establish and the scope of the activity. That is, do they have the capacity, ability and other attributes to continually strive to attain their goal of financial success and increase, or at least strive to maintain that level of success throughout the life or the existence of the institution? It is not possible that every person on earth will be a millionaire and live a life of luxury. Jesus confirmed that there will be poor among us always. Recognizing this, it is important for each of us to attempt to maximize the returns which are at our disposal.

For one person the Biblical concept of having 'more than enough' entails being able to build a mud hut, have a number of cows which can provide enough milk which can be sold and provide enough money for the family to live on. For another person it is being able to earn enough money to build a comfortable house and have it furnished modestly and be able to finance the education of all of the children, earn enough money to meet daily expenses and have enough saved to meet their financial needs when they retire. For another person it entails living in a mansion, having several villas in different countries, having a private jet and other luxuries. What is yours?

Many persons fail to achieve their desired level of financial success since they fail to recognize that they may be trying to achieve a level which may not be consistent with the will of the Lord for their life. This statement is made with reference to Jesus' parable in Matthew 25:14-30. **It should be noted that the master allocated the talents most likely in accordance with his** *perception of the ability of the respective servants. In the same way the Lord expects us to maximize the returns on the assets which He has placed at our disposal and to successfully accomplish the tasks which He has given us the ability to achieve.*

The servants who were given five and two talents and who generated 100% return were commended by the master. The servant who hid his talent and accused the master of impropriety was punished and his talent was given to the servant who was given five talents. We must recognize the level of return which the Lord expects to generate. In this example, every Christian is expected to operate either at the level of the servant who was given five or two talents. Deviations from this principle lead to much frustration.

A person who has the ability to operate at the five-talent level and fails to do so would suffer much frustration over the fact that he/she has underachieved. If the Lord has ordained that a person operates at the level of the two-talent servant and one strive to be a five talent achiever, it may also lead to much frustration since one may achieve financial success at the expense of other important areas of one's life.

We often find persons who earn a high salary and attain a high level of formal education, yet they are unable to amass as much wealth over their life time as a person who may not have acquired much formal education and who started a business venture with a smaller amount of capital, yet was able to acquire much material wealth. This is an illustration that it is not only the assets which we have at our disposal but more importantly how we use them and the amount of money we are able to save and invest prudently and consistently over an extended period. There are several other factors which determine the level of financial success which a person acquires. These include:

- (a) The empowerment to prosper, of the Lord on the life of a person. It should be noted that a blessing is determined by character, faith and knowledge rather than some prejudice which the Lord decrees. Some of the characters which attribute specific types of blessings are highlighted in the 'Beatitudes' which links various character traits to specific types of blessings.
- (b) A passion to achieve success,
- (c) The willingness to learn and apply the principles learnt to generate the required level of returns,
- (d) The ability to harness and utilize effectively and efficiently the resources necessary to achieve the desired level of financial success,
- (e) The ability to work with others and/or have others work for you to generate the level of financial success required.

For many persons, the journey from where we are to where God wants us to be is quite a distance. Similar to the persons who accomplished great exploits in the Bible, it often entails an almost total transformation of who we perceive ourselves to be, to what God has already invested in us, to enable us to received 'more than enough.' Many Christians will never be able to say at the end of their lives that they have truly enjoyed the abundance of material blessings which the Lord has promised the righteous since they have not correctly applied the Biblical principles of managing finances as directed in the Word.

It is important to identify what can be classified as being in a state of enjoying 'more than enough.' Most persons at the lower end of the income scale whose primary source of income is from a **salary will not enjoy a very high standard of living unless they have mastered**

the art of managing their net income. Most persons in this category are primarily living from pay check to pay check, living on credit and are trying to 'keep their head above the water' or living above their means. Their home may be poorly built and/or heavily mortgaged and their lifestyle may also be one of impoverishment or a little above the poverty level. Many such persons may engage in some other form of income generating activity in an attempt to service. Many Christians in this category do not enjoy the state of abundance of financial status, even though they may be quite happy and live a content life.

It is usually more financially rewarding when a person seeks to generate passive income (additional income along with one's main stream income) from investing on the stock exchange, investing in real estate, selling produce from one's garden and/or other business ventures. It is true that inflation and other external factors can render the investment unprofitable, but it is at lease more secure than going to work one day only to be fired because one's services is replaced by a younger and more energetic employee, or one's pension is mismanaged by a crocked pension plan manager, as is so common today.

The financial status of the majority of persons can be classified into one or more of the following segments:

(a) **The unemployed/poverty stricken;** classified as persons who survive on handouts from relatives, friends, the church, government, NGOs and/or other support groups in order to survive. Many persons use such support as a stepping-stone to assist them to emerge from this state, while others live and die as paupers.

(b) **The salaried earner;** persons who survive primarily on the salary which they earn from working for someone else or a corporate, government or other agencies. Such persons, particularly those at the lower end of the salary range, engage in meagre amounts of savings and investment.

(c) **Self Employed;** persons who earn an income from utilizing skills which they have acquired and/or by using the skills and assets to generate their income. Persons who are self-employed usually have better command over their income than a person who is a mere employee, even though they may not have the cushion of a contributory pension from an employer and other fringe benefits. Among the advantages of this category of income earners over the salaried earner are:

(i) They often have excess cash flow which they can save and invest. This often leads to the position where they expand by hiring additional employees and/or invest in real estate, stocks and other areas.

(ii) Persons in this category have the advantage of maximizing their returns and the benefits of their input accruing directly to them.

(iii) Very often such persons maintain customer loyalty because of the high quantity of service which they provide to their customers.

Among the primary disadvantages of this category are:

(a) If there are major problems in their operations, they will also directly suffer from the negative effect of low income or their service may become obsolete,

(b) Their operations may be closed or at least their income stream may cease when they are ill or go on a vacation,

(c) It is often difficult for such persons to expand since finding another person to provide the same or higher quantity of service may be difficult and expensive. Even when an apprentice is hired, he may be there primarily to master the skill then to start his own business. This feature is common in professions such as mechanical engineering, joinery, carpentry and other skilled labour techniques. In many instances the self-employed persons have to revert to seeking employment if their business fails.

Entrepreneurs are persons who own one or several business entities from which their primary source of income is derived.

> Contrary to the gambler who puts his money on a game of chance where he cannot determine whether or not he will win, an investor injects capital in the form of money, time and other assets in mastering an activity where his skill in making prudent business decisions determines the level of his success.

Investors are classified as persons who invest personal and/or corporate assets independently or with the assistance of professionals in a particular area of expertise and generate returns from their investment. Investors include persons who undertake trading in stocks and shares, property developers, money lenders, and investors in government securities such as debentures and treasury bills. They also include the 'mega-rich' who may have even inherited assets which are generating returns which is sufficient for them and their family to live on and to keep expanding their investment.

This list is not exhausted, since there are many persons who do not fit any of these categories exactly but may be operating in one or more of them. There are also the mega-rich persons, who have received a very large inheritance, who won a lottery or receive a large payment from a law suit, who may have so much money at their disposal that they may not even have to invest it but they have enough money to live on the principal amount, or even the interest for the remainder of their lives and a substantial amount will also be left for their inheritors.

One of the primary secrets of achieving financial success is investing in one, of a small number of business opportunities and/or financial instruments which consistently generate lucrative returns. This is usually not a story of overnight success, but as we are instructed in the Bible, we have to diligently nurture the resources which God has placed at our disposal so that His blessings will overshadow them.

Each sphere of financial state, as highlighted in Diagram 6.1, has unique characteristics and **it is often difficult to move from one category to another unless one is prepared to effect major changes in one's lifestyle (unless of course a miracle occurs, and even so, unless one maintains or retains the conditions which would enable us to 'keep the miracle,' even that can be lost)**. For most persons the change is gradual, as they increase their investments and make use of other opportunities and are able to realize more and more positive returns.

Two popular maxims states that:
- *"Success comes when preparation (working smartly) meets opportunity."*
- *"Winners see an opportunity in every risk, while losers see risks in every opportunity."*

Most persons fall into the category of being an income earner. They include many farm workers, domestic and factory workers, civil servants and member of the arm forces.

Salaried earners are persons who are employed by another person or institution and are paid for the level of service provided as governed by the policy of the employer. They range from non-skilled, semi-skilled to skilled persons. This category is generally classified as the poorest of the self-employed entrepreneurs and investors since a high level of performance is demanded for as little pay as the employee can afford, or is forced by government and other statutory bodies to pay. There are many persons at the top end of the salary scale such as Chief Executive Officers for some companies and other professions who earn very large wages and are able to live a very affluent lifestyle.

Some of the common traits of persons at the higher end of the bracket of income earner are that they acquire a 'good' academic education, technical and other skills and secured a job which they feel comfortable with, marry, purchase a home, acquire some means of transportation and save for old age. However, along the way they are acquiring more and more debt to the point where unless they work harder they will lose much of what they had acquired.

All of us are not born to be entrepreneurs and expert financial investors, nor are we all able, or prepared to acquire the necessary skills, financial and other resources which would enable us to become mega rich. It is thus important for us to identify where we are, what we are desirous of achieving and what we have to do to get there. Even though we are all leaders in some area of our lives, not all of us have the necessary ability to manage people and financial and other assets which would lead to much wealth. Therefore, most of us are satisfied to work for others, earn a pension, where possible, retire and hope that there is enough pension and other resources to enable us to have a relatively comfortable old age. This is not a reality for most persons, since old age for a large number of persons is plagued with serious sickness resulting in huge medical bills, and other disasters which cause many them to have to depend on governmental and other support systems.

> *Many persons become materially rich not by working hard physically, but by strategizing and pursuing a highly successful business venture, acquiring the franchise of one or several lines of business and/or product, and/or by investing wisely in one or small number of financial instruments.*

Similar to Jacob in Laban's household (Genesis 30:27), the blessings of the Lord accrues directly to you. They include persons who choose to, or who are unable to, secure income in any other way. It is important that persons who are able to do so prudently, should create an income stream whereby the blessings of the Lord come directly to them. These include:

(a) **Professionals** who use their skills to earn money independently, under a business name or as a company. This category of employers has the advantage of managing their time and resources and they derive the level of returns as they inject into it and demand for their services and/or product increases. This category includes medical doctors, lawyers, dentists, taxi drivers, mechanical engineers, various categories of consultants, and farmers who choose to work independently. Even though the blessing comes directly to them, their income stream is dependent primarily on their ability. Therefore, even though their level of independence is usually greater than the self-employed, they may still be restricted in their scope of operations.

(b) **The entrepreneur,** owns his own business and employs the service of others to work with and/or for him. The advantage of this category of persons is that the returns which they derive are not only dependant on their own level of output but also on that of others and on the returns from the capital invested. There are generally three types of businesses:

 (i) **The traditional business** where one or several persons and/or agencies pool their resources to form and manage a business venture,

 (ii) **A person or company purchases the franchise of a business** operation and operates within the framework of the system established by the franchise owner. (A franchise is the system whereby the owner of a patent (or at least a business model) allows another person or organization to duplicate the product, production process or system which was invented, designed or created by the owner),

 (iii) **A network operation** where one or several products are supplied by the controlling body. In this system the business owner secures a profit from the sale of the product and also a commission for the sale made by others whom he recruited to market the products of the organization.

(iv) ***The entrepreneur enjoys the privilege where he may not necessarily be working with the institution, yet he enjoys the profit and other benefits from the business,***

(v) ***The ownership, management and the assets of the company can be passed down from one generation to another,***

(b) ***The Investor***; utilizes his personal and/or corporate resources to generate additional returns. He does not necessarily have to work for the institution but his investments generate revenue for him. This is the category where most rich persons, successful businesses and other entities are operating in. The responsibility of the investor is to ensure that he has enough personal and/or corporate finance or access to it, effect the investment and enjoy the net income from his investment. The investments can be from areas such as real estate, natural resources and financial instruments. Most successful investors tend to derive more than 70% of their income from their investments and even if they are salaried earners it is usually from managing their own businesses.

Most persons do not just awake one day and become successful investors. The transaction is usually from a high earning salaried employee, a self employed or business owner who accumulates much positive cash flow over a number of years. Most investors start from a small beginning and expand their investment as they become proficient in one or several areas of investment.

(c) Successful investors usually have a large amount of capital to invest and competent financial advisors who assist them to channel their investment into one or a small number of investment opportunities which generate high returns. Eventually, they should be able to master the art of making prudent investment decisions independently. Contrary to the gambler who invests his money in a game of chance, an investor invests his money, time and other assets in mastering an activity where his skill in making prudent business decisions determines the level of his success.

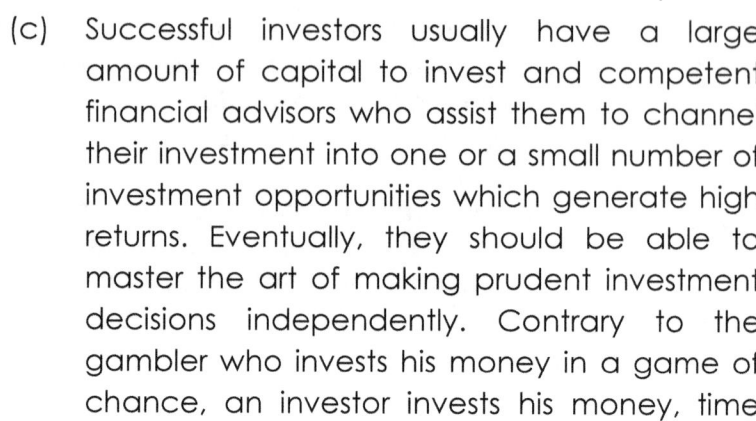

Becoming a successful investor usually require more than merely managing money. One must develop the knack to differentiate between a good investment from one which is merely appealing to the eye, emotion or where a good sales person or even financial advisor is not telling the whole truth. Even though having formal training in financial management and other academic disciplines usually aid the process, this awareness usually comes after undergoing a number of failed or not so successful investment deals. Even so, wordy experience is not superior to diligently following Biblical financial management and other principles.

The four aspects of the investment system can be summarized as follows:
   (a) **Salaried earners** work for the system,
   (b) **The self employed** creates parts of the system,
   (c) **Entrepreneur** manages and may even own a part of the system,
   (d) **Investors** invest capital into creating parts of the system without necessarily working in the system,

One of the primary reasons why many Christians remain poor all of the days of their lives is because of the fear of losing money if they invest. This fear often begins when parents inject negative thought in their children. Many parents and other adults are poor role models for others to follow since they are poor financial managers of personal finances and other resources. Some of these negative thoughts may include:

(a) **They emphasize on the importance of their children obtaining a 'good education' in order to find a secure job with benefits such as a sizable pension plan, medical insurance and other 'comforts.'** Unless a person can be at the top of the employment level and is paid a large salary and receive other lucrative fringe benefits, one is likely to be poor or at the most, at the middle income level of society.

(b) **They do not set good investment examples for their children to follow since they are burdened with debt,**

(c) **Children see so many persons fail in business ventures that they are afraid to get involved in business and investment,**

(d) **We feel that it is too risky to invest and one or both spouses may not support the idea that they can do more than merely earn a salary,**

(e) **The failure to identify an area in which one is comfortable to invest.** It is true that there are not many high return investment opportunities available to small investors in many societies. Even so, if a number of small investors are able to pool their resources they can benefit from the returns on their investment.

(f) **They rigidly hold on to investment funds which are earmarked for the education of the children and/or other long term plans, instead of investing and generating higher returns in the near future to meet these and other financial demands,**

(g) **We are not educated in the management of investment and feel insecure to trust even professionals in these areas to guide us along these paths,**

(h) **The fear of failure in this vital area, which can dramatically transform the life and that of members of the family and larger community.** It is sad that many of us take serious risks which cause disaster, rather than to invest in a business venture which has a higher probability of generating substantial returns thereafter, adding quality to our standard of living. One of the most common mistakes is to secure large amounts of credit primarily for consumer items when we have little control of what may happen to us in the future. Very often we allow our emotions to take us deeper into debt rather than invest in a viable business which may give us the ability to pay cash for the item in a year or so and still continue to generate profit in the future. This principle is tantamount to a farmer eating all of the seeds instead of planting them and reaping a bountiful harvest.

Another way of reviewing the categories of persons is to identify their relationship to financial returns depending on their access to capital, their level of education on investment strategies and their attitude towards investment. Some of these activities may overlap. They include:

(a) **A survivor** who has little resources and has little access to high earning investments,

(b) **A saver** who accumulates small amounts of money over time and would invest in 'safe' opportunities which they can afford as they arise,

(c) **A borrower** who accesses money from moneylenders, financial institutions and other sources to invest. Even though his return may be high, the high interest rate which he usually has to pay would absorb much of his profit,

(d) **A partnership** where two or more persons pool their financial and/or other resources in order to generate higher returns from their higher combined resources,

(e) **The rich may employ the services of a number of** financial advisors to invest on their behalf and/or master the art of investing on their own. Because of the size of their investment, they may be able to invest in business transactions which generate returns in excess of 50% of their input.

(f) **The mega-rich** can be classified as the few investors who have the capacity to generate huge profit from their investments because of the magnitude of their investment. Such persons are usually at the upper 5% of the economic system of a country. Their investment may be so large that the stock market of the country, and even the foreign exchange position of the country, may be affected by their investment. They include oil barons, majority shareholders in multinational corporations, and persons who may have inherited a huge fortune from their ancestors.

A person can be operating in two or more of these financial levels at the same time. He may be a salaried earner, for example, but is investing his surplus cash flow into a private business venture and/or in financial instruments. Similarly, a professional may have established a business of which he is also practicing his professional skills. He is thus earning a salary while he is benefiting from the net income of the business as a result of the employment of other persons to man other aspects of the business. Most persons fall into the category of salary earners.

The following table illustrates some of the general differences between rich and poor people:

No.	Indicators	Poor	Rich
1	Source of wealth	Primarily from income earned	Primarily returns from investment
2	Attitude towards money	Earn to live	Their money and other assets and employees work for them
3	Percentage of salary retained	Low	High
4	Percentage of taxes paid	High	Low
5	Payment of taxes	Deducted before salary is received	Determines how much is paid
6	Management of workload	More time spent working as salary increases	More time for leisure and other non-work related activities as returns on investment increases
7	Attitude towards financial risks	Avoids risks. Hence, they are unable to retain financial and other assets during their working life to be able to enjoy a high standard of living after retirement	Risk takers, and usually have enough money and other assets to enjoy a comfortable retirement
8	Management of one's career path	Other persons determine promotions, salary, working hours etc.	Manages the level of success and returns achieved
9	Management of debt	Increases as salary increases	Decreases as returns increases
10	Life style	Live above their means	Live below their means
11	Accumulation of pension	Limited access to manage personal contribution and that of employer which keeps declining after retirement	Increased returns on assets continue to grow even after 'official' retirement
12	Ability to leave an inheritance	Achieves very little surplus and may only leave a small amount of assets for future generations	The assets invested continue to generate returns, possibly for several generations, once they are managed
13	Relationship with laws such as taxation and other business related issues	They are unable to take full advantage of the statutes of the law in order to increase their salary	Uses the statutes of the law to their advantage
14	Management of Cash Flow	Decreases, even when salary increases due to the application of poor cash flow management strategies	Increases astronomically as net income increases

Table 6.2 Comparison of the Life Style of the Poor and the Rich

Prudent investments in opportunities such as the following have enable millions of persons to achieve financial success:

(a) **The acquisition of academic, technical and other forms of education.** Even though many persons who are educated are able to utilize the skills which they acquire to earn enough money to live a comfortable life, the reality is that very often an entrepreneur who is far less educated than they are, hires the academic and technically qualified person and uses their expertise to amass a huge amount of wealth.

Most persons do not apply the academic and/or vocational knowledge and skills which they acquire for the maximization of their personal returns. Rather they become a salaried employee of an institution for which they may not even be a shareholder. It is true that many persons who are not academically qualified in a specific discipline such as financial management use what they may classify as a 'gut feeling' about a business decision and earn lucrative returns as a result of their decision. For the Christian who is 'in tune with the Father,' this is usually the Holy Spirit nudging them on to make a wise financial decision.

(b) **Owning their own business**; the reality is that many persons do not take the time to study what they are getting into before starting a business. It is not a good enough reason that merely because a person is a good cook or loves to style hair, and/or is desirous of becoming wealthy, for example, that the person should establish a business. It is first important to study what one is getting into, acquire the managerial skill, finances, employees, large enough market and other prerequisites needed to ensure its success, before commencing the operation.

(c) **Investing in securities, mutual funds and other financial instruments which generate high returns**. It is important to be conversant with the intricacies surrounding the financial instruments which one is desirous of investing in before engaging in the investment.

(d) **Investing in real estate is an excellent form of investment in most countries.** Many persons and businesses purchase old buildings and rebuild or repair them and/or purchase a plot of land and build one or several houses and sell them or rent them at a handsome profit.

(e) **The production of a commodity and/or the provision of one or several types of services,**

It is important to establish and expand our cash flow and utilize this excess to invest in areas which generate lucrative financial returns. It would not be long before we begin to realize significant expansion over a short time. As a person begins to reduce unnecessary expenditure and expand his investment he may be termed as being mean, a miser and other derogatory terms by those who are observing him. One also has to guard against persons who would seek to provide misguided advice and make offers which would result in a loss or minimal financial returns. They are also robbers and tricksters who are intent on depleting us of our hard earned assets.

> Similar to other areas of life, persons who are not prepared to take advantage of well calculated risks, usually achieve very little financial successes. **People who take risks create changes;** sadly, this is not always for the better.

We have seen from Chapter 3 that the categories of investors are:

(a) **Risk adverse investors,** whose desire is to take on as little risk as possible. As a result they save their money and may only engage in investments where they are sure that they will receive at least their full capital back.

(b) **Cautious investors** who employ the service of investment managers such as brokers and/or financial advisors who, independently or with the consent of the investors, allocate the investment. Unless the amounts invested is very large and the returns very high, such investors do not maximize their returns as if they were knowledgeable enough to invest on their own. This is because they have to pay commission to the fund manager and the investment might be on a diversified portfolio rather than on a single or a few high earning securities.

(c) **Gamblers** have the disadvantage of 'investing' in activities where the probability of securing high returns from this game of chance is disproportionately high against them. It is true that some gamblers do 'strike it rich' and they may be rich for the remainder of their lives and have enough money remaining for future generations. Gambling is also a sinful activity.

(d) **Investors who study the market in which they are investing, and make wise financial and other business decisions, which generate lucrative returns,**

> For the unwise, money is like an addictive drug; they are happy when they have much of it, sad when they are broke, and would figuratively and literally kill themselves and others if necessary, to have more of it. As Christians, we should not allow our material things to dictate our lives. Our Source, Provider and Sustainer is Jehovah.

Most persons do not have the financial resources, managerial skills and other prerequisites to operate a successful large business. Therefore, it is usually better to start on a small scale and expand under favourable conditions. Before expansion is undertaken conditions such as the following should be present:

(a) Management should become proficient or able to acquire the increase inputs to manage at that expanded level,
(b) The profitability of the business should increase as the efficiency in the production and delivery process of the product and/or service increases,
(c) Demand for the product and/or service of the business should be increased in proportion with the desired level of expansion,

Many persons who are desirous of starting a business on their own and do not have the necessary inputs to do so, choose the option of forging **an alliance with other person/s to form a business entity**. This is the major system used by corporate entities where a small number of persons purchase the shares of a company or they are sold to the public. Another option which is used by some persons is to **secure the franchise, and/or become an agent for an established entity**. Established companies such as McDonald's, Kentucky Fried Chicken, Hilti, Pepsi and Coke would authorize other business entities to lease their franchise where they agree to adhere to the system which the parent body established. This would include building the restaurant or other entity the same way, using the same system of preparation of their product and/or implementing the management and other system as the terms and conditions as stipulated by the franchise.

It is usually very expensive to secure permission to use the patent of an established product and the parent body would send inspectors on a regular basis to ensure that their systems are being maintained. In this way they secure the methodology and other prerequisites which have already been successfully used by the parent body. After overseeing the success of the management of a franchise, some entrepreneurs may establish similar systems on their own and/or increase the number of franchise holdings which they have.

Millions of persons have also invested into an existing **network marketing** system where they receive items from an established agency such as Amway Inc., and Avon, and sell the items on a commission. This system is used by millions of persons who sell toiletries, pharmaceuticals, groceries and other items in a small way or on a large scale. This is often done in a small way by persons who sell items to colleagues at work and to neighbours during their spare time. As their profitability increase, many persons incorporate the assistance of other family members and even hire the services of other persons and expand their operations. Many persons and companies conduct telemarketing and other methods to advertise their services and organize an effective delivery system. This system has assisted many persons to develop their marketing, managerial and other skills to expand their operations and/or establish other methods of conducting business as their capital increases.

> Many persons are **wealthy** from the stand point that the returns from their savings and investments would ensure that they do not have to worry about being able to meet their financial and other material needs for a number of months or even years. Yet, they may be burdened with the responsibility of having to work very hard in a stressful environment in order to maintain it. The **financially successful** person on the other hand, have the benefit of having enough financial and other resources to meet their needs but without the worry and pressure to achieve and/or maintain them.

In some ways we have to learn the techniques which are needed to guide us in making wise financial and other decisions and apply them prudently. The failure to take well-guided risks is a primary reason why many persons remain poor financially and otherwise and do not achieve their full potential in this and other areas of their lives. There are several things which we usually have to do before we can move to the path of the financial abundance which God has already decreed for us. These include:

(a) **Be in the place where you can hear from God as to what area/s He wants you to invest in.** We must be in the place where we are committed to give of our time, talent and treasury to see the fulfilment of His will in our lives. We should also recognize that the level of abundance which He has for each of us would be dependent on His purpose for our lives; some one hundred fold, some sixty fold etc. Similar to King Solomon, once we are committed to 'building the tabernacle' then He will also provide abundant resources to enable us to 'build our own palace.'

1 Kings Chapters One to Ten describe the blessings which Solomon received even as he was willing to follow Jehovah and to build the temple of the Lord. We are also instructed in Proverbs 3:5, 6 as follows: "*⁵Trust in the Lord with all of your heart, and do not rely on your own insight. ⁶In all of your ways acknowledge Him, and He will make straight your paths.*"

Be educated in the area where He directs you to invest in.

Areas where we can be educated to achieve financial success include academic qualifications and technical training which would enable us to secure the desired job, be competent in managing our business, and make prudent investment decisions. It is also useful to attend trade fairs and seminars on leadership, marketing, human resources and other disciplines which are relevant to the success of our business. Also subscribe to magazines and other literature which provide information on the local and international market in which you operate and align yourself to persons who can be a mentor in various aspects of the investment program. It is important to keep abreast with events surrounding the activities which you are desirous of investing in.

(b) **Formulate and keep abreast with the personal vision of the owner/s or the corporate entity.** It is also important that even small investors are conversant with issues such as the preparation and interpretation of financial statements such as the income statement, balance sheet and cash flow statements. This knowledge is useful for an investor to know where he is, where he desires to be and how to achieve his goals.

(c) **Secure the necessary finances needed to undertake the desired level of investment.** A good way to commence this process is to adopt a disciplined lifestyle including budgeting wisely and to consistently increase the amount of money we can save from our salary and other sources of income. This process may entails one or more activities such as avoiding unnecessary debt, investing in high return projects, forming a partnership or other forms of business alliances, and where necessary, secure credit from a financial institution and/or other sources.

When the amount of capital cannot be raised privately, external funding must be sought. The ability to access an adequate amount of cheap capital at the time when it is needed and other factors of production are basic ingredients to help one achieve the desired level of financial success. Too little, and too expensive, factors of production as well as the unavailability of essential inputs when needed are classic causes of the failure for many businesses.

(d) **Harness the necessary skills needed to take you to where you are desirous of being.** As we progress up the road to financial success, it usually demands that we are better able to manage people, systems and other assets, in order to achieve the desired level of success. It is a fact that many persons can prepare more tasty food items than many of the popular successful eating-houses. However, unless they are able to access the level of capital and operate better systems than these institutions, they will not be able to generate the level of profits as these established agencies. This includes the location of the factory, distribution centre and/or other buildings, the deportment of staff towards management and customers, the standardization of the output and the image projected in the advertisement of the product and/or service provided.

(e) **Accept change and be adequately prepared to take advantage of the benefits which change creates.** If we review the number of areas which we have seen significant changes over our lifetime alone, we will recognize several significant changes which have occurred. Many persons who are creative are able to invent, design or produce items, patent them and derive much financial and other forms of success from the sale and/or rental of the patent, franchise, brand name or other systems and/or from marketing the product or services.

Other persons are able to create new products, improve on the efficiency use of various items, and/or production processes, improve the efficiency of a system and in other ways are able to benefit from the introduction of new and improved products and services. Bill Gates, the Rockefeller family and other famous entrepreneurs have been able to take advantage of increased demand for cheaper, faster, and more efficient products and services provided.

(f) **You must be prepared to take well-calculated risks.** The maxim which states "**nothing ventured, nothing gained**' must be heeded. It is often useful to start on a small scale and expand as management is fully equips to optimize returns.

(g) **In order to optimize sales, steps must be taken to ensure that factors such as the quality of the product, the cost, standardization, efficiency of the supply system, packaging, advertising and other market related issues are managed.** It is important to market the concept that '**good things are usually not cheap (expensive) and that cheap things are usually not good. Therefore, the selling price of an item should as far as possible be reflective of the quality and other prerequisites of the product (such as demand, supply).**

(h) **Equip yourself with the necessary resources needed to enable you to maximize your returns.** This is essential since many persons accept mediocrity simply because they do not take time to acquire the necessary knowledge to empower them to succeed. This may also entail seeking prudent advice from financial planners, consultants and other knowledgeable persons in a specific field.

Depending on the type of investment, many successful investors generate huge profit since they are able to benefit from economies of scale, tax and other advantages, by operating on a large scale.

(i) **The necessary infrastructure must be in place to take full advantage of the financial, human and other resources which are needed to achieve the desired objectives.** It is important to master the system which would enable you to utilize the resources available in an efficient way to generate the desired level of returns. The investors must have mastered the art of generating the desired level of returns in that particular endeavour independently or with the assistance of other persons who are knowledgeable and are committed to inject the necessary inputs to make the investment a reality. This may include other investors, financial advisors, employees and/or other persons and institutions.

(j) **Even if a person feels secure as an employee, his income should be complemented with interest from savings in high yielding financial instruments such as mutual funds, dividends from shares, rental income from real estate, profit from investment in business venture and other returns on their investment.** At the same time, they should seek to abstain from, or incur as little additional debt as possible while they are controlling unnecessary spending, increasing their income and expanding their saving and investment thrust.

(k) **Entrepreneurs and other investors have to take advantage of business opportunities, information and other benefits which are available on the internet.** It is increasingly being recognized that the new frontier of 'offshore' business is in cyberspace. Billions of dollars change hands each day on the internet. Many of these transactions are far cheaper than purchasing from 'regular' stores, since they often do not attract the high taxes and other charges.

(l) **We must secure the necessary advice from persons who are experts in the desired area of investment.** They may include stock brokers, financial planners, real estate agents and other professionals who would at least assist us to understand the intricacies of the business and guide us to master them. Depending on the nature of the advice it may be necessary to befriend such persons or where possible to hire their service at least until we become competent in managing the operation independently.

(m) **It is important to be prepared for disappointment.** Many persons are so scared of being disappointed that they would stay in a dead-end job since they are afraid of being exposed to financial and other losses when a better opportunity materializes. Weak managers often avoid making important decisions as they are afraid of facing the consequences of failure. Some other reasons why we experience failure are due to ignorance, or not being diligent enough to apply the correct Biblical principles in the execution of a particular task and/or not listening to the wise council.

Once our ways are committed to the Lord and He is directing our path, even if He allows us to fail in a particular area it is only for our betterment in some way. We should be diligent and committed enough to learn from our mistakes and to use failure as a stepping stone for success.

(n) **Specialize in one or a small number of areas of investment.** Most persons derive more profit from investing in areas in which they are knowledgeable and for which they have a love and a passion, instead of merely doing it for the sake of accumulating riches. The concept of diversification is usually not as profitable as specializing in an area which one is knowledgeable of and/or is able to employ other persons to assist in the process. This may include hiring specialist advisors and other categories of persons. In some instances a decision is made that the emphasis of the business would be on having a low mark-up in order to enjoy a high level of turnover, as is common on most items in supermarkets and the sale of non-luxury items. The converse occurs where there is a high mark-up on high end item such as the sale of jewellery and luxury cars. Failure to manage sales is a primary reason why a large percentage of businesses fail.

(o) **Master the art of managing people.** Most persons who achieve financial success have done so by utilizing the services of others such as employees, and professional advisors. Unless such persons are stimulated by factors such as their job security, financial rewards and a conducive working environment, then they may not provide the service to cover their cost of working and generate the required level of returns for the investor. Some persons use force, bribery and other unscriptural methods to achieve their financial success. The result of such actions may be that their operations are adversely affected by strikes and other industrial actions by employees and court actions by the state since their activities may be investigated for illegal activities.

(p) **Patent inventions, musical and other recordings, books and other items.** This would result in the accumulation of royalties and other fees when persons use the item for commercial purposes. It is true that many items which are patented are used without the users even paying the necessary royalties. A common example of this is persons and companies who download music from websites on the internet, burn CDs and record audio and video cassettes without the permission of the holder of the copyright for these recordings. The legislation to prosecute such persons is not well defined in many countries, while they are not rigidly enforced in many others.

(q) **Ensure that you are living within your means and not merely living in an illusion.** Many persons are of the opinion that earning more money would solved their financial problems only to find out that as they earn more, their expenses are still more than their income since their consumption pattern increases more than their income can afford. (The economic jargon which is used to describe this phenomenon is that 'the propensity to consume is a function of your income.'

As the average person receives an increase in income, they very often increase their purchase of consumer items and live a lifestyle which is beyond the level of increase in their income). The answer to this problem is usually to first learn to manage your cash flow and ensure that you have a positive cash flow each month, which would enable you to save and invest the difference. This principle is needed by the owners of businesses and investors who live a lavish lifestyle, instead of investing their retain earnings until they can really afford to live at the desired standard of living.

If, for example, a farmer eats the seeds for the next crop instead of planting them, then he would not have the desired harvest. It may be necessary to spend a part of the profit from one's salary or net income from a business venture. At the same time, a prudent person would seek to save and invest/reinvest a part of the earning in order to generate higher returns in the future. Similarly, if a person perpetually spends as much or even more than he earns, he will not be able to save and invest as much as he would have if he had managed his cash flow. This would have disastrous consequences when an emergency arises.

As a person masters the art of managing his cash flow, and as returns from investments increase, he would be able to gradually increase his affluence, consistent with his true level of financial freedom. This process is facilitated by reducing personal and/or corporate debt, emphasizing on saving and investing in areas which generate high returns, planning and executing long term goals.

> *We should not only seek to live within our means, but also to increase our means.*

(r) **Do not quit when the goal is just around the other corner.** This issue goes back to the mindset of the investor. We are reminded of the maxim which states that; **quitters never win and winners never quit**. This is not suggesting that we should jump around like 'three blind mice,' for a similar fault would result when a poor investment decision is made and because of pride, we would not abandon it.

An investor with a sound business and/or investment concept, which has been ratified by the experts in the area of their investment, must have the strength of character to see it through to a successful completion. Of course, if implementation of the project has gone severely wrong and we have done all that is within our means to make it work and it is still unsalvageable, and after consulting competent advisors and the Lord we are not given the clearance to continue, then, in wisdom we should allow it to die. This usually occurs when exogenous factors (which are beyond our control) have a negative effect on the projects.

(s) **Avoid the quest for instant gratification and instead pursue long-term objectives.** As we focus on the long-term, we will be challenged to make wise decisions over the short and medium terms in order to fully achieve the abundance which we expect from the execution of our long-term goals. **A vital part of this process is benefiting from the principle of compounding when saving at a commercial bank, which generates interest on the principle and interest accumulated, instead of losing when the money is kept at home in a safe of hidden somewhere else.**

(t) **Our financial priority should be in the area of investing rather than merely providing financial security, primarily at the initial stage of the investment.** Persons with their house and/or car as their largest 'investment' are usually not prepared or able to invest in income generating activities which have a significant effect in taking them to the desired level of financial liberation.

(u) **We should seek positive role models from persons who have achieved success in the endeavour in which we are pursuing, and in other positive areas.** This does not infer that we should shun even persons who are financial failures, for even they can be an impetus to challenge us to succeed. However, we should seek mentors who would guide us to achieve financial and other forms of success.

(v) **Take control of the aspects of your life which the Lord has entrusted into your care.** Even when you fail, do not blame others for failures which were due to your ignorance, incompetence and/or other defects. Failures should be used as an educational experience which should encourage you to rethink your strategy and propel you to retool and overcome these challenges. There are times, however, with the prompting of the Holy Spirit and advice from genuine persons when you are directed to chart a new course.

(w) **Invest in a business venture and/or investment opportunity in which you have a passion.** One of the primary reasons many businesses fail is that the owner/s is/are not committed to its success. Even if a project is generating high returns and management does not have the passion to see it grow to its full potential, there is a high probability /that it would fail. For this reason it is important to know what the Lord wants us to be and the investment area that He wants us to be involved in.

> If we cannot manage our cash flow by budgeting wisely, increasing our income, decrease expenditure and/or apply other methods and generally living within our means, then we would have to pay others to do so in the form of interest on credit and other cash outflows.

(x) **You have to acquire the necessary knowledge to equip you to take advantage of prudent investment opportunities.** Focus on the area which you desire to invest in and acquire the knowledge necessary to execute it successfully. If you are desirous of purchasing property, and renovating it for resale, for example, you must be knowledgeable of factors such as being able to secure the best:
   (i) Purchase arrangement, such as a low purchase price and being able to negotiate the most advantageous mortgage package. The legal and other costs associated with closing a mortgage are very high at some financial institutions.
   (ii) Contractors who would provide the required level of renovation to the property or construction of the building within your budget.

Millions of persons are mislead into believing that pursuing an academic career, securing a job which has benefits such as a pension upon retirement and medical insurance and other forms of job security is the panacea to achieving financial success. An increasing number of such persons are being forced to recognize that this path often leads to frustration and a life of mediocrity in terms of the quality of life they can afford to live. **Financial freedom from a secular perspective is primarily achieved when a person:**
   (i) **Enjoys a high level of income from their profession** and is able to save and invest prudently and are able to meet their current, medium and long term financial needs,
   (ii) **Receives a 'windfall'** such as a large inheritance from a deceased relative, a substantial law suit settlement, lottery, bingo or other games of change. (For the dishonest – from robbery,

fraud, tax evasion and other unscrupulous acts – for which they will be prosecuted if convicted),

(iii) **Is a share owner** in one or several corporate entities,

Even though this is a satisfactory state, it is important that we ensure that this and every other aspect of our lives are in keeping with the will of the Lord. The latter principle is highlighted in the parable of the 'Widow's Mite,' where the widow experienced financial freedom in that among other things she recognized that Jehovah was her source, and even if she gave all the money that she had to Him, He would have provided for her in ways which far surpassed the value of the coin which she gave to His work.

> Financial freedom from a secular perspective is being in the state where a person can enjoy the desired standard of living when his money is working for him rather than working for money. This may contrast with the spiritual connotation of financial freedom, which is having enough financial resources to enables a person to fulfil the will of the Lord for his ministry; personally, within the family, and further a field.

(y) **Accumulating the necessary capital to be able to invest at the level required:** For many persons this is accumulated as they purpose to live within their means and increase their savings. The strategy of consistently saving, even a little each month over a number of years is often successfully used by many persons to accumulate much money.

The money accumulated over time often provides them the opportunity to acquire the necessary knowledge and expertise to enable them to be successful when they decide to invest. This process is usually more promising when they begin to save a little at a time and are challenged as they realize how much their financial resources have grown, to increase their savings and investments.

Many persons who are in the coveted position of enjoying financial prosperity, are individuals or families who have their own business, private owners of large corporate entities and persons who are generating huge returns from personal and/or corporate investments. One of the significant benefits from a corporate entity is the tax concessions which can be derived.

The disposable income of the **salaried employee** is shown as follows:

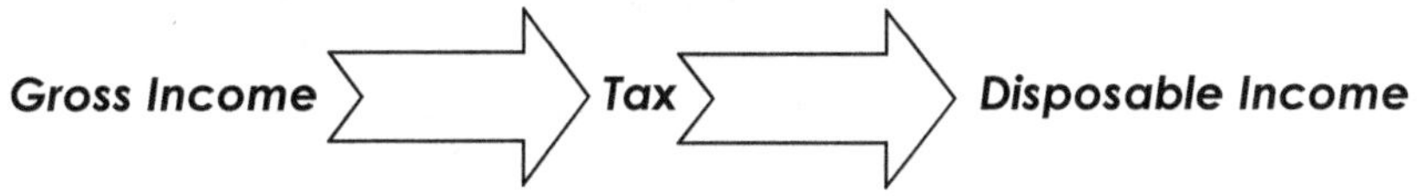

Gross Income ⟹ *Tax* ⟹ *Disposable Income*

The disposable income of the **business or corporate** entity is shown as follows:

Disposable Income ⟹ *Spending* ⟹ *Tax*

<u>Diagram 6.1   A Comparison of the Disposable Income of the Salaried Earner and the Owner of a Business.</u>

It is interesting to note that many of the expenses which are normally attributed to the income of the

Manager/owner and other employees can be included in the bi-laws of the company. Among the benefits which can be derived from this practice are:

(a) Expenditure such as the purchase and maintenance of the car used by the Manager/owner can be incorporated into the expenses of the business,

(b) The home in which the family lives can be bought in the name of the company. Vacations, which the family goes on can also be expensed as benefits of the Manager and other senior staff,

(c) In some countries even items such as the education of the children may be expensed as contribution made by the company or included under other categories, and expensed before the taxable income of the company,

> **Salaried workers and the self employed** earn most of their money from their income. They usually pay in excess of 30% of their gross salary as income tax in many countries. **Business owners and investors** earn most of their money from their assets and pay little or no income tax on their earnings. It is no wonder that persons from the latter group are richer. Which group would you prefer to be in?

Persons who are salaried earners and those who are self employed are often subjected to racial, sexual and other types of prejudices much more than entrepreneurs and investors. In addition, the higher up persons are in the social ladder, the more their money and position will 'speak' for them and the less their presence as individuals is felt.

The balance sheet and income statement of a person or organization with a managed portfolio verses one which is unmanaged as follows:

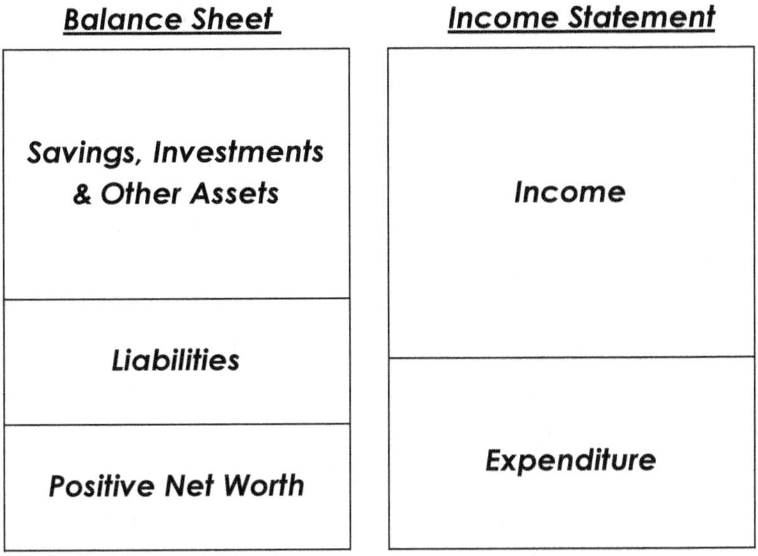

Balance Sheet

Savings, Investments & Other Assets
Liabilities
Positive Net Worth

Income Statement

Income
Expenditure

Notes:
4. Negative Net Worth denotes bankruptcy
5. When the level of expenditure cannot be supported by income generated by the business, the deficit is usually financed by credit and/or equity finance.

Diagram 6.1 Showing a Schematic Balance Sheet and Income Statement of a Managed Portfolio

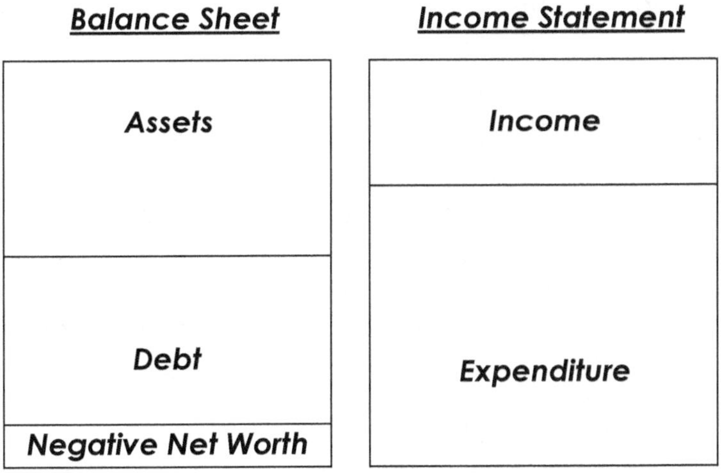

Balance Sheet

Assets
Debt
Negative Net Worth

Income Statement

Income
Expenditure

Notes: A person or company with a negative net worth is generally classified as being bankrupt.

Diagram 6.2 Showing the Schematic Balance Sheet and Income Statement of an Unmanaged Portfolio

Many persons take advantage of establishing a business venture while the company which they worked for decides to outsource specific arms of their operations, in an attempt to cut cost. Such persons may have been employees of the organization who settle for a retirement package which they can invest to purchase the equipment, rent factory space or secure other assets to conduct their operations. Depending on the type of operation it may be possible to convert one or several rooms of their home into office space or workshop to conduct their business.

If a person attempts to lie to himself and to others that he can live comfortably at a certain standard of lifestyle when in fact he is living on excessive amount of credit which he cannot afford, for example, then it is only a matter of time before he will become bankrupt or have to engage in dishonest practices in an attempt to maintain his inflated lifestyle. Many persons secure loans and run up huge credit card bills and other debts primarily in an attempt to maintain a standard of living which they cannot afford. The result is that the obligation to meet the loan payments results in many persons living from one pay check to another and even being in poverty. Truth on the other hand creates wealth. Some of the areas where this principle is manifested are:

(a) Recognizing that Jehovah is the source of all true wealth and that we can achieve all that He has already provided for us, and applying this fundamental principle to every area of our lives.

(b) **'Manna still falls from heaven**,' from the perspective that God often performs miracles to enable us to achieve financial and other forms of success, He has also provided us with the principles in His word which we can use to guide us along the path of success in our financial and every other area of our lives.

(c) We have to learn the necessary techniques and apply them in the correct way to enable us to achieve success,
(d) Once we manage the resources needed for success, unless we allow the 'cankerworm' (which may include inflation, theft, and a net loss) to eat away at our investments by not guarding them with faith, prayer and other instruments which the Lord has placed at our disposal, then we will achieve financial success,

A person who lives a lie, be it living above their means in order to impress others, and believing that their wealth provides ultimate happiness, will end in poverty. Even if it is not material poverty it will be spiritual poverty, that is, separation from Jehovah in this life and in eternity.

It is important to note that the blessings of the Lord go beyond our capabilities and what we can achieve on our own. Biblical examples of this include:

(a) The Lord revealed to Jacob a creative method to multiply livestock,
(b) The favour of the Lord on the lives of the Hebrew caused the Egyptians to give jewellery and other gifts to the Children of Israel as they left Egypt,
(c) The Lord granted success and much spoil to King David and other leaders in many battles even when their armies were outnumbered,
(d) Even though Peter and the other disciples toiled the whole night they did not catch any fish. When they obeyed the Lord, they caught so much fish that their boat was almost sunk and they had to solicit the assistance of other fishermen to help them to collect the abundance of fish which they had caught. This is an indication that the blessing of the Lord in financial and other areas of our lives goes beyond our abilities. Miracles are common in the lives of Christians and even

non-Christians since Jehovah is a God of love and mercy.

We are reminded of Psalm 49:10 which states: "**¹⁰When we look at the wise, they die; fool and dolt perish together and leave their wealth to others.**" This is confirmation that Christians often receive inheritance and other favour from being in the will of the Lord.

One of the important financial choices which each of us has to make is whether or not we are prepared to enjoy financial security or financial freedom. Persons who are desirous of enjoying financial security would usually be a salaried earner in a 'secure' job. Such persons are usually scared and/or unable to invest much money and other assets and thus, remain very poor. On the contrary persons in pursuit of financial freedom would acquire the knowledge, financial and other prerequisites, start their own business utilizing their skills, finances and other inputs, invest wisely, enabling them to generate the desired high returns on their investments. The level of success begins with the mindset of the investor/s. The way we think will challenge us to make the required preparation. We are reminded of Proverbs 23:7 states that a man is what he thinks in his heart.

Lies = Poverty
- **Lies** create poverty, while **truth** enables us to take advantage of opportunities which would enable us to obtain material and other resources.
- Why should we lie to ourselves that we can live a lavish lifestyle when we know that we are 'deep over your head' in debt which we cannot even pay.
- It better to be truthful and live on a budget on which we can afford material comfort? In this way, over the medium and long run we will have achieved far more material resources than if we remain in perpetual debt due to not having or seeking to implement an unrealistic budget.

Many persons have the misconception that buying a large house, fancy car and other trappings of the rich would make them happy, only to find that these things only make life more difficult since they have to do several jobs and may even engage in dishonest practices in order to survive. It is better to implement the principles of the Bible in order to achieve success in financial and other forms of success which lasts, and which can be enjoyed. These includes living on a well structured budget, executing long term plans, saving and investing prudently and increasing their affluence gradually at the level they can comfortably afford and which is consistent with their long term success. Throughout the process we have to rely on the Lord for wisdom, strength, favour and other blessings which are needed to execute these mandates, while we are fulfilling our responsibilities in areas such as giving of our tithes and offering, and assisting the poor, for example.

The path to Biblical financial and other forms of success as experienced by many persons can be illustrated as follows:

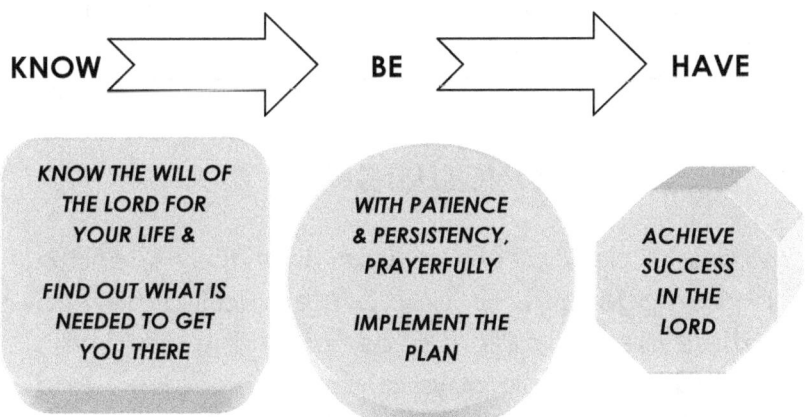

Diagram 6.4 Illustration of the Path to Biblical Success

The following table presents hypothetical examples of the application of the above principles:

Know	Be	Have
To be the head of an international missionary body.	Attend Bible school, affiliate yourself to, or establish a local church and train, become a missionary and establish affiliation with other missionary bodies,	Send missionaries to other countries and also finance missionaries from other church bodies who are willing to work with your ministry,
Accumulate a million dollars before age fifty.	• Secure a high paying job and save and invest prudently, • Establish a viable business entity within two years of employment, • Invest in property development and on the stock exchange,	A significantly growing cash flow and new worth,
Have a happy family life.	• Seek the Lord for His will on whom to marry, • Spend quality time nurturing a loving relationship with your spouse and children,	A stable and loving family where each member of the family is fulfilling the calling of the Lord on their lives,

Table 6.5 Strategies to Achieve Goals

The above table provides some broad parameters which can be used to guide us along the path of achieving our goals in life.

CONCLUSION

Millions of persons are so poor that they spend a large percentage of their day contemplating how to survive. There are also millions of persons in the world who have passed their prime days and may be retired and are about to die from old age and/or due to infections such as HIV, AIDS and cancer, who are unable to contribute much materially for themselves and others.

However, for those of us in the most productive stage, of our lives, who are either preparing to enter or are in the income earning stage, we have a responsibility to maximize the returns on the assets at our disposal.

Many persons seek **job security** since they are risk averse:
1. In an attempt to decrease their likelihood of not having enough money to cater for their material needs,
2. A job which offer benefits including medical insurance coverage and a contributory pension, from their income and a percentage from their employer,
3. Many persons who are dependent on the state as their primary source of income are usually burdened by huge debt, a limited pension and if there is a huge medical bill, their insurance coverage is usually not adequate to cover it. Sadly, less than five percentage of the population of the world are in the category of persons who can truly enjoy **financial freedom** where they have access to so much money and other assets that they do not have to worry about meeting basic materials needs.

Once we are obedient to the Lord as it relates to financial matters and other aspects of His Word, then we will reap the abundance which He has promised His children. We are not expected to do everything for ourselves, for it is He who gives us the power to become wealthy. As we 'put our hands to the plough' in obedience to His Word and will for our lives, He grants the increase. He has made available to us His Word, the Holy Spirit and the Spiritual Gifts, other believers, the medium of prayer and other forms of support to us so that we will succeed in all of our undertakings which are in accordance with His will. He is not slack concerning His promises for our wellbeing. We have an obligation to be diligent with the tools which He has placed at our disposal so that we can achieve the level of success which He has already decreed to us.

Achieving and Maintaining Success
- The first stage of success in any area of our live is to align ourselves to the will of Jehovah. If this is not done, even if we achieve the trappings of success, they will not last for very long and we will also not achieve the eternal reward of the good steward; that of spending eternity with Jehovah.
- The second stage is to change our mindset to one which takes on the mentality, attitude and other attributes which guarantees continual success. This will not come 'overnight,' for it requires that we:
  - Stay continually faithful to Jehovah,
  - Acquire the necessary tools and,
  - Aligning ourselves to persons who would assist us along the path to success.

Once this is achieved, we will begin to look for and receive the opportunities which will enable us to optimize the use of the material and other resources at our disposal to spread the Word of God and in other ways to bless others.

NOTES

SELECTED REFERENCES

Burkett, Larry: **Money Matters**, Thomas Nelson Publishers, USA, 2001.

Kiyosaki, Robert T. and Lechter, Sharon L.: **Cash Flow Quadrant**, TechPress Inc., USA, 1999.

New Revised Standard Version, **The Holy Bible**, World Bible Publisher, Inc., USA, 1989.

Orman, Suze: **The Road to Wealth,** Penguin Putnam Inc., USA, 2001.

World Bible Publishers Inc.: **The Holy Bible, New Revised Standard Version** USA, 1989.

APPENDIX

POWER POINT PRESENTATION AT SEMINAR ENTITLED:
THE MAN, HIS MONEY AND HIS MASTER

TOPIC: Enjoying More Than Enough

PRESENTOR: Gladwin B. Williams PhD.

THE PEOPLE'S CATHEDRAL MINISTRIES,
BRIDGETOWN, BARBADOS

MAY 11, 2003

INTRODUCTION

Malachi 3:10 states: "*[10]Bring the full tithe into the storehouse, so that there may be food in my storehouse, and thus put me to the test, says the Lord of Host, see if I will not open the window of heaven for you and pour for you an overflowing blessing.*"

Many aspects of the **overflowing blessings** cannot be measured accurately in financial terms. They include:

(a) **Fulfilling the calling of the Lord on your life,**
(b) **Protection for sickness, accidents** etc.
(c) **Peace of mind,**
(d) **Harmony in our home,**
(e) **Our children growing in the fear of the Lord and fulfilling their career and other Godly objectives,**

What constitutes financial success for a person is usually dependent on factors such as:

(a) **The norms of the society in which they live,**
(b) **Their personal goals,**
(c) **Their exposure to the lifestyle of persons from other communities,**
(d) **The fulfilment of the will of the Lord in their life,**

Specific areas which many persons use to measure their level of financial blessings include:
- (a) **The type of house they live in, their mode of transportation and general lifestyle,**
- (b) **Their earning capacity,**
- (c) **The amount of money they have saved and invested,**
- (d) **Their ability to enjoy leisure activities,**
- (e) **Having enough money to be able to assist the needy and conduct other spiritual and other activities.**

What method do you use and how much success have you achieved in fulfilling your financial goals?

There are several factors which can prevent us from enjoying the '**overflowing blessings.**' They include:
- (a) **We are not cheerful givers** – the Lords love a cheerful giver,
- (b) **We do not ask, knock and/or seek,**
- (c) **Our tithes are not brought to His storehouse,**
- (d) **We do not work smart** – while it is, for example, more effective to cut a tree using a sharp, rather than a dull axe. However, it is more expedient if one has access to use an electrical chainsaw but more efficient).
- (e) **Many persons fail to achieve their desired level of financial success since they do not recognize that they may be trying to achieve a level which is inconsistent with the will of the Lord for their life.**
- (f) **We are not in the place to utilize the blessings of the Lord.**

Methods of receiving the financial blessings from the Lord include:
- (a) **Receiving special favours directly from the Lord,**
- (b) **Inheritance from parents and/or other persons,**
- (c) **High returns as a result of working smartly,**
- (d) **From the unrighteous,**

(e) **Receive high returns from savings and investments,**

Where are you in the scale of financial affluence?

The financial status of the majority of persons can be classified into one or more of the following segments:

(a) **Unemployed/Poverty Stricken** depends on the system for their existence,
(b) **Salaried earners** works for the system,
(c) **The self-employed** create a part of the system,
(d) **Entrepreneur** manages and may even own a part of the system,
(e) **Investors** inject capital into creating parts of the system without necessarily working in the system,

> Many persons become rich not by necessarily working hard but by strategizing and pursuing a highly successful business venture, franchising one or several lines of business and/or product and/or by investing wisely.

Methods which can be used to formulate a business entity include:

(a) **The traditional business** where one or several persons and/or agencies pool their resources,
(b) **A person or company purchases the franchise of a business** operation,
(c) **Entering into a network** line of business,

One of the significant benefits from a corporate entity is the tax advantage which can be derived.

The disposable income of the **salaried employee** is shown as follows:

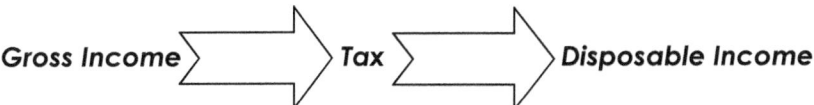

Gross Income ⟹ Tax ⟹ Disposable Income

The disposable income of the **business or corporate** entity is shown as follows:

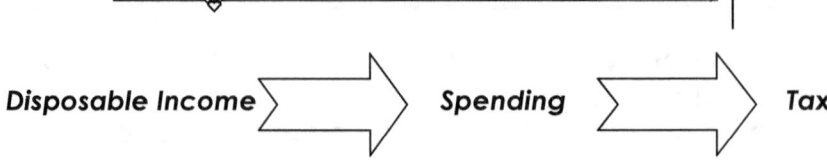

Diagram 1: Comparison of the Disposable Income of the Salaried Earner and the Owner of a Business.

Some of the factors which differentiates between the rich and the poor:

No.	Indicators	Poor	Rich
1	Source of wealth	Primarily from income earned,	Primarily from returns from investment,
2	Attitude towards money	Earn to live	Their money and other assets and employees work for them,
3	Percentage of salary retained	Low	High
4	Percentage of taxes paid	High	Low
5	Payment of taxes	Deducted before salary is received,	Determines how much is paid,
6	Management of workload	More time spent working as salary increases,	More time for leisure and other non-work related activities as returns on investment increases,
7	Management of Cash Flow	Decreases, very often, even when salary increases, due to the application of poor cash flow management strategies,	Increases astronomically as net income increases,
8	Management of one's career path	Other persons determine promotions, salary, working hours etc.	Manages the level of success and returns achieved,
9	Management of debt	Increases as salary increases,	Decreases as returns increases,
10	Life style	Live above their means,	Live below their means,
11	Accumulation of pension	Limited access to manage personal contribution and that of employer which keeps declining after retirement,	Increased returns on assets continue to grow even after 'official' retirement,

No.	Indicators	Poor	Rich
12	Ability to leave an inheritance	Achieves very little surplus and may only leave a small amount of assets for future generations,	The assets invested continue to generate returns possibly for several generations, once they are managed,
13	Relationship with laws such as taxation and other business related issues,	Do not, or are unable to take full advantage of the statutes of the law in order to increase their salary,	Uses the statutes of the law to their advantage,
14	Attitude towards financial risks	Avoids risks, thus, they are unable to retain financial and other assets during their working life to be able to enjoy a high standard of living after retirement,	Risk takers, and usually have enough money and other assets to enjoy a comfortable life during their working life and after retirement,

Prudently managed strategies such as the following have enable millions of persons to achieve financial success:

(a) **The acquisition of academic, technical and other forms of education to be able to secure high paying jobs and apply their knowledge to creating some form of direct income,**

(b) **Own and/or manage a highly successful business where they derive highly lucrative financial and other benefits,**

(c) **Investing in securities, mutual funds and other financial instruments, real estate and/or other forms of investment. The production of a commodity and/or the provision of one or several services.**

> For many of us, money is like an addictive drug, we are happy when we have much of it, sad when we are broke, and would figuratively and literally kill ourselves and others if necessary, to have more of it.

Some facets which have enabled many persons to achieve financial success are:

(a) **Be in the place where they can hear from God as to what area/s they should invest,**
(b) **Be educated in the area where He is directing them to invest in,**
(c) **Formulate and keep abreast of the personal vision of the owner/s or the corporate entity,**
(d) **Secure the necessary finance needed to undertake the desired level of investment,**
(e) **Harness the necessary skills needed to take them to where they are desirous of being,**
(f) **Accept change and be adequately prepared to take advantage of the benefits which change creates,**
(g) **Be prepared to take well-calculated risks,**
(h) **Equip themselves with the necessary resources needed to enable them to maximize their returns,**
(i) **Ensure that adequate systems are in place to optimize production, sales, profits etc.**
(j) **Keep abreast of developments and other information on the sector which they operate,**
(k) **Secure the necessary advice from persons who are experts in the desired area of investment and implement prudent methods,**
(l) **Be prepared for disappointment and use them as a stepping stone for future success,**
(m) **Specialize in one or a small number of areas of investment,**

(n) **Master the art of managing people and other assets at our disposal,**
(o) **Patent inventions, recordings, books and other items,**
(p) **Do not quit when success may be just around the other corner,**
(q) **Avoid the quest for superficial short-term success since they usually have serous negative consequences over the medium and long-run,**
(r) **Seek positive role models from persons who have achieved success in the endeavour which they are pursuing and in other positive areas,**
(s) **Take control of the aspects of their life, finance, business and other areas which the Lord has entrusted into their care,**
(t) **Invest in a business venture and/or investment opportunity for which they have a passion,**

CONCLUSION

From the above presentation we can deduce issues such as:

(a) Seek the Lord for direction and pursue His will in every area of your life,
(b) Budget wisely, plan long-term and execute your plans prayerfully and with discipline,
(c) Increase your Cash Flow to be able to maximize your savings and investments,
(d) Achieve the status where 'your money' (or more accurately, the Lord's money over which you have been made a steward) is working for you to the extent where you can achieve financial abundance,

The path to Biblical success as experienced by many persons can be summarized as follows:

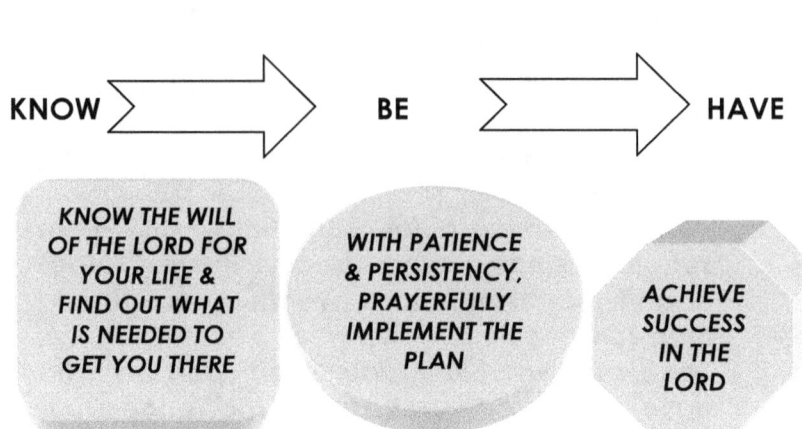

Diagram 2 Illustration of the Path to Biblical Success

ABOUT THE AUTHOR

Gladwin B. Williams is a Christian Counsellor who specialized in Pre-Marital and Financial Managing Counselling. He has fellowshipped with the Full Gospel Fellowship in Guyana, the Assemblies of God in Bangor, Wales, UK; in Maryland, USA; and in Guyana, and with the Abiding Word Ministries, The Gambia, West Africa and the People's Cathedral Ministries, Barbados, West Indies. He is also a graduate of the Banjul Bible School.

Gladwin was a lecturer with the University of Guyana, South America, and has worked with several national and international organizations. He has functioned in the noble office of an elder of the Stanleytown Full Gospel Fellowship, Guyana and as a Pre-Marital Counsellors for the Fellowship. He has also served in this capacity with the Abiding Word Ministries in The Gambia, West Africa. He is currently fellowshipping with the People's Cathedral in Barbados, West Indies.

Other books by Gladwin B. Williams include:
(a) **From Genesis To Destiny**
(b) **Using Money Wisely**
(c) **From Genesis to Destiny**
(d) **What Does Sex Have to Do With It?**

For further information, the author can be contacted by email at: gladwilliams@yahoo.com

www.ingramcontent.com/pod-product-compliance
Lightning Source LLC
Chambersburg PA
CBHW051849170526
45168CB00001B/34